Giulia **Parola**

Europe in Green:
European
Environmental
Democracy

Versita Discipline:
Language, Literature

Managing Editor:
Margherita Poto

Language Editor:
Laura Isakoff
Paul Fraccaro

Published by Versita, Versita Ltd, 78 York Street, London W1H 1DP, Great Britain.

ISBN (hardcover): 978-83-7656-061-8

ISBN (paperback): 978-83-7656-060-1

ISBN (for electronic copy): 978-83-7656-062-5

Managing Editor: Margherita Poto

Language Editor: Laura Isakoff
                 Paul Fraccaro

Cover illustration: ©iStockphoto.com/iconeer

www.versita.com

To my mother Earth, to my mother
to my father Sky, to my father

To my dears friends Emi, Meg and Osindra

From Earth to Olidori and back

Contents

Abbreviations 9

Introduction 12

CHAPTER 1

Environmental Democracy in a European Context 15

    1.   "Democracy" and "Environment" in the European Union 15

    2.   Environmental Democracy in Europe...53

CHAPTER 2

Implementation of Environmental Rights and Duties in Europe.......... 82

    1.   Environmental Democracy at the EU Level...84

    2.   Environmental Democracy at National Level...126

Conclusion...160

Index 164

Bibliography..168

Detailed Table of Content...252

Abbreviations

C	Case
CFCA	Community Fisheries Control Agency
CFI	Court First Instance
COM	Communication
CONF	Conference
CSOs	Civil Society Organisations
Doc.	Document
e.g.	Exempli Gratia
EC	European Community
ECE	Economic Commission for Europe
ECFESD	European Consultative Forum on the Environment and Sustainable Development
ECHR	European Convention on Human Rights
ECJ	European Court of Justice
ECOSOC	Economic and Social Council
ECR	European Court Reports
ECtHR	European Court Human Rights
ed.	Editor
eds.	Editors
EEA	European Environmental Agency
EEA	European Energy Agency
EEC	European Economic Community
EFSA	European Food Safety Authority
EHRR	Essex Human Rights Review
EIA	Environmental Impact Assessment
EIoP	European Integration online Papers
EMSA	European Maritime Safety Agency
ETF	European Transport Workers' Federation
ETI	European Transparency Initiative
ETS	European Treaty Series

EU	European Union
EU-OSHA	European Agency for Safety and Health at Work
EUF	European Focus
f.	Following
FAO	Food and Agricultural Organisation
G.A.	General Assemble
ICJ	International Court of Justice
IPCC	International Panel on Climate Change
IPPC	Integrated Pollution Prevention and Control
ISSN	International Standard Serial Number
IUCN	International Union for Conservation of Nature
MS	Members States
NGO	Non Governmental Organisation
OECD	Organisation for Economic Co-operation and Development
OJ	Official Journal
OSCE	Organisation for Security and Cooperation in Europe
p.	Page
Para.	Paragraphe
pp.	Pages
PPP	Polluter Pay Principle
PRTR	European Pollutant Release and Transfer Register
REACH	Registration, Evaluation, Authorisation and Restriction of Chemicals
RMA	Resource Management Act
S.I.	Statutory Instruments
SEA Directive	Directive on Strategic Environmental Assessment
TEC	Treaty establishing the European Community
TEU	The Treaty on European Union
TFAJ	Task Force on Access to Justice
TFEU	Treaty on the Functioning of the European Union
UK	United Kingdom
UN	United Nations
UN/ECE	United Nations Economic Commission for Europe
UNCED	United Nations Conference on Environment and Development

UNECE   United Nations Economic Commission for Europe
UNEP   United Nations Environment Programme
UNESCO   United Nations Educational, Scientific and Cultural Organization
UNGA   United Nations General Assembly
UNTS   United Nations Treaties Series
UNU-IAS   United Nations University-Institute of Advanced Studies
           (UNU-IAS)
US   United States
Vol.   Volume
WFD   Water Framework Directive
WWF   World Wildlife Fund
WWF-EPO   WWF European Union Environmental Policy

Introduction

The growing environmental crisis is pushing the citizens of Earth to realise that the world is one and that it has to be protected. This situation increases the pressure for a more universalistic, inclusive creation of a new form of democracy based on an environmental approach. Therefore a variety of questions arise: how can the environmental crisis be resolved? Or, from a legal point of view, how can political and legal structures contribute to the avoidance of environmental damage and threats of an ecological crisis? How can international, national, and local authorities and citizens act and organise themselves to answer to the current ecological crisis?

In my previous book, "*Environmental Democracy at Global Level*", I suggest an answer to the aforementioned questions through the construction of an Environmental Democracy (Parola, 2013). This new form of democracy comes from the attempt to seek a theoretical legal solution without twisting the political system, and finding a different way to use the democratic concept and tools. What is necessary now, rather than the legally asserted and protected rights to the environment, is to put more emphasis upon the adoption and exercise of responsibilities towards all forms of life and a special responsibility to care for the planet. Every individual has to rediscover what environmental rights are; this stems from the fact that s/he exists as a human being and that even without their explicit granting, those rights nevertheless exist a priori. Such moral and ethical acknowledgement has to be included also in the legal concept of the individual, in particular in the notion of citizenship. The new citizenship comprises two aspects: first, environmental citizenship, which entails environmental rights, and second, ecological citizenship, that covers ecological duties.

From a spatial perspective, environmental democracy should be set up at the global level, through international environmental law, and at the local level, through regional and national regulation, to manage global and local ecological problems. The Aarhus Convention on Access to Information, Public Participation in Decision-Making and Access to Justice in Environmental Matters is moving in this direction, and has set up this new form of democracy at the global level.[1]

At the regional level there are also problems which can be resolved only at this level through collaboration and coordination between the states which compose this region.

In the light of the results pointed out in my book, regarding the theoretical construction of environmental democracy and its elements, this book examines environmental democracy at the local level. A complete overview of environmental democracy at the local level would have been too extensive for the framework of this book. Therefore, I have decided to explore environmental democracy in depth by referring to European Union law. As will be analysed in detail, the European Union (EU) is a useful example to explain how the region has found and is still seeking various solutions to the several environmental problems related to the European region and is still working to transform Europe into a Green Europe.[2]

The European Union is the only region which has as its official objective the promotion of economic development, social cohesion and environmental protection at the same time. In fact, there is no other model in the world which brings together the three pillars of sustainability "as ensuring peace, transboundary peaceful cooperation and integration, democracy and elements of an open society, under the government of the rule of law" (Krämer, 2006b, p. 555). Indeed, the EU has developed a number of steps towards positive environmental integration, and, as it will be shown, also towards the construction of an environmental democracy at a local level.

The Aarhus Convention was signed by the European Commission on behalf of the European Community with the intent of ratifying it; however, before this

---

1   See Convention on Access to Information, Public Participation in Decision- Making and Access to Justice in Environmental Matters, Participants, June 25, 1998, 38 I.L.M. 517 (1999), entered into force Oct. 30, 2001.
See in particular about global level: Parola, 2013, Wates, 2005b, p. 393.

2   For instance, the Water Framework Directive is based first on the recognition of the local environmental problems. The recitals also remind us: "In Europe depletion of the water resource has been a continuous process for forty years. Human water uses have increased all over the period, without any consideration of sources initially imagined as self-purifying" (Recital 4 of the WFD). Second this local problem can be solved by "developing an integrated Community policy on water" (Recital 9 of the WFD). Directive 2000/60/EC establishing a framework for Community action in the field of water policy as amended by Decision 2455/2001/EC and Directive 2008/32/EC. See in general about WFD: Aubin, & Varone, 2002, p. 28; Boscheck, 2006, p. 268; Bouleaul, 2008; Kaika, & Page, 2003, p. 314; Kaika, 2003, p. 303; Ker Rault, & Jeffrey, 2008, p. 241; Kostas Bithas, 2008; Moss, 2008; Naddeo, Zarra, & Belgiorno, 2007, p. 243; Peuhkuri, 2006; Rodriguez, 2006.

occurred, the European legislation was necessarily adapted to the rights and obligations contained therein.

In line with this, the three specific rights, called Access to Information, Public Participation in Decision-Making, and Access to Justice, which were set out in the Aarhus Convention, have also emerged and have been implemented by the Member States[3] as well as at the EU level (Douglas-Scott, 1996, p. 109).

Chapter I focuses on the implications of environmental democracy for the EU. It begins by exploring if there is democracy and which kind of democracy exists in the EU, further scrutinising the relationship between Europe and the environment and finally analysing whether a theoretical model of environmental democracy exists in European law; in other words whether the environmental rights and ecological duties can be considered as already existing, and if so, whether there is the basis to construct an environmental and ecological citizenship.

Based on the results of Chapter I, Chapter II gives an overview of the implementation of the substantive provisions in its three pillars' rights, and of the attempts to implement ecological duties, firstly at the EU level and then at the Members States' level.

The goal of Chapter II is not to explain the legislations in detail since the work has already been covered already by numerous scholars, but rather to put emphasis on the fundamental elements regarding the implementation of both the environmental rights and duties emerging from the surface of the different environmental legislations.

---

3   Each EU Member State signed, and with the exception of Ireland has ratified, the Aarhus Convention. Individual member States are therefore obliged to bring their own national legislation into compliance with the Aarhus Convention's requirements. Thus, there is in many cases national legislation implementing the Convention in addition to the EU directives. See in general Krämer, 2006b, p. 555; Roy, 2006, p. 51; Gourtin, 2006, p. 13.

CHAPTER 1

Environmental Democracy in a European Context

Section I: Environmental Democracy in the European Union

"If citizens' participation is the "lifeblood" of democracy,
then the European Union suffers from anaemia and is in desperate need for a
remedy" (Abels, 2008).

1. "Democracy" and "Environment" in the European Union

1.1. "Democracy"

As it is well known, the EU is a new type of organisation:4 it is not a state nor is it a nation, but it is more than a common market and it is not merely an intergovernmental organisation that solves the problems of the Member States.

When the European Economic Community was created in 1957, the question of the democratic nature of the new organisation was not a matter of serious concern and could be assumed to be "absorbed" by the democratic credentials of the delegating Member States.[5] In fact, the initial European Communities

---

4   There is, in fact, a considerable body of literature on the nature of the Community, how it has evolved, and its future direction. See, on this point, Craig, & De Burca, 2008; Cremona, 2004, p. 553; See also Bankowski, & Christodoulidis, 1998, p. 341. On the European constitutionalization process: Von Bogdandy, 2005, p. 913; Wessels, & Diedrichs, 1997.

5   There are also disagreements among scholars about its nature. "Is it a functional intergovernmental cooperation mechanism between Member States? Is it a 'supranational community' of shared values and 'constitutional tolerance'? Maybe an experiment in the cosmopolitan ideals of a 'post-national' or a 'pluralistic' polity? Or is it a technocratic

were based on a *"permissive consensus"* (Lindberg, & Scheingold, 1970, p. 41; Smismans, 2009), and since then, little by little, it has become a polity which performs functions that affect the interests and identities of the European citizens as well as the Member States. Hence, the EU started to feel a lack of democratic basis and understood that it could no longer draw on indirect legitimacy. Consequently, it tried to establish direct links with its citizens, increasing its structures and processes in a more democratic way, in particular through participatory mechanisms.

The intention here is not to advocate one of the myriad approaches to democracy in Europe, but to try to identify how EU law is dealing with the problem of democratic deficit, or as some authors have called it with an "infringed popular will" (Zampetti, 1995, p. 11), and which solutions it has already found (Balme, & Chanet, 2008).

1.1.1. Democratic Deficit in the EU

To start, it is interesting to recall what Beck wrote arguing that "if the EU were to apply for membership of the EU it would be rejected because of its lack of democratic structures!" (Beck, 1998).

This joke comes from a real deficit of democracy, which has been remarked upon for a long time by most scholars,[6] who define democratic deficit, even if not by all,[7] as a "myth propagated by eurosceptic circles" (Moussis, 2009, p.

'problem-solving agent' established to solve the transnational governance problems of an economic and technocratic nature? The technocratic vision has indeed, for a long time, dominated both the public and scholarly debate on the EC/EU: is it an elite game in the hands of economic interests and bureaucrats?": see Rodriquez, 2008, p. 24.

6   The public debates on democracy became prominent in the period preceding and immediately following the negotiations for the Maastricht Treaty, which "notwithstanding high hopes, and indeed some progress, notably failed to address these questions" (De Burca, 1996, p. 349) and eighteen years later, the debate is as lively as ever. Lee, 2003, p. 195.

7   A word must be said about the position which denies a democratic deficit. Following two approaches there is no democratic legitimacy deficit: firstly the community only executes closely circumscribed functional decisions, which member states have agreed to by democratic means. This view has been defended by Majone who consider the EU as a 'regulatory state' (Majone, 1996) "Regulatory policies, such as competition policy, the removal of trade barriers or monetary policy, are destined to address and redress market failures. For those policies to be effective, they have to be taken in an undemocratic fashion in the sense that they are excluded from the adversarial power play of parliamentary, majoritarian politics. Otherwise, decisions would be unduly politicised whereby their credibility and Pareto-efficient effects would be undermined and the Eu's (out) legitimacy would suffer". (Majone, 2000, p. 273; Majone, 2002, p. 319).

For H.-Peter IPSEN the then EC constitutes a regulatory agency "our fourth branch of government which fulfils clearly specified functional goals and hence offers no room for

145). Nevertheless, most authors judge that even though democratic structures are in place at the EU level, such as a directly elected parliament, the EU has a democratic deficit. Dahl, one of the most famous democratic theorists even calls it "gigantic" (Dahl, 1998, p. 115).

Although the term "democratic deficit" encompasses a number of different features,[8] for current purposes it is worth noting that it is possible to identify two principal elements, one linked to the other and both underpinning the democratic deficit of the EU: first there is the issue relating to transparency and second to the legitimacy of decisions.

The transparency problem emerged from the influence of the "administrative tradition of continental Europe" (Jendroska, 2006, p. 63) where access to governmental information and public participation in decision-making was not known to many European administrative cultures and where their custom of secrecy was used to block a possible citizens' involvement.

The role of the individual was narrow, merely entailing the right to vote: and this was the only kind of relationship between the state and its citizens. In fact, the state was considered for a long time as "a structure which expresses and creates the unity of the nation rather than as a forum for the competition of

---

political discretion". (Kohler-Kock, & Rittberger, 2007b, p. 4); secondly some authors assert individuals are better off from a rights perspective. According to Ernst-Joachim Mestmacker the community is set up on an economic constitution which derives its legitimation from the creation of a free market and the notion of free movement which empowers individuals as it extends their individual rights and freedoms (Mestmacker, 1994, p. 615). Mestmacker concludes that "as long as political procedures are consistent with existing national democratic practice and have a prima facie normative justification [...] we cannot draw negative conclusions about the legitimacy of the EU from casual observation of the non-participatory nature of its institutions". Mestmacker, 1994, p. 622.
See also Majone, 1998, p. 5; Crum, 2005, p. 452. On the matter, see also Craig, 1997, p. 105.
8   In 1996 Craig and Burca (1999, p. 23) distinguished among a number of reasons to explain what it was democratic deficit: "There is what may be termed the distance issues. The existence of the Community has involved the transfer of competence on many issues to Brussels and away from the nation state. This has meant that, in a literal sense, matters are further removed from the citizens. It has also been a factor in questioning the Community's legitimacy: Why should 'those people over there be making decisions which affect me over here?' [...] An equally important facet of the democracy deficit argument is the executive dominance issue. The transfer of competence to the Community enhances the power of the executive at the expense of parliamentary bodies. [...]. A third feature of the democratic deficit is the by-passing of democratic argument. This is applied most frequently to the operation of the EC's complex committee structure, known generally as comitology. Many technical, but important, regulations are made by committees established pursuant to a delegation of power to the commission [...]. A fourth aspect of democracy deficit can be termed the transparency and complexity issue. Traditionally much of the decision-making of the community, particularly that of the council has taken place behind closed doors. In addition the very complexity of the legislative procedures means that it is virtually impossible for anyone, other than an expert to understand them".

different interests of individuals, social groups and organisations" (Jendroska, 2006, p. 63).

Consequently, the law was understood as a "common interest"; in other words, the interest of the whole society and not an outcome of a social compromise between the interests of different groups. In fact, European societies were not accustomed to considering the relationship between the state and its citizens in "contractual terms" (Jendroska, 2005, p. 12).

Hence, this traditional approach has been maintained at the national level until not so long ago and still influences the European level (Roberts, 2002, p. 255). It has been proposed that the secrecy approach is not beneficial or justifiable anymore, in particular because almost all of the members which influenced this custom have already changed their own secrecy approach, responding to the new expectations and demands coming from society, and thus, they are moving towards a concept of open governance.

Nevertheless, it is worth noting that the perception that "secrecy leads to mistrust, and that openness is the way to regain public confidence in government action" has appeared also in EU discussions and policies concerning public participation for a long time (Roberts, 2002, p. 255). An example is the access to information in the EU, which has moved "from a culture of secrecy, relating to the diplomatic nature of international decision-making, through voluntary initiatives, to formal legal obligations of access to Community documents" (Lee, 2005, p. 127-128). Indeed the introduction at the EU level of legislation on general access to documents, as will be shown in the following sections, seems to assume that openness has an inherent value, and is related to making decisions close to the citizens' interests.

The second component of democratic deficit attributed to the EU as well as to domestic policy-making is essentially an "accountability and legitimacy deficit" (Heinel, 2007, p. 224). This is a complex debate, embracing different issues: first the European project itself does not have the support of the European people; and second, there is a concern that the methods and procedures by which the EU institutions reach decisions are not subject to democratic principles (Lee, 2003, p. 207).

The reason for the situation as described above is that at the time of its foundation and in the earlier stages of its development, European integration was "largely an elite project" (Lee, 2003, p. 207), hence, EU decision-making was a matter for high officials. Government ministers and citizens had no formal participatory role.

Nevertheless, the situation has started to change since the EU has been taking a deeper interest in the European citizens and also has introduced the theories of "Direct effect" and "Supremacy", as defined by the European Court of

Justice (ECJ).[9] The consequences of EU action in more policy areas and the daily

---

9   The EEC Treaty, signed in Rome on 25 March 1957, was mainly aimed at economic progress. Expression of other aims was, however, in its preambles, which posted economic integration as a means to a better end, rather than as the sole end in itself. The material limits of the Community jurisdiction were not precisely defined by the Treaty. Nevertheless, the relatively open provisions and the aims stated in the preambles of the Treaty gave the ECJ extensive possibilities for a broad and instrumentalist interpretation of Community Law. Mechanisms of enforcing EC laws have evolved in an attempt to provide ways which enable the law of this international Treaty to be respected by the signatory Member States (MS) and enforceable by the individuals in that State to whom these obligations and rights are applicable. These mechanisms began with Direct Effect whereby the primary laws of the Treaty could be given effect directly in the MS' domestic courts. The question regarding Direct Effect first arose in 1956 in relation to the ECSC Treaty, but was later posed on a much larger scale within the framework on the EEC Treaty, when the Court passed its ground breaking judgment Van Gend en Loos (Case 26/62, NV Algemene Transport- en Expeditie Onderneming van Gend en Loos v. Nederlandse Administratie der Belastingen [1963] ECR 1). The Court stated: "The Community constitutes a new legal order of international law for the benefit of which the States have limited their sovereign rights, albeit within limited fields, and the subjects of which comprise not only MS but also their nationals. Independently of the legislation of MS, Community law therefore not only imposes obligations on individuals but is also intended to confer upon them rights which become part of their legal heritage. These rights arise not only where they are expressly granted by the Treaty, but also by reason of obligations which the Treaty imposes in a clearly defined way upon individuals as well as upon MS and upon the Institutions of the Community". Then the Court set up four conditions for the Direct Effect of Treaty provisions: it must be clear, unconditional, containing no reservation on the part of the Member State, and not dependent on any national implementing measure.

One year later, in the Case Costa v. ENEL (Case 6/64, Flamino Costa v. ENEL [1964] ECR 585.) the Court affirmed and developed its constitutional theory of the Community where the national law was in conflict with a provision of EC law. In this case the Court concluded that Community law had to be given primacy by national Courts over any incompatible national law Subsequently other cases developed the doctrines of Direct Effect and supremacy into firmly embodied foundations of EC law (Case 11/70 Internationale Handelsgesellschaft mbH v. Einfuhr- und Vorratsstelle für Getreide und Futtermittel [1970] ECR 1125; Case 106/77, Amministrazione delle Finanze dello Stato v. Simmenthal SpA [1978] ECR 629, [1978] 3).

Subsequently also the enforcement mechanisms of Direct Effect and Indirect Effect were not successful in ensuring EC laws were being upheld and observed, and the distinction between Horizontal Direct Effect and Vertical Direct Effect was "causing potential embarrassment for the validity of this method of enforcing EC rights" (There was then the extension of doctrine of Direct Effect to secondary laws such as Directives (Spa SACE v. Italian Ministry of Finance, Case 33/70) [1970] ECR 1213), but limited to the Vertical direction; this was followed by the enforcement mechanism of Indirect Effect (Von Colson v. Land Nordrhein-Westfalen (Case 14/83) [1984] ECR 1891), which was necessary as a consequence of the ECJ not allowing Direct Effect to be used Horizontally and is a process of purposive statutory interpretation (Litster v. Forth Dry Dock and Engineering Co. Ltd 1 All ER 1134; [1990] 1 A.C. 546"). In fact the 'useful effect' (from the French effet utile) rationale for Direct Effect requires a remedy where private individuals fail to respect provisions of EC law. The ECJ recognised problems it had in ensuring EC law was being followed as required and had been widely criticised by academics and other commentators for denying Horizontal Direct Effect. It hence established the alternative remedy of State Liability to alleviate these criticisms. To circumvent the limitations of the doctrine of horizontal Direct

impact of the European integration process put forth evidence that merely the EU structure remains unsatisfying for addressing the legitimacy of the European construction (Smismans, 2009).

Until the need to participate at an EU level and the possibility for citizens to exert influence over the policies which affect their daily lives is recognised, the democratic deficit will continue to persist (Parry, 2010).

1.1.2. The Remedies of Democratic Deficit

So, how can this European democratic deficit be remedied? The democratic deficit approach is divided between doctrines which see the democratic deficit "virtually insurmountable given the inherent limitations in the EU's democratic capacity" and those "who claim that it can be resolved or at least attenuated through constitutional engineering in the short to medium term" (Kohler-Kock, & Rittberger, 2007a, p. 1).

The EU has tried to answer to the democratic deficit by undertaking different paths. In particular, two measures have been put into place to implement the slogan 'Europe closer to the citizens'[10]: first, the extension of control through representative tools, and the extension of the roles of the National Parliament and European Parliament in decision-making. The second involves deliberative and participative measures to increase the opportunities for public involvement in EU decision-making (Hallo, 2008, pp. 10-11). For instance, internet consultations as well as other measures to grant the participative right via the right of access to documents held by Community institutions.[11]

As will be explained in the following section, it was only recently that Europe started with these above-mentioned ways, reforming the system and consequently departing from the traditional "thin democracy" towards a more

---

Effect, the ECJ developed a general principle of state responsibility for compliance with EC law. State liability derives from the fact that EU MS, or emanations of the state, are responsible for the creation and above all for the implementation and enforcement of EC law. Many EU rights, particularly those in the many Directives in the fields of employment and industrial relations, are enforced through the doctrine of Direct Effect of Directives. This doctrine was created by a case in the field of employment rights: Francovich and Others v. Italian Republic. (Cases C-6 and 9/90 Francovich and Bonifaci v. Italy [1991] ECR I-5357. See Caranta, 1993, p. 272; Craig, 1996, p. 399; Harlow, 1996, p. 199; Parker, 1992, p.181; ROSS, 1993, p. 55. See also Anagnostaras, 2001, p. 281; Thorvaldsson, 2002.

10   The slogan has been mentioned in the programme Europe for Citizens available at www.europeforcitizens.ie

11   This right was introduced to the EC Treaty in 1999, Article 255, and specified in Regulation 1049/2001 regarding public access to European Parliament, council and commission documents, OJ 2001, L 145, p.43. Hallo, 2008, pp.10-11; Hallo, 2007; See also Heinelt, 2007, p. 224.

open government. This changed approach, more deliberative and participatory, was influenced by many factors, one important factor being the need for environmental protection. As has been underlined, it is not a coincidence that environmental law was the first to recognise procedural rights within the EU (Jendroska, 2006, p. 63).

1.1.2.1. Representative Democracy Tools

Whether representative democracy is the ultimate legitimation of the legislative and administrative process or a symbol of governance according to the will of the people (Mathiesen, 2003, p. 36), both the European Parliament and National Parliaments are potential reform targets to "alleviate the democratic legitimacy deficit" (Rittberger, 2007, p. 133).

Thus, the initial concern for the 'democratic deficit' of the EU focused on the need of a popular involvement via the European Parliament. Such direct parliamentary representation of European citizens was introduced by direct elections for the European Parliament in 1979, and subsequent changes increased its powers – budgetary and legislative powers (from consultation to co-operation and co-decision procedure), and control over the Commission.

Moreover, the Parliament has increased its influence in the European law-making process, through expansion of the co-decision procedure under former Article 252 of the EC Treaty, which has become the standard procedure through which regulations and directives are deliberated and decided upon, and in which the Parliament is assigned a veto power, and in that sense, a co-legislative role.[12] Furthermore, a significant change made by the Lisbon Treaty[13] concerns an extension of the decision-making powers of the European Parliament as well. Co-decision is henceforth known as the ordinary legislative procedure and has been expanded to more policy areas leaving few over which the Parliament only enjoys a consultative role.[14]

Although the expansion of the role of the European Parliament to decrease the democratic deficit was useful, an element is missing: namely, a European

12   Rodriquez, 2008, p. 24; On this issue, see amplius Menendez, 2005, p. 105. On the co-decision procedure, see Pennera, & Schoo, 2004, p. 531. On the co-decision procedure as laid down in the Treaty establishing a Constitution for the Union, see Daswood, & Johnston, 2004, p. 1481. On this issue, see Farrell, & Heritier, 2002.

13   As of the Treaty of Lisbon (2007) (OJ 2007 C 306/01), in force 1 Dec. 2009, the European Union replaces and succeeds the European Community.

14   Although most environmental policy is already subject to co-decision making environmentally related areas in which the new 'ordinary legislative procedure' applies include aspects of transport, energy, fisheries, external trade, regional and agricultural policy. Benson, & Jordan, 2008, p. 280.

demos which could provide the basis for a parliamentary expression of democracy. Indeed, the parliamentary model is based on an expression of the general will and in order to deduce such, the governed who are represented in parliament should have a certain level of social unity and a common identity; that is, a general acceptance of the 'idea of Europe' and "a commitment to the shared values of the Union as expressed in its constituent documents" (Kaelble, 1994, p. 27; Weile, 1997, p. 249).

For some authors, there is no such common identity in the EU, and, as Article 1 of the EU Treaty states, the EU is still based on a process of integration "*among the peoples of Europe*". The creation of a common identity seems to crystallise very slowly (Risse, 2002), and because of this a European 'public sphere' in which citizens are informed on, and take part in political discussions does not exist; also, a truly European media remains lacking. Communication on European issues which is not nationally coloured is a further default, complicated by being split into different languages.

Moreover, European political parties are weak and turnout in EP elections is uneven and low (Smismans, 2009; 2003, p. 473; 2004, p. 122). Although interest groups ought to expand their action to the European level, they remain mainly national interest groups.

Some authors see the expansion of the control and role of National Parliaments as a remedy for this democratic deficit, constituting a growing involvement of National Parliaments in EU policy-making. The main reason of this idea is that the National Parliaments should formulate the will of the Member States' people (Auel, & Benz, 2007, p. 57)[15] and it is "the most important mechanism linking the citizens to the EU, because it translates the views of the citizens into European policy" (Andeweg, 2007, p. 102). Furthermore, since the Lisbon Treaty has been ratified, National Parliaments have a more direct role, as they can block European legislative initiatives for not respecting subsidiarity. However, the threshold for them to be able to do so is high because one third of all National Parliaments need to vote in this sense within a short time limit of eight weeks.

Despite all of these means found within the representative democracy model being somewhat useful in avoiding part of the democratic deficit, they are nevertheless insufficient to improve and create democratic accountability in the European Union (Smismans, 2009). Indeed, the improvement of representative democracy in Europe addresses only part of the issues relating to the democratic deficit. A territorially elected parliament cannot represent the whole of its electorate's personalities and interests, given that individuals are potentially

---

15 See also Maurer, 2007, p. 75.

infinite in their purpose and wills, in particular if this election is a European election.

Thus, something more is therefore needed: democracy must become more inter-active with citizen participation in the current debates. In this respect, a continuous role of individuals is vital and the involvement of civil society organisations (Smismans, 2003, p. 473)[16] may also constitute a step towards greater and more effective participation in the EU and an improvement of openness (Parry, 2010). If in a democracy, sovereignty ultimately rests with the individual citizen, then their political leaders have a duty to involve them in what is happening in their name.

Then the most efficient tool to decrease the democratic deficit and strengthen the link among citizens is to increase public participation with the final aim of creating the basis for constructing a European *demos*. The Lisbon Treaty, which in some way is taking this path, reinforces the significance of 'participation' in political life generally.

In summary, it can be said that participatory mechanisms through which citizens are able to act can serve as a complementary mechanism to traditional parliamentary representation. (Smismans, 2009)

1.1.2.2. Participatory and Deliberatory Tools

Before starting, it is necessary to note that a broad meaning of public participation is appropriate and at the EU level includes "open and transparent procedures and decisions, consultation or more intense involvement in decisions, which could encompass also the element of deliberative democracy" (Lee, 2005, p. 114). Recent years have seen a remarkable consensus concerning the need for participatory democracy in decision-making at the EU level.

---

16   European civil society can be described as multiform, multi- dimensional and multilevel". Armstrong, 2002, p. 113. By multiform, "we refer to a pluralistic understanding of the forms of civil society moving from the civic participation of the individual, through loose networks of actors, to formalised and enduring organisational structures. By multidimensional, we can think of the different roles played by civil society actors from the promotion of political deliberation, through more, or less, structured processes of consultation and participation (participatory democracy), to direct roles in the de- livery of governance. By multilevel, we mean the inclusion of the diverse structures and traditions of national civil society actors, together with any sub-national and transnational actors. A narrower definition of European civil society would encompass only some of these elements". See Rodriquez, 2008, p. 24. See also Armstrong, 2008. The author recalls the Craig civil society concept: "Civil society, connoting in this context networks, movements, etc., which organise to assert interests outside state-based and controlled political institutions, is accorded an important role in the deliberative process. Participatory democracy is thus seen as starting from the bottom up, from 'groups of people dedicated to the disinterested search for the public interest in society": Craig, 1999, p. 41.

Despite some authors denying this,[17] the path towards more participatory procedure is now seen as a possibility to improve the legitimacy of decision-making, possessing the potential to provide a response to the disputed democratic deficit of EU law and effectiveness at the EU level. The involvement of individuals in the decision-making process at the European level aims at decreasing the democratic deficit by: "expanding the knowledge base to increase the quality of EU policies; making public administration accountable to society as a whole; achieving an all-embracing mobilisation of political interests and enhancement of direct participation of citizens; creating a trans-national democratic public sphere" (Kohler-Kock, 2007b, p. 255).

Given the limits of understanding EU democracy merely in terms of the parliamentary model, participatory democracy can contribute to EU democracy. Although instances of direct citizen participation will be limited in impact, they are desirable for contributing to a European public sphere. Thus, the objective is therefore to "make Europe more relevant to its citizens", "to regenerate a European spirit" and "to give incentive for a shared willingness to bring forward the European project" (Kohler-Kock, 2004, p. 5).

Indeed there are numerous proposals for the enhancement of democracy by involving the public, and attention is given to a range of alternative participatory instruments, as well as explicit appeals being made for deliberative processes. In order to increase the level of democracy, the creation of a political means that could provide citizens opportunities for participation, influence and control has been suggested (Dahl, 1998, p. 115).

Among different deliberative instruments, the most interesting for this discussion are citizens' forums and citizens' initiatives. One example has been called e-democracy, which by use of electronic consultation processes allows for a new form of direct citizen involvement. The second citizens' initiative will be analysed later.

A collective political identity shared by the peoples in Europe could be necessary, according to some scholars who have commented on introducing these tools, and who also consider that Europe still doesn't have this characteristic, since European states have distinct "national histories each with its own interpretations of the past and own languages" (Kohler-Kock, & Rittberger, 2007, p. 1).

---

17   Some scholars held that there is no consensus in Europe on the legitimacy of representation outside of political *parties* and the electoral process and that "without wider agreement, voluntary associations and interest groups should not be given a court-enforced right to participate [...] in Community policy- making", Bignami, 2004, p. 61; See also De Leeuw, 2007, p. 295.

For other scholars, the above-mentioned deliberative instruments could enhance democracy and civil dialogue. Concerning civil dialogue, it may be noted that European institutions have set up the European Commission and the European Economic and Social Committee which have to achieve this aim.[18] Civil dialogue is, in fact, considered another "instrument to revitalise civil society, to encourage more social interaction and to create an open and transnational public space, which together form the prerequisite for a European wide civil society". A transnational public space and a "vibrant Pan-European civil society would therefore be the very basis for a thriving European democracy" (Kohler-Kock, 2004). Thus, enhanced consultation procedures are perceived as a means to remedy also the situation of "governance without government" (Getliffe, 2002, p. 101) that Demmke (Demmke, 1998) describes as the "post-parliamentary age" whereby decisions are taken by committees made up of national civil servants, resulting in reduced levels of transparency.

---

18   "The origin of civil dialogue is to be found in detail in the development of EU social policy. The language of civil dialogue emerged from debates surrounding the Commission's Green and White Paper on European Social Policy of the early 1990s and the desire for a broader forum for discussion on the future of social policy. The result was the convening of the first European Social Policy Forum in March 1996. This is often viewed as the start of civil dialogue, bringing together over 1,000 participants mainly from NGOs in the social sphere. The Forum is considered "the launch of a new policy objective: the building over time of a strong civil dialogue at European level to take its place alongside the policy dialogue with the national authorities and the social dialogue with the social partners" (Commission, 'Communication on Promoting the role of voluntary organisations and foundations in Europe', 6 June 1997, COM (97), 241 final). "In its 1997 Communication on Promoting the Role of Voluntary Organisations and Foundations in Europe, the Commission indicated the importance of the Forum for the development of a civil dialogue with the aims of: a) ensuring that "the views and grassroots experience of the voluntary sector can be systematically taken into account by policymakers at the European level so that policies can be tailored more to meet real needs"; b) disseminating "information from the European level down to the local level so that citizens are aware of developments, can feel part of the construction of Europe and can see the relevance of it to their own situation, thus increasing transparency and promoting citizenship". In its Communication on Strategic Objectives (2000-2005), entitled Shaping the New Europe, the Commission claimed that it: Wants to find a new synergy between all the European Union's democratic bodies, as part of a broader improvement of European governance. We want to strike a new balance between action by the Commission, the other institutions, the Member States and civil society. Our aim is to bring Europe much closer to the people. In 2000, the Commission published a Discussion Paper: "The Commission and non-governmental organisations: building a stronger partnership". The paper found its place within the context of an administrative reform of the European Commission established by Commission President Prodi and Vice-President Kinnock in response to problems of legitimacy crisis. It stressed the valuable NGO contribution to the development of legitimate European governance and specified some considerations about the cooperation between the Commission and NGOs and about the role of these organisations", Rodriquez, 2008, p. 24.

1.1.3. The Treaty Instruments to Participate

As a response to the slim victories and defeats in some referenda which were held in the aftermath of the Maastricht Treaty negotiations and the decreasing popular support for the European integration project,[19] the European Institutions have tried to find other means of improving democracy. The heads of states and governments called for "a Union closer to the citizens",[20] because they were aware that classical arrangements, such as political parties, parliamentary assemblies, or other representative bodies, and also the lack of public space,[21] could no longer provide sufficient mechanisms of democratisation in terms of representing the will of the people.

One initiative which proves this new goal was the well-known "Commission White Paper on European Governance" 2001.[22] The message was the necessity to reform European governance connecting "Europe with its citizens" and renewing "the Community method by following a less top-down approach and complementing its policy tools more effectively with non-legislative instruments".[23]

In fact, the White Paper contains elements which "strongly mirror the tenets of the model of advocacy democracy by emphasising the prominence of non-electoral channels for citizens participation" (Kohler-Kock, & Rittberger, 2007a, p. 10). In particular, the White Paper recognises five principles underlying the notion of good governance: Openness, Participation, Accountability, Effectiveness

19   This data was indicated by the Eurobarometer surveys since the early 1990s.

20   Turin Council: White Paper on the 1996 Intergovernmental Conference, 29 March 1996, Vol. II, internet.

21   "A 'Public Space' is defined as an arena of communication in which those who govern and those who are subject to governance in a given legally constituted polity gather and express particular interests, concerns, and expectations that interfere with political decision making. So the public space thus initiates a process in which political decision making is mediated through public opinion and collective will formation. In this sense a public space provides a mechanism of democratization. The way in which it distributes chances of access, arena of debates, and links to the institutionalized system of political decision making finally indicates a polity's degree of democratization". See for this definition Eder, & Trenz, 2007, p.167.

22   On the definition of the term "governance", see European Commission Work Programme, white Paper on European Governance: Enhancing Democracy in the European Union, SEC (2000) 1547/7, 11 October 2000. See Wind, 2009; Jørgensen, 1997; Schout, & Jordan, 2005, p. 201; Möllers, 2006, p. 313.

23   "The Commission already adhered to that principle when preparing and launching the White Paper: In the preparatory phase it engaged in extensive consultations with representatives of organised interests and the academic community, it organised and stimulated a broad public debate after publication, and since then provides incentives for more thorough investigations on the conditions of the linkages between European citizenship, civil society and EU democracy", Kohler-Kock, & Rittberger, 2007a, p. 10.

and Coherence.[24] The first two are most important because they are the main ground on which participative and deliberative democracy can develop and are also the principles to which the White Paper mainly refers in order to assure good governance: Openness, which primarily means active communication by the institutions as well as making governmental decisions more accessible and understandable.

Better information and transparency of EU policy-making shall be supplemented by improving consultation and dialogue not just with territorial and functional interests but also with civil society groups and individual citizens. A range of instruments is suggested and has been put into practice in the last few years: for instance, "the opening up of advisory committees to civil society, business test panels, and venues for ad hoc and on-line consultation" (Kohler-Kock, & Rittberger, 2007a, p. 10). Thus, Openness in terms of improved transparency is, in fact, a prerequisite for public accountability, and openness in terms of better access to decision-making bodies is a pre-condition for political participation" (Rodriquez, 2008, p. 61).

The second important principle is the notion of Participation. This element is mainly ensured through wide involvement throughout the whole policy process; as it has been argued, the fundamental importance of this principle is that it "should help policy makers to stay in touch with European public opinion, and could guide them in identifying European projects which mobilise public support". Moreover, the role of the European civil society is viewed as support to representative democracy through the European Parliament, rather than as an alternative.

As the Commission put it: "the aim is for participatory democracy to be reconciled as much as possible with representative democracy in order to increase the acceptability and effectiveness of European decisions". In the following years, other statements about the necessity to enhance openness, transparency and participation have been launched; however a detailed analysis of these issues remains outside the scope of this book.[25]

---

24   Accountability entails that institutions and Member States explain their actions and take the necessary responsibility for such actions; Effectiveness requires that policies are effective and timely, with clear objectives, and evaluation of their future and past impact, and are pursued at the proper level and implemented in a proportionate way; Coherence necessitates that policies and actions cross the boundaries of sectorial policies, are performed with a clear view as to overall consistency and are more easily understood. See also Heldeweg, 2005, p. 3.

25   See the European Transparency Initiative" (ETI) November 2005. The Initiative is intended to "build on a series of transparency-related measures already put in place by the Commission, in particular those taken as part of the overall reforms being implemented since 1999 and in the White Paper on European Governance. Major achievements in this

Nevertheless, what is crucial to summarise is that the suggestions made by the White Paper represent an innovative theoretical construction; also in practice, the mechanisms of deliberative and participatory democracy have remained rather "rudimentary" (Shaw, 2000, p. 382).

It is clear that the White Paper does not give the answer to all issues. However, in spite of its shortcomings it is, at least, a beginning; indeed, a trend towards democratisation through strengthening the role of the European citizen can be found since the Treaty of Maastricht up to the recent Lisbon Treaty. The participatory instruments introduced at the EU level to resolve the democratic deficit can be identified: firstly, access to information, secondly, public participation and finally, access to justice.

1.1.3.1. Access to Environmental Information

The call for more transparency and democratisation (Frost, 2003, p. 89) of the EU's decision-making process was met by the publication of a Commission paper on Openness in the Community,[26] which in turn led to the Code of Conduct on access to documents, later implemented by two decisions: one by the Commission[27] and another by the Council.[28]

Later, the Treaty of Amsterdam[29] provided further steps to complete the regime on access to the Institutions' documents by inserting former Article 255 into the EC Treaty. This Article stated that "*Any Union citizen and any natural or legal person residing or having a registered office in a member state, shall have a right of access to European Parliament, Council and Commission documents*".

---

field are: a) the "access to documents" legislation, which provides the framework for access to the unpublished documents of the EU institutions and bodies through register of documents or following individual requests. b) the launch of databases providing information about consultative bodies and expert groups advising the Commission; c) wide consultation of stakeholders and in-depth impact assessments prior to legislative proposals; d) the Commission's "Code of Good Administrative Behaviors", which is its benchmark for quality service in its relations with the public. Moreover, the Commission adopted a new "Green Paper on a European Transparency Initiative" on May 3rd 2006. The Commission emphasized, in particular, that 'inherent in the idea of partnership is consultation and participation'. By the same token, the Commission stressed the importance of a 'high level of transparency' to ensure that the Union is 'open to public scrutiny and accountable for its work'. Rodriquez, 2008, p. 61.

26   COM (93) 258 final, OJ C 166/5, 2 June 1993.

27   Decision 94/90, (1994) OJ L 340/41.

28   Decision 93/371, (1993) OJ L 340/43.

29   Treaty of Amsterdam, OJ C 340 of 10.11.1997. The Treaty was signed on 2 October 1997 and entered into force on 1 May 1999.

It further established that a new legally binding regime on access to documents should be implemented by May 2001. Indeed, as will be analysed in the following paragraph, legislation, namely the "Transparency Regulation", was adopted on May 30, 2001 and entered into force on December 3, 2001.[30]

Ex Article 255 EC, in granting this right, has given citizens increased protection. In fact, it is an explicit implementation and manifestation of Article 1 of the Treaty on the European Union when it states: "*This Treaty marks a new stage in the process of creating an ever closer union among the peoples of Europe, in which decisions are taken as closely as possible to the citizen*" (Schram, 2005, p. 24).

The Nice Treaty[31] did not change anything further but moved on in the same direction and introduced a non-legally binding Charter of Fundamental Rights[32] which establishes in its Article 42 that "*Any citizen of the Union, and any natural or legal person residing or having its registered office in a Member State, has a right of access to the European Parliament, Council and Commission's documents*" (De Abreu Ferreira, 2007b, p. 399).

The scope of both Article 42 and former 255 is narrow: first, it excludes non-citizens and non-resident natural or legal persons from the access to information, and secondly, existing commitments to transparency under former Article 255, in this first version of the provision, covered only the Commission, Council and European Parliament and not all European institutions and bodies (Kiss, 2008, p. 161).

1.1.3.2. Public Participation in Environmental Matters

1.1.3.2.1. White Paper on European Governance
Some steps have been made to increase participation as well, and important steps were taken through the measures used to implement the White Paper on European Governance, although with limited outcome (Heldeweg, 2005, p. 2). For instance, the Economic and Social Committee[33] has successfully launched

---

30   Regulation (EC) N° 1049/2001 of the European Parliament and of the Council of 30 May 2001 regarding public access to European Parliament, Council and Commission documents, OJ L 145, 31.5.2001, p. 43, available at www.eur-lex.europa.eu/LexUriServ/LexUriServ.douri=CELEX:32001R1049:EN:TML.
See Von Unger, 2007, p. 440.

31   Treaty of Nice, OJ C 80, 10 March 2001. The Treaty was signed 26th February 2001 and entered into force on 1 February 2003.

32   Charter of Fundamental Rights of the EU, OJ C 364/1, 18 December 2000. The Charter of Fundamental Rights is the result of a joint proclamation, by the Council, the European Parliament and the Commission at the Nice Council.

33   This role for EESC is recognised in former Article 257 EC which gives EESC the role of representing "the various economic and social components of organised civil society". "In

different kinds of initiatives; it has pressed ahead with the opening up to a broader and mainly EU-level public audience, which serve both as platforms and contact points for advocacy networks (Kohler-Kock, 2007b, p. 260).

The Committee has introduced the instrument of online consultations as well. Thus, every proposal that is to be decided upon is made public, "every citizen and every organisation is invited to comment, every petition can be read online, and the Commission reports about the results at the end of the process" (Kohler-Kock, 2007b, p. 260). But unfortunately, those forums of consultation do not live up to the expectations of participative democracy and deliberative democracy.[34] For instance the European Consultative Forum on the Environment and Sustainable Development (ECFESD) was scarcely consulted by the Commission and, during its first four years of existence, only on two occasions was able to reach out to the larger public (Kohler-Kock, 2007b, p. 255).

1.1.3.2.2. Constitution for Europe and the Following Plan "D"

The idea of the White Paper to give citizens a voice and to open civil dialogue influenced the development which followed it toward a participatory and deliberatory democracy in the EU Treaty. In particular, an important step in this direction could have been the inclusion of the principle of participation in the 2004 Treaty establishing a Constitution for Europe.[35]

Indeed the Constitutional Treaty in its first part 'the democratic life of the Union' contained a provision on representative democracy: "*the functioning of*

September 1999, EESC produced an own-initiative opinion on the role and contribution of civil society organisation in the building of Europe in advance of the First Convention of civil society organised at European level, arranged by EESC in October 1999. The 1999 Opinion is interesting in setting out a broad overview of the multiform, multidimensional and, to a more limited extent, multilevel nature of European civil society. Of particular interest are the attributes which the Opinion attaches to civil society in terms of its pluralism (the self-organisation of society into diverse social group), autonomy (the free-will of individuals to engage in social action, albeit framed by the wider constitutional framework of the state), solidarity (action in the common interest), public awareness (creation of a climate of social communication), participation (within and outside the political system)": Rodriquez, 2008, p. 67; Armstrong, 2002, p. 113.

34 For example the European Consultative Forum on the Environment and Sustainable Development (ECFESD): "even though its structures meet the demands for equal geographical and political representation, openness and transparency, it neither lived up to the standard of deliberation not did it bring about increased participation of interested actors". See Kohler-Kock, 2007b, p. 262.

35 Among the others, see Fossum, & Menendez, 2005, p. 380; Barbi, 2005; Birkin-Shaw, 2004, p. 57; Cremona, 2003, p. 1347; Tizzano, 2003, p. 249; Kokott, & Rüth, 2003, p. 1315; Closa, 2005, p. 145; Daswood, & Johnston, 2004, p. 1481; Peters, 2004, p. 37; J. Bering Liisberg, 2010; Abromeit, & Wolf, 2005.

the Union shall be founded on representative democracy" (Article I-45),[36] and a provision on 'participatory democracy'(Article I-46) which explicitly mentioned: *"The Institutions shall, by appropriate means, give citizens and representative associations the opportunity to make known and publicly exchange their views in all areas of Union action"* and Paragraph 2 affirms *"The Institutions shall maintain an open, transparent and regular dialogue with representative associations and civil society".* The adoption of the principle of participation was interpreted by scholars as a new effort to integrate the idea of direct and close cooperation between EU institutions and European civil society (Kohler-Kock, 2007b, p. 255).

Other important elements introduced by the European Constitution, were citizens' initiatives, which reflect the idea of deliberative democracy, as also held by the Lisbon Treaty, into the overall representative structure of the EU.[37]

This instrument was new for the EU democracy, but unfortunately very weak since the initiatives can only invite the Commission to consider it without a mandatory obligation to follow it, and they are also restricted to issues which are required for the purpose of implementing the constitution (Kohler-Kock, & Rittberger, 2007a, p. 1). Moreover, as some commentators have pointed out, there is "a significant danger that political and economic elites (could) drive, if not manipulate the process, weakening rather than enhancing legitimacy" (Lee, 2005, p. 120).

Lee has underlined another weakness linked to the protection of minorities: "the minimum number of Member States whose citizens are involved in the initiative, and the number of citizens from each member state, need to be filled out by highly sensitive legislation. The difficulty is that the emergence of a European public for the purposes of participatory democracy is no more imminent than is a European public for the purposes of representative democracy" (Lee, 2005, p. 120). So, this norm only provides a limited contribution to moving beyond the democratic deficit.

---

36   See par. I: "The functioning of the Union shall be founded on representative democracy"; par. II: "Citizens are directly represented at Union level in the European Parliament. Member States are represented at Union level in the European Parliament. Member States are represented in the European Council by their Heads of State or Government and in the Council by their governments, themselves democratically accountable either to their national Parliaments, or to their citizens", and par. III: "Every citizen shall have the right to participate in the democratic life of the Union. Decisions shall be taken as openly and as closely as possible to the citizen".

37   See Peters, 2004, p. 37, in Article p. 44. The author considers the citizens' initiative laid down by Article I-47, par. 4, as one of the few real novelties presented by the Treaty: "Independent of actual future resort to that instrument, the mere option might become an important symbol of genuine, bottom-up democracy. It seems apt to over- come the citizens' feeling of powerlessness vis-à-vis a gigantic European bureaucracy, while at the same time preserving the Commission's monopoly of legislative initiative".

The persistence of the lack of power of European citizens and the increased gap between them and the EU was clearer after the negative French and Dutch referenda on the Constitutional Treaty.[38] The Commission understood that more democratisation was necessary for the future of Europe and consequently the Member States embarked on a 'reflection period' about how to remedy the failed Constitutional Treaty. In 2005, Commissioner Margot Wallströ launched a new initiative called Plan "D" as in Democracy, Dialogue and Debate.[39]

The Plan was about debate, dialogue and listening with the goal of stimulating a wide public debate and building a new consensus on the future direction of the European Union. Nevertheless, it is clear that the emphasis on dialogue and debate is not sufficient because, to be truly democratic and to help identification with the European project, "not only interest groups but also the citizens themselves should be encouraged to participate in genuine debates before final decisions are taken, although this is primarily a task for civil society organisations and political parties" (Parry, 2010).

Thus, in 2006 the White Paper on European Communication Policy[40] tried to complete this approach by developing tools and initiatives for citizens' involvement. The Commission's "A citizens' agenda for Europe", adopted on 10 May 2006[41] stressed the need to shift to a "policy agenda for citizens" drawing upon continued dialogue with the public via the implementation of Plan D (Barnard, 2007, p. 271).

The last step undertaken by the EU to improve participation was the Treaty of Lisbon which recognised the necessity to make the EU "*more democratic, meeting the European citizens' expectations for high standards of accountability, openness, transparency and participation; more efficient and able to tackle today's global challenges such as climate change, security and sustainable development*".[42]

1.1.3.2.3.   Treaty of Lisbon

The purpose of the Lisbon Treaty has been to simplify the institutional structure and the decision making process in order to increase efficiency, coherence and

---

38   Snyder, 2004, p. 255. See also Schwarze, 2006, p. 199. On the failure of the constitutional referenda in France and the Netherlands, see specifically Hurrelmann, 2007, p. 343. Recently, see also De Burca, 2006, p. 6; Joerges, 2006, p. 2. On the 'period of reflection' on the future of Europe after the failed referenda, see: Editorial, 2007a, p. 561.

39   Available at www.speakupeurope.eu/plan_d.html.

40   Available at www.epri.org/epriknowledge/contents/Material_2nd_EPRI_workshop/white_paper_en.pdf.

41   Available at www.eur-lex.europa.eu/LexUriServ/LexUriServ.do?uri=CELEX:52006DC0211:EN:NOT.

42   For more information see the website: www.europa.eu.int.

democratic legitimacy. The Preamble establishes that the aim of the Treaty is: "*to complete the process started by the Treaty of Amsterdam and by the Treaty of Nice with a view to enhancing the efficiency and democratic legitimacy of the Union and to improving the coherence of its action*" (Clientearth, 2009).

The Treaty reconfirms the reliance on the Nation-State model of representative democracy,[43] nevertheless it may be possible to identify some changes moving towards participatory and deliberatory democracy.

The first one is relative to the access to information: the Lisbon Treaty expands the number of institutions subject to transparency stating that "*Any citizen of the Union [...] shall have a right of access to documents of the Union institutions, bodies, offices and agencies*", Article 15(3), but does not do likewise concerning the subjects who possess the right.[44] There are also exemptions, with the European Court of Justice, the European Central Bank and the European Investment Bank falling thereunder except where "*exercising their administrative tasks*" (Benson, & Jordan, 2008, p. 280).

Another step towards more democratisation is the inclusion, or better the 're-inclusion' in the Treaty of Lisbon, of the participation principle. Indeed Article 11, like the Constitution before it, picks up on the 'democratic' possibilities of 'participation'. One of the striking differences between the Constitutional Treaty and the Lisbon Treaty is that the latter no longer mentions the concept of 'participatory democracy'.

Nevertheless, it includes exactly the same provisions which described 'participatory democracy' in the Constitutional Treaty: however, without a title. Some authors have criticised the disappearance of this concept from the text because it "illustrated the sensitivity around the question whether 'participatory democracy' should be a normative model for European governance" (Smismans, 2009). Other scholars have argued: "contrary to the constitutional Treaty (which) had "pompously" announced as the principle of participatory democracy in the Union, at minimum the Reform treaty is a bit more "honest": it does not boast about any principle, but only replaces the old paragraph 4 of I-47, stating that there is a European citizens' initiative" (Pichler, & Giese, 2008, p. 117).

However, also without an explicit mention, Article 11 calls on the participatory mechanisms of citizens' initiatives, establishing: "*not less than one million*

---

43   Article 8a refers to the principle of representative democracy, stating that "citizens are directly represented at Union level in the *European* Parliament. [...] Every citizen shall have the right to participate in the democratic life of the Union. Decisions shall be taken as openly and as closely as possible to the citizen.. Political parties at European level contribute to forming European political awareness and to expressing the will of citizens of the Union".

44   Indeed the right is granted only to the EU citizens.

citizens who are nationals of a significant number of Member States may take the initiative of inviting the Commission, within the framework of its powers, to submit any appropriate proposal on matters where citizens consider that a legal act of the Union is required for the purpose of implementing the Treaties".

As under the Constitution, the details of this provision are to be filled out by legislation, and consequently Article 24 establishes that *"the European Parliament and the Council, acting by means of regulations in accordance with the ordinary legislative procedure, shall adopt the provisions for the procedures and conditions required for a citizens' initiative within the meaning of Article 11 of the Treaty on European Union, including the minimum number of Member States from which such citizens must come".* The European Parliament has already indicated some criteria for its implementation arguing that any initiative should be admissible if it concerns EU competence and if it is not contrary to the general principles of the Treaty, and it should not take more than two months to decide on its admissibility.

Apart from such citizens' participation, the new Treaty allows the participation of representative associations: *"The institutions shall, by appropriate means, give citizens and representative associations the opportunity to make known and publicly exchange their views in all areas of Union action. The institutions shall maintain an open, transparent and regular dialogue with representative associations and civil society"* (Holtz, 2008).

1.1.3.3.   Access to Justice: Former Article 230

Access to justice is an important instrument of participation because its role is to protect the other two rights. As will be examined in detail in the following, the Lisbon Treaty has amended access to justice, with a new paragraph 4 in Article 263 (formerly 230): *"Any natural or legal person may, under the conditions laid down in the first and second paragraphs, institute proceedings against an act addressed to that person or which is of direct and individual concern to them, and against a regulatory act which is of direct concern to them and does not entail implementing measures".*

Before this amendment, a person or business could only challenge the legality of certain EU acts directly before the Court, if it could be shown that the act was of "direct and individual concern" to that person or business. The Court has been heavily criticised for interpreting the notion of 'individual concern' in a strict manner; in fact, in other respects the ECJ has applied teleological interpretations of Article 230. Thus, the strict standing rule in Article 230(4) EC has not been so much due to its wording, as due to its strict interpretation (Ballesteros, & Luk, 2010). The only way of opening the doors for these individuals and ensuring their right to effective judicial protection at an EU level was to amend the EU Treaty.

Thus, there is no longer any requirement for "individual concern" in respect to a "regulatory act" which "does not entail implementing measures" (Lee, 2008, p. 135). This can cover certain regulations which previously were almost impossible to challenge. Individuals may challenge the legality of those acts if they can show 'direct concern'.

Already in 1995 the ECJ suggested that the Member States should change the wording in Article 230(4) EC and introduce more liberal standing rules.[45] This suggestion was not followed in the Nice Treaty. The ECJ interpreted that position as a signal not to liberalise Article 230(4). Only with the Treaty Establishing a Constitution for Europe, and then the Treaty of Lisbon, the Member States decided to follow the ECJ suggestion.

The impact of the change proposed in the Lisbon Treaty is not measurable at the moment since there is no clarity on what kind of a regulatory act at an EU level is within the framework of the new hierarchy of acts. In fact, the wording "regulatory act" is not mentioned anywhere else in the Treaty, and survived from the Constitution; but the Lisbon Treaty does not pick up on the Constitution's re-categorisation of EU laws and procedures into legislative acts and non-legislative acts. The doctrine has already suggested that this term refers to a normative act of general application, as opposed to an administrative act of individual scope (Pallemaerts, 2009, p. 30).

Nevertheless, the extent to which standing is relaxed depends on the judicial interpretation of this phrase (Lee, 2008, p. 1, 3, 5). As a matter of fact, as shall be discussed below, the main obstacle to accessing justice in order to challenge acts of Community Institutions which contravene EU Environmental Law is not "direct" but "individual" concern. The reforms of the standing requirements of Article 230(4), which result from the Lisbon Treaty, do not constitute a major step forward. At any rate it only applies to a limited sub-category of acts of Community Institutions (Pallemaerts, 2009, p. 30).

Moreover, in the same provision, the Treaty maintains the requirement that an act (other than regulatory acts) adopted by EU Institutions has to be of direct and individual concern for it to be challenged by a natural or legal person. These requirements have been interpreted to exclude environmental NGOs from having access to the ECJ (Ballesteros, & Luk, 2010). The issues concerning this Article are very complex and they will be explored in detail in the following discussion.

---

45   Report of the ECJ of Justice on Certain Aspects of the Application of the Treaty on European Union, Luxembourg, May 1995.

1.2. "Environment" in the European Community

To discuss Environmental Democracy from a European perspective, it is necessary to call for a synopsis of the relationship between Europe and environmental protection. Thus, this part briefly sets out the historical evolution of the "ecologisation" (McGillivray, & Holder, 2001, p. 139) of European governance in order to provide a background for the subsequent parts. Nevertheless, before starting it is necessary to analyse the term environment in the EU context.

1.2.1. The Definition of the Term "Environment" in Europe

Currently, what is considered as "European environment" is not clear since there is not a conclusive and uniform definition of environment in EU law. The environment is defined differently depending on the context and instrument in which it is being used (Kiss, & Shelton, 1993, p. 4).[46] The diverging definitions can be categorised into wide and narrow definitions and Environment may also have an anthropocentric or ecocentric character. The following overview shall first address the term "natural resources" particularly since they constitute part of both sets of definitions and second, an overview of the debate surrounding the definition shall be given.[47]

In the European context natural occurrences are listed as natural resources which are not human or man-made. According to several directives and regulations

---

46   See also Thornton, & Beckwith, 2004, p. 5.

47   Despite the vagueness of the term Environment, it is possible to find two categories of definitions: one includes only natural elements, a narrow definition, and one includes also a social dimension, a wide definition. The following shall give an overview .over that. First, however, the term natural resources shall be addressed particularly since they constitute part of both sets of definitions.
One can categorise the definitions of natural resources on the international level into two sets (Reiners, 2009). It has been suggested that natural resources are naturally occurring materials that are useful to man (Skinner, 1986, p. 1). Another proposal is that natural resources are tangibles or intangibles which may be used in an economic manner or to create economic value and which are not manufactured or produced (Rosenne, 1986, p. 63). These definitions imply that the appearance in nature must have an economic value. This economically-valuing definition represents the first set of definitions.
The second category covers definitions of natural resources, which do not include an economic element (This approach is favoured by Schrijver, 1995, pp. 15-16. It was suggested that natural resources are all physical natural goods, as opposed to those made by man (Cano, 1975, p. 1). Hence, there are basically two sets of definitions, one requiring an economic value, the other one not. Nevertheless, both definitions agree on the fact that a natural resource is something nature given so to speak and not man-made. Moreover, they do not seem to include human beings.

natural resources comprise fauna and flora, natural habitats, groundwater[48] and surface waters,[49] soil,[50] oil, natural gas and solid fuels.[51] Sometimes their economic value is stressed,[52] but also elements without an economic value fall within the definition. Moreover, the EU is a party to the Convention on Biological Diversity[53] since 1993[54] and Article 2 of the Convention lists as natural resources air, water, land, flora and fauna and natural ecosystems.[55]

---

48   *E.g.* Step 1(j) of Annex I to the Directive 2009/31/EC of the European Parliament and of the Council of 23 April 2009 on the Geological Storage of Carbon Dioxide and Amending Council Directive 85/337/EEC, European Parliament and Council Directives 2000/60/EC, 2001/80/EC, 2004/35/EC, 2006/12/EC, 2008/1/EC and Regulation (EC) No 1013/2006, OJ 2009, L 140/114.

49   *E.g.* Groundwater and surface waters Preambular 28 of Directive 2000/60/EC of the European Parliament and of the Council of 23 October 2000 Establishing a Framework for Community Action in the Field of Water Policy, OJ 2000, L 327/1; fresh water Article 2(2)(g) of Regulation (EC) No 1638/2006 of the European Parliament and of the Council of 24 October 2006 Laying Down General Provisions Establishing a European Neighbourhood and Partnership Instrument, OJ 2006, L 310/1; water in general Preambular 12 of Commission Regulation (EC) No 889/2008 of 5 September 2008 Laying Down Detailed Rules for the Implementation of Council Regulation (EC) No 834/2007 on Organic production and Labelling of Organic Products with regard to Organic Production, Labelling and Control, OJ 2008, L 250/1; Article 13(1) of Regulation (EC) No 1905/2006 of the European Parliament and of the Council of 18 December 2006 Establishing a Financing Instrument for Development Cooperation, OJ 2006, L 378/41.

50   *E.g.* Preambular 12 of Commission Regulation (EC) No 889/2008 of 5 September 2008 Laying Down Detailed Rules for the Implementation of Council Regulation (EC) No 834/2007 on Organic production and Labeling of Organic Products with Regard to Organic Production, Labeling and Control, OJ 2008, L 250/1.

51   *E.g.* all three Preambular 2 of Directive 2003/30/EC of the European Parliament and of the Council of 8 May 2003 on the Promotion of the use of Biofuels or other Renewable Fuels for Transport, OJ 2003, L 123/42; Preambular 2 of Directive 2002/91/EC of the European Parliament and of the Council of 16 December 2002 On the Energy Performance of Buildings, OJ 2003, L 1/65; only oil Preambular 1 of Directive 2009/33/EC of the European Parliament and of the Council of 23 April 2009 on the Promotion of Clean and Energy-Efficient Road Transport Vehicles, OJ 2009, L 120/5.

52   *E.g.* Preambular 5 of Council Directive 1999/13/EC of 11 March 1999 on the Limitation of Emissions of Volatile Organic Compounds Due to the Use of Organic Solvents in Certain Activities and Installations, OJ 1999, L 85/1.

53   Convention on Biological Diversity of 5 June 1992, 1760 UNTS, p. 79.

54   See available at www.cbd.int/countries/?country=eur.

55   See further on these examples not mentioning the term natural resource explicitly but describing the natural environmental elements, not human and not man-made Article 2(1)(c)Council Directive 67/548/EEC of 27 June 1967 on the Approximation of Laws, Regulations and Administrative Provisions Relating to the Classification, Packaging and Labelling of Dangerous Substances, OJ 1967, L 196/1 Article 2(12) of Council Directive 91/414/EEC of 15 July 1991 Concerning the Placing of Plant Protection Products on the Market, OJ 1991, L 230/1.

Hence, at the European level natural resources are also nature given occurrences which are not man-made and do not include human beings. Furthermore, they have numerous appearances that include air, water, land, flora and fauna, natural ecosystems, oil, gas and fossil fuels.

1.2.1.1. Wide Definition of "Environment"

Some definitions of the environment found at the European level are wide. A wide definition is one which comprises not only natural resources but, in addition, humans or man-made things or even both.[56]

The "Declaration on the Environment" adopted by the Heads of State and Government in 1990, at the defining of Treaty negotiations which led to the adoption of the Treaty of Maastricht is interesting. The Declaration lists numerous elements: a "*clean and healthy environment: the quality of air, lakes, coastal and marine waters, the quality of food and drinking water, protection against noise, protection against contamination of soil, soil erosion and desertification, preservation of habitats, flora and fauna, landscape and other elements of the natural heritage, and the amenity and quality of residential areas*".

The concept of the environment is an all-encompassing term including economic, social and aesthetic elements, including the preservation of natural and archaeological heritage and the man-made as well as the natural environment (Krämer, 2003b). This notion can be considered to be evolving and open to development in the face of new discoveries, technical advances and greater societal interest in, and understanding of, the subject matter (Comte, 2006, p. 190).

No explicit legal definition of the environment is found in the Treaty of the European Communities. However, former Article 174(1) and former Article 175(2) of the EU Treaty[57] imply that the European environment comprises natural resources such as the natural element water, man-made elements such as waste and human beings themselves (Thornton, & Beckwith, 2004, p. 4).

Thus, the EU Treaty seems to give a broad definition of the environment. Another example of a European document implying a broad definition is the Helsinki Final Act of 1975.[58] There the co-operation in the environmental field comprises air, water, land and soil, genetic resources, rare animal and plant

---

56   A definition of an ordinary dictionary for instance defines the environment as the circumstances, objects or conditions, by which somebody or something is surrounded, (ed.) Allen, 2000, p. 465.

57   OJ 2006, C-321 E/39.

58   Conference on Security and Co-Operation in Europe Final Act of 1 August 1975, 14 ILM 1992, p. 1292.

species, natural ecological systems, human health and waste.[59] Still a broad definition, although slightly narrower, is the definition contained in the Lugano Convention of 1993.[60]

Its Article 2(10) defines the environment as comprising "*natural resources both abiotic and biotic, such as air, water, soil, fauna and flora and the interaction between the same factors, property which forms part of the cultural heritage; and the characteristic aspects of the landscape*".

This definition does not include humans, but natural resources and man-made elements (Thornton, & Beckwith, 2004, p. 5). Moreover, it also comprehends the relationships between the elements. Other definitions that comprise also the relationship between the environmental elements are enshrined in Directives, though excluding man-made things.[61] In particular, Article 2(1)(a) of Directive 2003/4/EC[62] which implements the Aarhus Convention comprises as environmental elements air, atmosphere, water, soil, land, landscape, natural sites, biological diversity and its components, including genetically modified organisms, and the interaction among these elements. Several Directives do not provide for a definition of the environment, but list for example humans and the environment next to one another and thereby imply at least that the environment does not comprise humans but might include man-made things.[63]

---

59   Conference on Security and Co-Operation in Europe Final Act of 1 August 1975, pp. 28-29.

60   Convention on Civil Liability for Damage Resulting from Activities Dangerous to the Environment, Lugano Convention of 21 June 1993, ETS 150.

61   Listing "water, air and land and their inter-relationships as well as between them and any living organism" Article 2(1)(c)Council Directive 67/548/EEC of 27 June 1967 on the Approximation of Laws, Regulations and Administrative Provisions Relating to the Classification, Packaging and Labeling of Dangerous Substances, OJ 1967, L 196/1; Article 2(12) of Council Directive 91/414/EEC of 15 July 1991 Concerning the Placing of Plant Protection Products on the Market, OJ 1991, L 230/1; another example for a wider definition not including man-made things is to define the environment to be the natural surroundings of or the complex of external factors that acts upon an organism, an ecological community, or plant and animal life in general, Allen, 2000, p. 465.

62   Directive 2003/4/EC of the European Parliament and of the Council of 28 January 2003 on Public Access to Environmental Information and Repealing Council Directive 90/313/EEC, OJ 2003, L 41/26.

63   Preambular 6 of Directive 1999/45/EC of the European Parliament and of the Council of 31 May 1999 Concerning the Approximation of the Laws, Regulations and Administrative Provisions of the Member States Relating to the Classification, Packaging and Labelling of Dangerous Preparations, OJ 1999, L 200/1; Article 1 of Council Directive 1999/32/EC of 26 April 1999 Relating to a Reduction in the Sulphur Content of Certain Liquid Fuels and Amending Directive 93/12/EEC, OJ 1999, L 121/13; Article 1 of Directive 2001/18/EC of the European Parliament and of the Council of 12 March 2001 on the Deliberate Release into the Environment of Genetically Modified Organisms and Repealing Council Directive 90/220/EEC, OJ 2001, L 106/1; Article 6(5) of Directive 2000/76/EC of

Hence, several documents at the European level provide a wide definition of the environment which seems to include natural resources and sometimes human beings, man-made things or all of the above.

1.2.1.2. Narrow Definition of "Environment"

Some of the definitions of the environment found at the European level are narrow, however. A narrow definition will only include natural resources but exclude man-made things and human beings.

For the European Environment Agency,[64] which periodically assesses the state of the European environment, the definition of the European environment in these reports is a cluster of environmental issues, such as quality of air, water and soil. Of course this approach is limited and narrow because it takes into account only the indicators and not the complexity of this concept.

Examples of definitions representing a narrow approach are less frequent. Other examples of a narrow definition are found in the Habitats Directive of 1992 which only comprises habitats and wild fauna and flora[65] and the Wild Birds Directive of 1979 which only comprises wild birds.[66] A narrow definition is also found in several other directives. Again, they do not expressly define the environment but from listing the environment next to man-made things, humans or other elements it can at least be concluded what the environment does not comprise. For instance, some directives list humans and animals and the environment.[67] They, hence, seem to exclude humans and animals from the

---

the European Parliament and of the Council of 4 December 2000 on the Incineration of Waste, OJ 2000, L 332/91; Article 1(7) of Commission Directive 2001/59/EC of 6 August 2001 Adapting to Technical Progress for the 28th time Council Directive 67/548/EEC on the Approximation of the Laws, Regulations and Administrative Provisions Relating to the Classification, Packaging and Labelling of Dangerous Substances, OJ 2001, L 225/1; Article 4(2) of Council Directive 2002/55/EC of 13 June 2002 on the Marketing of Vegetable Seed, OJ 2002, L 193/33; Article 1(a) of Directive 2009/41/EC of the European Parliament and of The Council of 6 May 2009 on the Contained Use of Genetically Modified Micro-Organisms, OJ 2009, L 125/75; Article 1(1) of Directive 2008/50/EC of the European Parliament and of The Council of 21 May 2008 On Ambient Air Quality and Cleaner Air for Europe, OJ 2008, L 152/1.

64   See for example EEA: Environment in the European Union at the Turn of the Century, Copenhagen 1999.

65   Preambular 1 of Council Directive 92/43/EEC of 21 May 1992 on the Conservation of Natural Habitats and of Wild Fauna and Flora Official Journal 1992, L 206/7.

66   Council Directive 79/409/EEC of 2 April 1979 on the Conservation of Wild Birds Official Journal 1979, L 103/1.

67   Article 2(1)(b) of Directive 98/8/EC of the European Parliament and of the Council of 16 February 1998 Concerning the Placing of Biocidal Products on the market, OJ 1998, L 123/ 1; Preambular 6 Directive 2000/16/EC of the European Parliament and the Council

ambit of the environment. Even though the definitions only including natural resources are narrower than the ones above, their importance is not to be underestimated especially due to the above-shown wide range of occurrences falling under the term natural resources.

Thus, the narrow definitions that only comprise natural resources also have a wide scope of application. It is also possible to identify several definitions at the European level. For example, a text of the Council of the European Community includes "*water, air and land and their inter-relationship as well as relationships between them and any living organism*".[68]

The term "environment" could be said to cover "*all those elements which in their complex inter-relationships form the framework, setting and living conditions for mankind, by their very existence of by virtue of their impact*".[69]

The EU Treaty indicates, without expressly interpreting the term, in conformity with former Article 174 (1) and (2), that the shape of the environment extends to human beings, natural resources, land use, town and country planning, waste and water. Thus, in principle this includes almost all areas of the environment, in particular fauna and flora and climate. The inclusion of town and country planning underlines the fact that the environment includes man-made as well as natural elements.[70]

---

of 10 April 2000 amending Council Directive 79/373/EEC on the Marketing of Compound Feedingstuffs and Council Directive 96/25/EC on the Circulation of Feed Materials, OJ 2000, L 105/36; Article 6 of Directive 2002/32/EC of the European Parliament and of the Council of 7 May 2002 on Undesirable Substances in Animal Feed, OJ 2002, L 140/10

68   Council Directive of June 27, 1967, 1967 O.J.; See: Kiss, & Shelton, 2000.

69   EEC, OJ C 115, May 1976, p. 2. See also: Larsson, 1999, p. 121.

70   Thornton, & Beckwith, 2004, p. 1. Other definitions that encompass the link between the environmental elements are provided in Directives which keep out man-made things. Listing "water, air and land and their inter-relationships as well as between them and any living organism" Article 2(1)(c)Council Directive 67/548/EEC of 27 June 1967 on the Approximation of Laws, Regulations and Administrative Provisions Relating to the Classification, Packaging and Labeling of Dangerous Substances, OJ 1967, L 196/1; Article 2 (12) of Council Directive 91/414/EEC of 15 July 1991 Concerning the Placing of Plant Protection Products on the Market, OJ 1991, L 230/1; another example for a wider definition not including man-made things is to define the environment to be the natural surroundings of or the complex of external factors that acts upon an organism, an ecological community, or plant and animal life in general, Allen, 2000, p. 465. In particular, Article 2(1)(a) of Directive 2003/4/EC (Directive 2003/4/EC of the European Parliament And Of The Council of 28 January 2003 On Public Access to Environmental Information and Repealing Council Directive 90/313/EEC, OJ 2003, L 41/26) which implements the Aarhus Convention comprises as environmental elements air, atmosphere, water, soil, land, landscape, natural sites, biological diversity and its components, including genetically modified organisms, and the interaction among these elements.

1.2.2. Anthropocentric and Ecocentric Character of Environment in Europe

The Environment mainly has an anthropocentric character in Europe, so that the focus is on protecting the health of humans rather than protecting the environment for its own sake (Parola, 2013). This can be seen for instance in the Habitats Directive, in which the destruction of a habitat for development is provided for, so long as certain procedural requirements are fulfilled. The anthropocentric orientation of EU environmental law and its practical expression in legal instruments implicitly reject ecological thought.[71]

Nevertheless, this strong statement should be moderated, because on several occasions the EU has led action in certain fields which entail a more ecocentric and global approach.

An example can be found concerning the Animal welfare which was introduced in a Protocol annexed to the TEC by the Amsterdam Treaty.

The Lisbon Treaty has amended the existing wording of the Protocol and added the amended Treaty (Article 13). The changes brought by the Treaty to the existing text include references to fisheries, technological development and space policies, and in particular, the classification of animals as "*sentient beings*". Recognising "*animals as sentient*" is symbolically important and may also have potential legal and policy implications. Both EU institutions and Member States "consequently have to pay full regard to animal welfare in formulating and implementing policy in these sectors" (Benson, & Jordan, 2008, p. 283).[72]

Another important example is the action in the fight against Climate Change which demonstrates how the EU also pursues ecological objectives. During the negotiation of the Constitutional Treaty, Climate Change was not such a "hot topic" (Lee, 2008, p. 133) but it has become a new objective in the Lisbon Treaty. This adds proof to the EU's awareness of that topic as a "global environmental problem", which has to be resorted to at the global level; but reaffirms that concrete action has to be undertaken also at regional and national levels.

This Article can be linked also to the new provisions relating to "Energy policy" (Corazza. 2009) as contained in the new Article 194. The reasons for the link are: firstly, scientific and technological advance and the aim to "promote energy efficiency and energy saving and the development of new and renewable forms

---

71   McGillivray, & Holder, 2001, p. 143.
    Ecocentric approach which originally comes from the first and ancestral relations between Nature and man and which is still present in some religious and philosophical views around the world, gives a different concept to the "Environment", one in which all organic existence in a single framework is united in harmonious interaction: Parola, 2013.
72   See also Camm, & Bowles, 2000, p. 195.

of energy", and secondly, because all of the objectives of energy policy should be pursued "with regard for the need to preserve and improve the environment" (Lee, 2008, p. 131).

In addition, it is interesting to note that the ECJ places huge importance on the relationship between environmental quality and human health; but also numerous decisions in which the Court in a situation of conflict between natural resources and other interests decided in favour of the environment exist, following an ecocentric approach. For example, *Lappel Bank* outlined that the Wild Birds Directive accords special protection to species which constitute "a common heritage of the Community".[73] Moreover, in two landmark decisions the Court explicitly ruled that environmental legislation designed to protect human health and the environment should be interpreted as creating rights and obligations for individuals vis-à-vis the environment.[74]

Thus, it should be underlined that, in particular, regarding the legislation on the protection of animals and habitats, this ecocentric approach has largely been ensured over the last twenty-five years through the jurisprudence of the ECJ,[75] which "fine-tuned the rather rudimental provisions of EU legislation, generally trying to protect the environment against the greed of administrations or economic operators" (Krämer, 2009, p. 195).

In conclusion, the approach to the environment by Community Law is in principle anthropocentric; however, some grains of the ecocentric approach have entered into EU environmental law provisions, in particular by ECJ jurisprudence.

1.2.3. Protection of Environment in the Treaty

The Treaty of Rome, which in 1957 created what was then the European Economic Community, did not contain any reference to the environment. At that time, the main scope of such Treaties was to establish functionally integrated markets in order to attain economic benefits.[76]

---

73   Case C- 44/95, R. v. Secretary of State for the Environment, (1996) ECH I-3805.

74   Case C-361/88, Commission v. Germany [1991] ECR I- 256; Commission v. Germany [1991] ECR I-825,7. see Jans, 1996; Ward, 2000, p. 137.

75   See for instance: ECJ Case 272/80, Biologische Produketen (1981) ECR 3277; Case 412/85, Commission v. Germany (1987) ECR 3503; Case C-322/86, Commission v. Italy (1988) ECR I-3995; Case C-355/90, Commission v. Spain (1993) ECR I-4221; Case C-365/97, Commission v. Italy (1997) ECR I-7773.

76   Indeed the original aim of the EEC was one of economic integration rather than protection of human rights or the environment. The legal regime of the European Union operates within three pillars. The first pillar, established by the Treaty of Rome (with subsequent amendments) organizes the European Community and addresses the economic objectives of the Community as well as social and environmental issues. The

Nevertheless, with the forceful support of the European Court of Justice starting decades ago, environmental protection has been elevated from a "position of neglect" to one of the "essential objectives" of the European Union.[77] In fact, it became clear that the creation of a common market and the development of economic growth could not be achieved without a policy for the environment and without an environmentally friendly orientation.

The first official mention of environmental protection came in a declaration made in October 1972 where the Heads of the Member States clearly expressed the political will to protect the environment: "Economic expansion is not an end in itself: its firm aim should be to enable disparities in living conditions to be reduced. It should result in an improvement in the quality of life as well as in standards of living. As befits the genius of Europe, particular attention will be given to intangible values and to protecting the environment, so that progress may really be put at the service of mankind".[78]

This was followed by the First Action Programme on the Environment in 1973.[79] Since then, five further Action Programmes have been produced and the

second pillar is the Common Foreign and Security Policy established under the Treaty of the European Union from 1992 (Maastricht Treaty). The third pillar addresses police and judicial cooperation in criminal matters. See EUROPA, The E.U. at a glance, Treaties and Law, available at www.europa.eu/abc/treaties/index_en.htm.

77   Which the relevant directive 'must be seen in the perspective of', *ADBHU*, Case 240/83 para. 13. We see here the use of the general goals of the EU in the interpretation of secondary legislation. See *inter alia* Jacobs, 2006, p. 185; Sjafjell, 2009.

78   See E.C. Commission, 6th General Report (1972) p. 8: see also Shelton, 1993, p. 557.

79   There have been six such programmes since 1973, the first four converging periods of four or five years. 1st Environmental Action Programme, 1973-1976 (1973) OJ C112; 2st Environmental Action Programme, 1977-1981 (1977) OJ C 139; 3st Environmental Action Programme, 1982-1986 (1981) OJ C46; 4st Environmental Action Programme, 1987-1992 (1987) OJ C328; 5st Environmental Action Programme 1993-2001 (1993) OJ C138; 6st Environmental Action Programme, 2002-2012 (2002) OJ L242/1. See Burnett-Hall, & Jones, 2009, p.14.

The 1st Action Programme set out 11 "Principle of a Community Environmental Policy" that continued to be supported in subsequent Programmes. These may be summarised as follows: (1) Pollution should be prevented at source rather than dealt with after the event; (2) Environmental issues must be taken into account at the earliest possible stage in planning and other technical decision making processes; (3) Abusive exploitation of natural resources is to be avoided; (4) the standard of knowledge in the EC should be improved to promote effective action for environmental conservation and improvement; (5) the polluter should pay for preventing and eliminating nuisances, subject to limited exceptions and transitional arrangements; (6) Activities in one country should not degrade the environment of another; (7) The EC and the Member States must in their environment policies have regard to the interests of developing countries and should aim to prevent or minimise any adverse effects on their economic development; (8) There should be a clearly defined long-term European environmental policy that includes participation in international organisations and co-operation at both regional and international levels; (9) Environmental protection is a matter for everyone in the EC, at all levels; their co-current Sixth Programme extends from 2002-2012 (Pedersen, 2010). The first Programme made the attempt to articulate a single environment policy for the EEC and it establishes two main principles still in use, the Polluter Pays Principle and the Preventive Action Principle (Collins, 2006, p. 98).

The awareness *vis-à-vis* the environment, as it will be seen, has been reflected gradually also in the Treaties. In fact, environmental protection was promoted to the level of the main objectives provisions of the EU Treaty by the Treaty of Maastricht, while the Amsterdam Treaty recognised environmental protection as an independent goal, 'rather than an incidental requirement of economic growth (Craig, & De Burca, 2008, p. 21).

Since then environmental protection has been a central issue in the EU, and so many huge steps on environmental regulations and policies have been made that the EU has been considered a largely successful experiment in regional environmental governance since the EU is "one of the world's most advanced examples of international cooperation' in the realm of environment and beyond".[80]

1.2.3.1. Single European Act

Although, until 1986, there was not an explicit Treaty basis for environmental action, with the fundamental support of the ECJ the Commission and Council

---

operation, and the harnessing of social forces, is necessary for success. Education should ensure the whole community accepts its responsibilities for future generations; (10) Appropriate action levels must be established -local, regional, optional Community and international – for each type of pollution and area to be protected; (11) Major aspects of national environmental protection policies should be harmonised. Economic growth should not be view for purely quantities aspects.

80   In addition to leading by example, the EU has also intentionally undertaken the project of actively promoting sustainable development and environmental protection at the international level, through such mechanisms as capacity building in developing countries, the conclusion of multilateral environmental treaties, and other forms of international diplomacy. See generally Commission Communication External Action of 16 February 2006, Thematic Programme for Environment and Sustainable Management of Natural Resources including Energy, COM(2006) 20, available at eur-lex.europa. eu/LexUriServ/ site/en/com/2006/com2006_0070en01.pdf. See also: Collins, 2007b, pp. 323-324; Smith, 2002, p. 241. "The EU has accorded preeminent importance to environmental protection, EU environmental law and policy has grown exponentially, and Europe has become an acknowledged world leader in sustainable development and also now in climate change politically, the EU has seen itself as a leader in this area. Climate change is perceived as an issue with great popular resonance, where the EU wishes to be seen to provide something obviously valuable beyond what the Member States can provide". See Somsen, 2002.

used former Article 100 (ex 94) and former 235 (ex 308) as a legal basis to develop a body of environmental legislation.[81]

The first Article provides for the approximation of Member State laws that directly affect the establishment or functioning of the common market and was the principal instrument for environmental regulation; former Article 235 provides for action necessary to attain, in the course of the operation of the common market, one of the objectives of the Community, where the Treaty itself has not provided for the necessary powers. This approach to environmental policy is explained by the idea that during that period this policy was instrumental to the market (McGillivray, & Holder, 2001, p. 139).

The protection of the environment was settled by an autonomous Community action: the Single European Act (SEA) of 1986, by which three new Articles (Articles 130r, 130s and 130t) setting out the basic principles of Community action on the environment, were introduced. The SEA codified the status quo on decision-making in the environmental arena by providing an explicit legal base for environmental protection.

The fundamental principles which control Community environmental policy are: firstly, a principle of incorporation, according to which the policy of the Community in every field of its competence must be shaped after the assessment of the requirements for the protection of the environment.

Secondly, there is the principle of subsidiarity[82] which, and in combination with, the possibility of the Member States to depart from the Community rules and regulations, gives "precedence to national legislation over community law of the environment and hinder(s) the latter's development to a full legislative system with harmonised and homogenous application throughout the EU" (Karakostras, 2008, p. 12).

The provisions offered not just a legal basis for the enforcement of measures by Community institutions, but they also included the fundamental principles which control their acts. These principles do not have the character of a guideline or of a general declaration of intent, but are fully legally binding. In other words, the acts of the Community institutions and of the Member States must be in compliance with them.

The environmental provisions inserted in the EU Treaty through the SEA have since been renumbered and amended by the Maastricht, Amsterdam and Nice Treaties (Pedersen, 2010). After the Maastricht Treaty, the Community ceased to

---

81   Case 92/79 Commission v. Italy (1980) ECJ 1115; Case 240/83 Procureur de la République v. Association de défense des Bruleurs d'huiles Usagées (1983) ECR 531.

82   A detailed discussion of the nature and scope of this principle is beyond the scope of the book. However in this topic, among others, Macrory, 1999, p. 363; Toth, 1992, p. 239; more recently, see Estella De Noriega, 2002.

have an economic-only orientation and was transformed into a multidimensional institution with wider powers to interfere with the legal orders of the Member States also in the environmental field.

This treaty enlarged, improved and integrated, for the first time explicitly, environmental protection in the principles and objectives of the Community in Articles 2 and 3 of the EU Treaty. The amended former Article 130 of the SEA elevated the Community's environmental action to Community policy. In other words, environmental protection is not just a component of other Community policies, but it "*must be integrated into the definition and implementation of the other Community policies*". Moreover, it is explicitly provided that the competent institutions for the implementation of Community environmental policy should aim at a high level of protection.

1.2.3.2.   The Treaty of Amsterdam

The few changes brought by the Treaty of Amsterdam were in agreement with the proposal to broaden the Community activities for the environment. Here for the first time environmental protection is elevated to a Community objective independent of economic development and growth and it is established as a general imperative that permeates the whole range of Community Action (Karakostras, 2008, p. 15). Indeed, Article 2 of the Treaty of Amsterdam "*sets forth the objectives of the Union, including those of achieving balanced and sustainable development, strengthening the protection of the rights and interests of the EU nationals and maintaining and developing the Union as an area of freedom, security and justice*".

Thus, the Treaty of Amsterdam has altered the objectives of the Community, making the promotion of the core environmental concept of "sustainable development" a central objective in the revised Treaty. What is important for the current purpose is that such a principle includes an inter- and intra-generational element, e.g. the main idea of the responsibilities vis-à-vis future generations; this will be dealt with below. The inclusion of the mentioned principle has also been seen "as a response to the Member States adopting sustainable development as a guiding principle in national legislation and policy documents, thereby discharging their obligations under international law" (McGillivray, & Holder, 2001, p. 148).

Finally, the Treaty introduced the environmental policy Integration Principle. This commitment was implemented by the Cardiff Process, launched by the heads of government in 1998, and it also underpins the Sixth Environmental Action Programme (Benson, & Jordan, 2008, p. 283).

Hence, the principle of integration is reinforced with its codification in Article 6, which states that environmental protection requirements must be integrated into the definition and implication of Community policies and activities referred to in Article 3, in particular with a view to promoting sustainable development.

Former Article 174 determines the objectives that Community policies on the environment shall pursue, and it reaffirms that such policies shall aim at a high level of protection taking into account the diversity of situations in the various regions of the Community, listing the principles on which it shall be based (Kiss, 2008, p. 166).

1.2.3.3.   The Constitution for Europe

The Constitution for Europe (Beyer, Coffey, Klasing, & Homeyer, 2004, p. 218) and the following Treaty of Lisbon did not have a prominent "green agenda", nevertheless some provisions could be interpreted in an environmental light and they could even have a big impact in the environmental field. In this context, the most important provision of the Constitution is Article I-47, which provided for participative democracy by ensuring the right of public participation and citizens' initiatives.

It is interesting to note that as of June 2007, the 18 European Citizens Initiatives that have been launched[83] have enjoyed great popularity on the home-pages and the online signature forms. Eleven of the sixteen were proposed by NGOs including well-known organisations like Greenpeace and Friends of the Earth. Unfortunately, none have been launched by individuals (Fischer, & Lichtblau, 2008, p. 333). The topic of the initiatives concerned different issues: EU-organisation/political process, economics, health care/social issues and environment protection, in particular addressing the problems related to nuclear power and genetic food.

The most important and interesting for this study was the initiative "1 million Europeans against Nuclear Power", supported by numerous NGOs which joined the initiative at different points in time. During the course of the constitutional debate in 2003, several smaller antinuclear organisations, like Atomstopp, became aware of the possibility of the European Citizens Initiatives. Consequently, at a French anti-nuclear demonstration in January 2004, the decision was made to make use of this new instrument as a political means for the struggle against nuclear energy, and the internet was selected as the main medium of communication.

In July 2005, Friends of the Earth and other smaller NGOs decided to support the initiative. Unfortunately, only 634,686 Europeans have signed against nuclear energy. The campaign failed principally for two reasons. Firstly, due

---

83   Available at www.citizens-initiative.eu.

to considerable problems in the procedure: in fact, each organisation has a different deadline for decisions. Secondly, other campaigns already have top priority, such as climate change, which has become a popular topic, and so the topic of nuclear power is losing attraction for NGOs.[84]

1.2.3.4. The Lisbon Treaty

The Lisbon Treaty largely maintains the *status quo* in its explicit environmental provisions. Nevertheless, it has been said that the Treaty has introduced "some limited", but "potentially broad ranging modifications to the environmental "rules of the game" in the EU" (Benson, & Jordan, 2008, p. 280).

The principles and objectives of environmental policy remain "virtually" the same (Lee, 2008, p. 131). Indeed, the provisions containing environmental content have not changed the terminology of the objective concerning environmental protection, namely that of achieving "*a high level of protection and improvement of the quality of the environment*" (Article 3(3) TEU). Then, the Lisbon Treaty includes the environmental provisions in former Articles 174 to 176 of the TEC establishing the legal basis for environmental legislation in Articles 191 to 193 of the TFEU. However, the environmental title in the treaty has been amended to specifically include the aim of combating climate change as one of the EC's objectives.[85]

Article 191 of the TFEU presents the objectives of the Union policy on environment stating that: "*Union policy on the environment shall contribute to pursuit of the following objectives: preserving, protecting and improving the quality of the environment; protecting human health; prudent and rational utilisation of natural resources; promoting measures at international level to deal with regional or worldwide environmental problems, and in particular combating climate change*"(Clientearth, 2009).

Concerning Sustainable Development, the Treaty introduces a new definition which is based closely on the wording of the Constitution and which amends former Article 2 of the TEU[86] (now Article 3 of the TEU). The sentence added that

---

84   Available at www.million-against-nuclear.net/. See also Lorenz, 2007; Egger, 2007.

85   The Art. 191(1) TFEU as amended, (formerly 174(1)) now states: "Union policy on the environment shall contribute to pursuit of the following objectives: —preserving, protecting and improving the quality of the environment, —protecting human health, —prudent and rational utilisation of natural resources, —promoting measures at international level to deal with regional or with regional or worldwide environmental problems, and in particular combating climate change".

86   The Union shall establish an internal market. It shall work for the sustainable development of Europe based on balanced economic growth and price stability, a highly competitive social market economy, aiming at full employment and social progress, and

to "*promote scientific and technological advance*" has to be read in accordance with the principle of Sustainable Development. This means that scientific and technological advances have to promote[87] Sustainable Development, identified as being achievable through meeting several new goals related to aspects of the internal market,[88] including raising living standards and the quality of life.

Moreover, amongst other core objectives of the EU, Article 3 also establishes that the Union shall in its dealings with the wider world "*contribute to peace, security and the sustainable development of the Earth. Finally the pursuit of Sustainable Development would become a specific policy goal in the external relations of the EU*".

Some changes in the Lisbon Treaty are not so explicit, but they have considerable potential to affect the future development of environmental regulation. An example is Article 11 concerning citizen initiative, which has already been examined. It should be said that for environmental purposes this instrument is welcomed, although there is a risk of manipulation by the elites, and of deepening divisions between different parts of the Union,[89] and there are many elements that need to be clarified.

The Treaty talks about "a million signatures" without specifying whether it requires signatures to come from a minimum number of countries or a minimum number per country involved, or the requirements for their collection, verification and authentication. It also does not define the meaning of the Commission being "invited" to make a proposal. Is it obliged to draw up a proposal or is it only invited to consider it? The Commission has prepared a Green paper where it proposes answers to these questions, recognising the Commission's responsibility to present conclusions and propose measures accordingly (Clientearth, 2009).

Among the implicit changes, there is also an amendment of Article 6: the new EU Charter of fundamental rights, signed 12 December 2007, become by

---

a high level of protection and improvement of the quality of the environment. It shall promote scientific and technological advance.

87   Sustainable development is also an element of Article 3(5) on external matters: "In its relations with the wider world, the Union shall uphold and promote its values and interests and contribute to the protection of its citizens. It shall contribute to peace, security, the sustainable development of the Earth, solidarity and mutual respect among peoples, free and fair trade, eradication of poverty and the protection of human rights, in particular the rights of the child, as well as to the strict observance and the development of international law, including respect for the principles of the United Nations Charter". Lee, 2008, p. 133.

88   For instance, "price stability", "highly competitive social market economy and "full complement".

89   "At this level, participation is likely to be restricted to organised pan-European interest groups; the contribution of 'participation' to 'democracy' in any familiar sense is by no means automatic". See Lee, 2008, p. 131.

reference binding in the same way as the treaty.[90] Secondly, the European Union shall accede to the European Convention on Human Rights.[91]

Concerning the first novelty, the Charter, through the Lisbon Treaty, would become a legally binding instrument[92] in particular its Article 37, under Title IV Solidarity, which states that "*a high level of environmental protection and the improvement of the quality of the environment must be integrated into the policies of the Union and ensured in accordance with the principle of sustainable development*".

This wording of the Article reflects and combines the provisions already present in the environmental chapter of the TEC and the TFEU.[93] The exact boundaries of the interpretation of this Article will have to be set by case-law. Nevertheless, as will be deal with below, the inclusion of the principle of a high level of environmental protection, per se, does not give citizens 'a right' to a clean environment or the right to claim positive action in courts by the EU Institutions or Member States.[94]

Regarding the European Convention on Human Rights,[95] after a long discussion over the possibility of accession, finally with the entering into the force of the Lisbon Treaty the EU has become a party to the Convention.[96] Accession to the

---

90   Charter of Fundamental Rights of the European Union, Dec. 14, 2007, 1007 O.J. (C 303) 1. The Charter represents a mixture of civil, political as well as economic, social, and cultural rights. See Butler, & De Schutter, 2008, p. 277.

91   Relating to the binding character of the Charter, it has to be noticed that England and Poland have opted out. See Protocol on the application of the charter of fundamental rights of the European Union to Poland and to the United Kingdom.

92   However, concerning the binding character of the Charter, it has to be noticed that England and Poland have opt-outs. See: Protocol on the application of the Charter of Fundamental rights of the European Union to Poland and to the United Kingdom. Available at www.eur-lex.europa.eu/LexUriServ/LexUriServ.do?uri=OJ:C:2007:306:0156:0157:EN:PDF. The reason England negotiated this, was to avoid major changes in their labour law; Poland was mostly concerned about but the possible equal treatment of homosexual and heterosexual couples. See Hectors, 2008, p. 165.

93   Indeed, Article 191 (2) requires the Union policy on environment to aim at a high level of protection. However the Charter Article is broader since it covers all Union policies.

94   How ONGs have suggested that provision "serve as a basis for a demand of a judicial review of legislative acts/omissions in cases where the EU Institutions or Member States would have manifestly breached their margin of discretion". See Clientearth, 2009.

95   The European Convention on Human Rights (ECHR) is an international treaty which was signed on 4 November 1950 in Rome under the auspices of the Council of Europe. It sets out a number of fundamental rights. To date, 47 countries across the European continent have ratified this convention, including all 27 EU countries. Available at www.lawsociety.org.uk/documents/downloads/guide_to_treaty_of_lisbon.pdf#17.

96   The long discussion over how to effectively protect fundamental rights in the EU had, inevitably, led to the consideration of a possible accession by the EU to the ECHR, as a way of creating an "international supplementary constitution" of the EU or, as the ECJ,

European Convention Human Rights means that the EU and its institutions will be accountable to the European Court of Human Rights for issues concerning the Convention. In other words, the EU institutions would be directly subject to the Convention and to the jurisprudence of European Courts which would be able to directly apply the Convention as part of EU law. Nevertheless, the Treaty of Lisbon and its Protocols state that accession to the Convention will not affect the EU's competences and that provision will be made for preserving the specific characteristics of the EU and EU law.

In conclusion, it may be said that through the explicit and implicit environmental provisions in the Treaty, the institutions of the EU have generated a vast amount of legislation relating to the environment.

---

put it in Rutili (ECJ, Case C-36/75, Roland Rutili v. Ministre de l'Intérieur, 28 October 1975. (Uerpmann-Wittzack, 2006) a source of "guidelines which should be followed within the framework of Community Law". But this possibility of an accession by the EU to the ECHR was for long time expressly ruled out by the ECJ in its (Opinion 2/94) and by the Treaties.

2. Environmental Democracy in Europe

"In Europe, as much as everywhere, humankind depends on Earth's ecosystems for the services they provide – for resources such as food, water, timber, fibre and fuel; for functions such as climate regulation, the absorption of wastes and the detoxification of pollution; and for protection as afforded by the atmospheric ozone layer".[97]

The intention here is not to repeat the Environmental Democracy structure theorised in my previous book, but to try to identify what EU law is doing with these concepts (Parola, 2013). Hence, it is now useful to observe, following the above presented overview of the scope of the terms "democracy" and "environment" at the European level, how those two aspects may be unified in the concept of Environmental Democracy.

2.1. Dimensions of European Environmental Democracy: Form and Space

2.1.1. Form

The first point to analyse is which form of democracy can be found at the EU level and if, implicitly or explicitly, it can be used to achieve environmental goals. To sum up this point through the outcomes emerging from above, it can be said that the representative form is the base of the EU, but a general movement towards a participatory and deliberatory democracy has been made in the last twenty years.

Features reflecting more participatory elements at the EU level can be found in ex-Articles 255 and 263 of the Treaty and in Articles 41 and 42 of the Charter of Nice, concerning access to information and access to justice. Also, the participation element has been recognised by the Lisbon Treaty when it introduced the novel instrument of a citizens' initiative. Thus the new Treaty recognised, even if merely in a small part, the model and mechanisms of "deliberative democracy".

---

97   EUROPEAN ENVIRONMENT AGENCY: The European Environment – State and Outlook 2005, Copenhagen, at p. 28.

Nevertheless, several points in this last element of the deliberative and participatory democracy are missing. Indeed, direct democracy in Europe is and remains "the eternal Cinderella" (Editorial, 2007b, p. 353). In fact, in the new TEU, as it has already been underlined, the measure to participate has been criticised (Allegri, 2008)[98] by most scholars mainly because the Article on citizens' initiative is too poor and weak, since it is principally based on dialogue and consultation and "doesn't include 'strong' participatory powers for citizens, like the right to promote referendums, to form European political parties, or other forms of participation" (Valvo, 2004, p. 27).

Also concerning these rights it is not even clear who the primary beneficiaries are, representative associations or civil society? What is clear, however, is that participation is meant by the Treaties as a "collective rather than individual opportunity".[99] Moreover, another obscure point is paragraph 4 of Article 11 which does not clarify whether European citizens "will be able to predetermine in detail the contents of proposals they will invite the Commission to submit, or if the definition of such contents will be up to the Commission itself" (Villani, 2005, p. 643). Further it has been argued that one million people are only 0,25% of the European population, which is "light years away" from a democratic majority (Pichler, 2008, p. 32).

The above measures are, of course, enough to satisfy the citizens' criticism of a lack of democracy or the lack of elements of participatory and deliberative democracy. The vagueness of the tools to participate has been interpreted as a sign, firstly "of mistrust of the European people or even as a sign of its inconsistency: in both cases future perspectives of European democracy look gloomy" (Allegri, 2008, p. 2), and then as a sign that the leaders of the Union's representative democracy "did not want to meet their citizens too much" (Pichler, 2008, p. 32).

From a more explicitly environmental point of view, despite this generally negative judgement concerning the tools to introduce the elements of participatory democracy at the EU level, it is possible to note a major "enthusiasm" towards the recall possibility to transform the EU into an environmental participatory democracy. Although the movement towards environmental participatory democracy does not appear in the Treaty provisions yet, it may

---

98   Although Europe is still constituted in a representative way, it should finally get involved with direct democracy "and not only simply playing around with it a bit". Pichler & Giese (2008): "Proposition for a European Initiative procedure—Incentives of founding Art. 8b (4) Treaty of Lisbon".

99   Although art 24 rules that every citizen has the right to petition the European Parliament, to apply to the Ombudsman, and to write to any of the institutions, bodies, offices or agencies of the Union in one of the official languages, receiving an answer in the same language.

be found in secondary legislative instruments, in a number of directives, in the signature of the Aarhus Convention, as well as in the directives and regulations which the EU has adopted to implement that Convention. Moreover, environmental rights and ecological duties have found a more or less important place in the EU system as well.

In conclusion it is possible to underline that, as will be discussed in detail in the following parts, there is a general movement towards an environmental participatory democracy in Europe rather than a general participatory or deliberatory democracy and this movement is amplified by the granting of environmental rights and duties to the European citizens.

2.1.2. Space

The second dimension is the spatial one. The spatial context of Europe, of course, is the territory of Europe. In the previous book, I wrote that Environmental Democracy has to be built at different levels, global and local, and the EU also recognises this as a way to try to resolve the environmental crisis (Parola, 2013). Indeed, the First Environmental Action Programme referred to five possible levels of action – global, local, international, regional and national – and the need "*to establish the level best suited to the type of pollution and to the geographical zone to be protected*". Thus, the EU acknowledges that the efficiency and effective action to protect the environment can be supported at different levels following the principle of Subsidiarity.[100]

Of course the initial insertion of this principle was to prevent an undesirable extension of Community competences but from an environmental point of view it can be used in the above approach: the environmental global problem needs a global or international action and local problems need local action, which can be divided again into regional and national problems and their corresponding solutions.

So in the context of the Environment the principle of Subsidiarity, introduced by the Single European Act, stipulates that environmental action should be

---

100   Principle of Subsidiarity "which has its most recent historical origins in the teachings of the Roman Catholic Church, but which is also to be found in political thought of the eighteenth and nineteenth century and can be traced back to earlier times, and which finds a more complete modern day expression in German Basic Law, declares that no action should be taken by a larger political entity unless its objectives cannot be effectively achieved by action of a smaller" political entity. See Emiliou, 1992, p. 383; Cross, 1995, p. 107.

taken at the Community level to the extent to which environmental objectives could be attained better at that level than at the Member States level.[101]

Another aspect of the spatial dimension is that at the regional level there are different problems which can be resolved just at this level, through collaboration and coordination between the States which compose this region.

For instance, the Water Framework Directive[102] is based first on the recognition of the local environmental problems, as the recitals also remind us: "*In Europe depletion of the water resource has been a continuous process for forty years. Human water uses have increased all over the period, without any consideration of sources initially imagined as self-purifying*".[103] Secondly, this local problem can be solved by "*developing an integrated Community policy on water*".[104]

Moreover, the success of this Directive "*relies on close cooperation and coherent action at Community, Member State and local level as well as on information, consultation and involvement of the public, including users*".[105] Furthermore, recital 18 goes on to affirm the fundamental importance of solving the problem at different levels within the Community: "*Community water policy requires a transparent, effective and coherent legislative framework. The Community should provide common principles and the overall framework for action. This Directive should provide for such a framework and coordinate and integrate, and, in a longer perspective, further develop the overall principles and structures for protection and sustainable use of water in the Community in accordance with the principles of subsidiarity*".

The objective of this directive is "*maintaining and improving the aquatic environment in the Community*".[106] In order to achieve this goal, recital 23 makes it clear that: "*Common principles are needed in order to coordinate Member States' efforts to improve the protection of Community waters in terms of quantity and quality, to promote sustainable water use, to contribute to the control of transboundary water problems, to protect aquatic ecosystems, and terrestrial ecosystems and wetlands directly depending on them, and to safeguard and develop the potential uses of Community waters*".

---

101   Article 130 r (4) before it was amended by the Amsterdam Treaty.

102   Directive 2000/60/EC establishing a framework for Community action in the field of water policy as amended by Decision 2455/2001/EC and Directive 2008/32/EC. See in general about WFD: Aubin,, & Varone, 2002, p. 28; Boscheck, 2006, p. 268; Bouleaul, 2008, p. 1747; Kaika, & Page, 2003, p. 314; Kaika, 2003, p. 303; Ker Rault, & Jeffrey, 2008, p. 241; Kostas Bithas, 2008; Moss, 2008; Naddeo, Zarra, & Belgiorno, 2007, p. 243; Peuhkuri, 2006; Rodriguez, 2006.

103   Recital 4 of the WFD.

104   Recital 9 of the WFD.

105   Recital 14 of the WFD.

106   Recital 19 of the WFD.

2.2. Actors of Environmental Democracy at a European Level: the Role for European citizens

This part assesses the development of norms which concern environmental rights and ecological duties within the context of the development of EU environmental law.

Before starting with the discussion on rights and duties, a word must be said about the importance of the role of European citizens *vis-à-vis* the protection of the environment.[107]

The recognition of the fundamental role of European citizens in the environmental field is clear in the EU environmental protection system. An example is the Sixth Environment Action Program namely "*Our Future our Choice: An Action Programme for the Environment in Europe at the Beginning of the 21st Century*". This title is significant because it emphasises the importance of the environmental choice of the single European citizen.

Thus, this Programme proposes five priority "*avenues*" of strategic action to "*help us meet our environmental objectives*".[108] For this book, a significant element of the programme is the fourth point entitled "*Empowering Citizens and Changing Behaviour*". This document mainly recognises that "*in recent years we have begun to play a more active role, as individuals, in environmental protection. Many people have started to make efforts to change their personal and family behaviour, for example, by recycling, buying environment-friendly products and installing energy efficient systems in our households*".

Then, the Action programme underlines that "*well-informed citizens who are actively involved in environmental decision-making are a powerful new force in achieving environmental results*". Moreover, practical information about the environment and which actions may protect or damage the environment, are fundamental since it helps people to choose and, for instance, buy alternative products and services that are energy efficient. Moreover, the Action Programme reminds us that more and more citizens are demanding a stronger voice in the decisions made at the community, regional, national and international level

---

107   Chalmers, 1999. On European citizenship, see also, recently, Besson, & Utzinger, 2007, p. 573; Jacobs, 2007, p. 591; Kostakopoulos, 2007, p. 623; Magnette, 2007, p. 664.

108   The first is to improve the implementation of existing legislation. The second aims at integrating environmental concerns into the decisions taken under other policies. The third focuses on finding new ways of working closer with the market via businesses and consumers. The fourth involves empowering people as private citizens and helping them to change behaviour. Finally, the fifth aims at encouraging better land-use planning and management decisions.

that affect our health and the quality of our environment. To be effective they "*need quality information that they can use and understand and they need the appropriate access to decision-makers to be able to express their views*".[109] Thus, the interpretation of the EU approach is quite clear at least at a theoretical level, and the fundamental step to achieve this goal is to provide instruments to push the people to feel like environmental and ecological citizens by granting them environmental rights and duties.

To exercise those rights and respect those duties they need to know and understand what the environmental issues are, what is needed to resolve them and how they can contribute. Thus, environmental education, information including indicators and maps, and awareness raising initiatives will be essential to this process. Those tools, hence, ought to aim at encouraging more sustainable lifestyles.

Besides, the efforts to develop this new role at a European level "have often been driven by the need for greater enforcement of existing EC environmental law" (McGillivray, & Holder, 2001, p. 163). On several occasions, the Communication mentions that citizens are often the first to discover breaches of Community environmental laws.[110]

Indeed, individuals and NGOs also play an important role in providing information so that the Commission can properly fulfil its watchdog function, and the bulk of former Article 226 EC cases are initiated by following up private complaints.[111] For example, the last report[112] shows that the majority of cases were initiated by following up private complaints, and only a minority of these were pursued on the basis of the Commission's own investigations.[113]

---

109   "Public participation in planning could be improved through more easily accessible and better quality information. Environmental reporting by companies and authorities needs to make information available at a local level so that people can easily obtain data on emissions from factories or other installations in their area". See the text of Sixth Environmental Action Program.

110   Commission Communication on Implementing European Community Environmental Law, COM (2008) 773 final, 18 November 2008, p. 6, Commission Communication on Implementing European Community Environmental Law, COM (2008) 773 final, 18 November 2008, p. 6.

111   Available at www.ec.europa.eu/community_law/infringements/pdf/25_annexes_1_to_4_en.pdf.

112   25th Annual Report on monitoring the application of Community law [COM(2008) 777].

113   Moreover the environmental sector generates by far the highest number of complaints and represented 43 per cent of the active complaints. Of course it has to be noted that apart from the most obvious breaches such as illegal landfill or acts against protected habitats or species, ordinary "citizens are not able to detect less visible infringements, such as excess emissions of invisible gas, discharges into water courses above permit limits, or a failure to install best available pollution control techniques. They

Thus, the question is now whether the important role played by individuals and recognised by the EU can transform the European citizenry into environmental and ecological citizens and whether this transformation will be similarly reflected in procedural and judicial rights and duties.

On 1 January 1993, as a result of the Maastricht amendments to the European Treaties, all nationals of Member States acquired under the Treaty something called citizenship of the European Union.[114] The concept of citizenship is clearly stated in the Treaty and involves a number of individual rights, including the right to move and reside freely, and the right to vote or stand as a candidate in municipal elections in the country in which he or she is residing.

Although citizenship at the EU level is mainly constructed for the purpose of free movement and equal treatment, nevertheless a new approach, which incorporates an environmental dimension, has begun to be constructed. As a matter of fact, a movement to grant environmental rights and duties has been emerging for more than five years in secondary law, although, as will be discussed in the following, at the Treaty level there is no explicit recognition yet.

2.2.1. European Environmental Rights

This part will attempt to give a general framework under which it may be seen whether environmental rights are granted in the European Union's legal order and whether there is any implementation of the rights approach of Environmental Democracy (Hayward, 2000, p. 164-165). At present, a substantive human right to the environment does not exist explicitly in European law, as in international law (Parola, 2013). Nevertheless, the focus for this part is on the question of whether the existing EU environmental and human rights provisions already provide implicitly the protection of the right to an adequate environment.

Then, this part will seek to identify the main environmental procedural rights currently enjoyed by European citizens within the EU, and to assess whether these are such as to render unnecessary the provision of a fundamental substantive right to an adequate environment, entrenched or binding at the constitutional level of the EU.

The following discussion will take into account the different provisions from the Treaty, the European Charter of fundamental rights and the European

---

generally lack resources such as analytical laboratories, and access to facility premises. The Commission cannot rely primarily on private citizens to detect and report infringements of Community environmental law. The Commission should be able to develop its own strategy for monitoring the implementation of legislative measures falling outside citizen's awareness". Ballesteros, 2009, p. 54.

114   Article 8 of Treaty Establishing the European Community.

Convention on Human Rights. The main reason concerning the analysis of the last two documents is that they have become very important since the Lisbon Treaty was signed and entered into force.

2.2.1.1. Substantive Environmental Rights

The Treaty in its present form does not provide any legal expression of a substantive environmental right. This does not mean that there were not some efforts to acknowledge this right. Indeed, since the late 1990s the institutions of the EU have started to discuss the necessity of such recognition. For instance, in preparations for an Intergovernmental conference, both the European Commission and a number of Nordic countries tried to promote the idea that EC law should contain an express inclusion of a right to a healthy environment or some similar right.[115]

Other proof of such efforts can be found in two statements of the Parliamentary Assembly of the Council of Europe, the first in November, 1999: "*in the light of changing living conditions and growing recognition of the importance of environmental issues, it considers that the [European] Convention [on Human Rights] could include the right to a healthy and viable environment as a basic human right*"[116] and recommended investigating the feasibility of amending the Convention to include such a right.[117]

Then the second declaration is a recommendation from 27 June 2003, 1614 (2003) on Environment and Human Rights: "*The Assembly recommends that the Governments of Member States: ensure appropriate protection of the life, health, family and private life, physical integrity and private property of persons in accordance with Articles 2, 3 and 8 of the European Convention on Human Rights and by Article 1 of its Additional Protocol, by also taking particular account of the need for environmental protection; recognise a human right to a healthy, viable and decent environment which includes the objective obligation for states to protect the environment, in national laws, preferably at constitutional level; safeguard the individual procedural rights to access to information, public participation*

---

115   The 1994 Rapport of European Parliament's Committee on Institutional Affairs proposed a model constitution for the European Union which included a title on Human rights Guaranteed by the Union. There rights included, *inter alias*, "Everyone shall have the right to the protection and preservation of his natural environment". Doc EN/RR/244/244403 27 January 1994. Macrory, 1996, p. 219.

116   Council of Europe, Standing Committee acting on behalf of P.A., 4 November, 1999, Texts Adopted, Recommendation 1431, online: Parliamentary Assembly <assembly.coe.int//Main.asp?link=http://   assembly.coe.int/Documents/AdoptedText/TA99/EREC1431.HTM>.

117   See Shelton (1997) citing Jacque, (1997) p. 70-71.

in decision making and access to justice in environmental matters set out in the Aarhus Convention".[118]

Despite the above mentioned expressions of awareness about the extreme importance of recognising a substantive right to environment, the EU has not yet explicitly enshrined it within the Treaty establishing the European Community (Shelton, 2001, p. 185). The only provision which could at least implicitly grant such a right is Article 37 of the Charter of Fundamental Rights of the European Union (Collins, 2007a, p. 143).

Nevertheless, there is a complex debate concerning the value and the interpretation to give to this provision. Thus, the question that will be at the centre of the following part is whether Article 37 contains a right to healthy environmental protection or whether it is rather a non-binding guiding principle. And, even more, if its legal significance has changed after the entry into force of the Lisbon Treaty which has declared the binding character of the Charter.

2.2.1.1.1.   Article 37 Codifies an Environmental Human Right
Article 37 proclaims "*A high level of environmental protection and the improvement of the quality of the environment must be integrated into the policies of the Union and assured in accordance with the principle of Sustainable Development*".

Some scholars have argued that this Article provides some "codification" of a right to environment. They point out the explanation given by the draft which says "*the principle set out in this Article has been based on Article 2, 6 and 174 of the EC Treaty, which have now been replaced by Articles III-3(3), III-4 and III-129 of the Constitution. It also draws on the protection of some national constitutions*".

This second part is the most important for the above interpretation. Most national Constitutions of the EU-27, hence, enshrine environmental protection as a fundamental right; therefore they grant to the Charter provision the status of a "formal" fundamental right (De Abreu Ferreira, 2007a).

The location in the national Constitution as well as the wording is varied; some appear under the heads of economic and social policy, while others under titles on fundamental rights, basic rights or individual rights. Concerning the wording, some of them proclaim it in a direct form as an individual right,[119]

---

118   See Council of Europe, P.A., 24th sitting, Texts Adopted, Recommendation 1614 (2003), online: Parliamentary Assembly<assembly.coe.int/Main.asp?link=/Documents/AdoptedText/ta03/EREC1614.htm>. No "hard law" instruments have codified the connection, but again, this is unnecessary since we are dealing here with rights that are already enshrined in existing Conventions.

119   For instance the Constitution of Belgium, where the right to "lead a worthy life of human dignity" includes "the right to protection of a sound environment"(art. 23(3)(4)) See Martens, 2007, p. 287; Spain where the Article 45 (Spain) Constitution states that "everyone has the right to enjoy an environment suitable for the development of the

while some constitutions oblige the state to protect the environment.[120] It has been underlined that the last obligation might have the same meaning as the recognition of an individual right "since the concerned persons can ask the State authorities to respect it" (Kiss, 2008, p. 167).

Several European countries have not explicitly recognised a substantive right to environment within their Constitutions, but some of the Constitutional Courts of these same countries interpreted their Constitutions as including the right[121] to protection of the environment" (Kiss, 2008, p. 167).

So according to those authors, Article 37 grants an implicit substantive right to the environment by the Constitutions of Member States; in other words, the legal ground of Article 37 is the national provision which recognises this right. Consequently the Article establishes a substantive environmental right.

Following, instead, the interpretation of another part of the doctrine, Article 37 has to be read in light of Article1 of the Aarhus Convention which, signed by the EU, affirms a substantive right to a healthy environment (Ermacora, 2003). On the grounds of this provision, binding for the EU, a general human right to a clean environment is acknowledged on the EU level, also including procedural rights (Jendroska, 2006, p. 66).

Following this interpretation, an attempt to express a more concrete formulation of this right was made by the Avosetta Group during the negotiation

---

person as well as the duty to preserve it."; Portugal where the Constitution asserts that "all have the right to a healthy ecologically balanced human environment and the duty to defend it" (CONSTITUIÇÃO DA REPÚBLICA PORTUGUESA [Constitution] Article 66 (Port.); Further north, the Finnish Constitution, adopted in 2000, states that the "public authorities shall endeavour to guarantee for everyone the right to a healthy environment".(Article 20 (Fin.), Article 20 stems from a constitutional reform taking place in the mid 1990s in Finland aiming at providing a more "coherent set of fundamental rights" in Finland. See Davies, 2007, p. 190). Likewise, the Norwegian Constitution, altered in 1992, contains a right to "an environment that is conducive to health". GRUNNLOV [Constitution] Article 110B (Nor.). Most recently, France joined the ranks of European nations possessing constitutional guarantees of the right to environment in February of 2005. The French Constitution was amended in 2005 and now includes a Charter of the Environment ("Charter"). The Charter affords all citizens of France the right to live in a "balanced environment, favourable to human health". In addition, a great number of Eastern European countries have altered or changed their constitutions to include a substantive right to the environment: Czech Republic, Estonia, Hungary, and Slovenia. For example, the Hungarian Constitution states, "Hungary recognizes and implements everyone's right to a healthy environment". Article18 (Hung.), see also Bandi, 1993, p. 43. In doctrine See: Kiss, 2008, p. 167; Pedersen, 2010.

120   Greece (Article 24(1), the Netherlands (Article 21), Sweden (Article 2(2), Germany (Article 20 (a) and 31) and Austria (Comprehensive Constitutional Law on Environmental Protection Article1) See: Kiss, 2008, p. 167.

121   An example is Italy the right to health recognised by the Constitution has been interpreted by the Constitutional Court: Article 9(2) and 32(1) interpreted by the Constitutional Court inter alia in a judgment, n. 5172 on 6 October 1976. See Kiss, 2008, p. 167.

of the Constitutional Treaty in 2003:[122] "Everyone has the right to a clean natural environment. This right is subject to reasons of overriding public interest. It includes the right to participation in decision-making, the right of access to the courts and the right to information in environmental matters. A high level of environmental protection and the improvement of the quality of the environment must be integrated into the policy of the Union and ensured in accordance with the principle of sustainable development" (Ermacora, 2003, p. 29).[123]

2.2.1.1.2.   Article 37 Does Not Codify an Environmental Human Right

Despite the above-mentioned scholars affirming that a substantive right already exists, most scholars deny this approach for the following reasons:

Article 37 has been defined by Kiss as the "poor parents" of the Charter, because it is drafted in a way that fundamentally differs from other parts of the Charter and its contents have "little in common with the other Articles" (Kiss, 2008, p. 161). This provision does not confer an individual right on the citizens and several points prove this interpretation.

Firstly, the right is placed in the Charter's Title IV on solidarity and not in Title V on individual rights. Indeed, the expressions used in the Charter to grant human rights and freedoms have different terms compared to the terms used in Article 37: for example, Article 2(1) provides "*everybody has the right or the freedom*" or Article 9 "*the right [...] shall be guaranteed*"; or concerning, for example, human dignity in Article10 (2) which stipulates "*the right is recognised*"; Article 34(2) says "*Everybody [...] is entitled*". Concerning the protection of the environment none of these terms has been used.

Other evidence may be found in the literal reading of the wording of the provision, in fact when it says "*A high level of environmental protection [...] must*

---

122   See Conference Report, 2003, p. 34.

123   This Avosetta idea took the suggestion from the proposal suggested by the Green G8: "The inclusion of environmental rights in the Charter of Fundamental Rights (to the Treaty)". Brussels (April 29, 2002) – The eight largest environmental NGOs in Europe, the "Green G8", have presented their initial contribution to the debate on the Future of Europe to the European Convention. The document, "The Future of the European Union, Environment and Sustainable Development", which is expected to be the first of a number of contributions towards the Convention, raised 12 issues for consideration by the Convention. For current purposes the significant issues are: "Include environmental rights in the Charter of Fundamental Rights. If the Charter is imported into the Treaty, the environmental Article must be amended to be phrased in terms of a right, as existing in several national constitutions and the Aarhus Convention. In no event, should existing Treaty Articles be replaced or modified by the Charter's provisions on environment as they stand now".
   Available at www.eeb.org/press/2002/Green_G8_on_Convention_29_04_02.pdf.

be integrated into the policies of the Union" the language demonstrates there is a clear obligation to achieve a high level of protection and not a right.[124]

Moreover, the Charter refers to environmental protection as a policy goal and not a right.[125] In this light, Article 37 seems to add little in terms of a substantive right and appears to merely confirm the objectives of the Community, as set out in the EC Treaty. In fact, it appears just as a reinforcement of former Article 174(1) Treaty (Macdonald, 2008, p. 213). Thus, it is not a right for the citizens but just Union policy, as the title of the Article also indicates: "Environmental protection" and not right (Kiss, 2008, p. 161).

The question could be why a Charter of Fundamental Rights speaks about policies. And why did they not want to proclaim such a right? Probably the EU did not want to go so far, because of the difficulty in the definition of this right (Parola, 2013).[126] So the EU's choice to classify it as a pure policy principle without legal content allowed them to find a way out of the aforementioned questions.

Nevertheless, according to some authors the definition problem is not a convincing reason not to act more in practice, because a "certain extent of vagueness is common to each human right".[127] Although the above exposed points reduce the weight of Article 37, nevertheless it is possible to affirm that the Charter represents at least a little progress since it recognised the impossibility of ignoring the question of protection of the environment (Lee, 2008, p. 131). The debate stems from the common feeling of the fundamental need in Europe and in the World that a clean environment is necessary for the enjoyment of basic human rights.

In conclusion, the following question shall be answered: if Article 37 does not install a right to a healthy environment, how can a way be found to integrate a right to environmental protection available for each individual? A solution to fill

---

124   As Collins has well noted "Interestingly, the ambiguity as to the rights aspect of this provision would presumably allow courts to adopt either an anthropocentric or an eco-centric approach, since the provision does not specify the source of the duty". Collins, 2007a, p. 120.

125   See Articles 2 and 174, (1) (2) ECT and Article 37, Nice Charter.

126   See also: Desgagne, 1995, p. 296.

127   Ermacora has argued that "In fact, there are several positive effects justifying the necessity of enshrining the human right to a clean environment: firstly, it would be to enhance the clarity of the meaning and the boundaries itself, providing legal certainty and concentrating the aspects of such a right into one clause; secondly, to increase awareness of such a right by individuals who could feel more concerned and take legal (court) action to defend their environmental basic right and finally, because it could establish the equal ranking of environmental interests with such as the right to property which could be invoked in order to defend economic interests". Ermacora, 2003 p. 29; of the same opinion is Heldeweg, 2005, p. 22.

the gap without having to wait on Charter revision action from the EU institutions could be through a procedural rights approach which has been developing since the entry into force of the Aarhus Convention. In other words, it could be the introduction of procedural environmental rights. It is worth remarking that a set of this kind of rights encompassing a right to access to information, a right to participation, and a right to access to justice has already reached a level of regional customary law in Europe through adoption of a number of regional legal instruments, agreements, and initiatives (Pedersen, 2010).

Another solution could be interpreting two Articles of the Charter in an environmentally friendly way: Article 37 could be read together with the right of access to documents provided by Article 42 and the right to an effective remedy provided by Article 47. The terms used in both provisions are quite vague, but it has been suggested that they could be greening in accordance with obligations emerging also from Articles 4 and 9 of the Aarhus Convention.[128] Concerning public participation, Article 6 of Aarhus and Article 11 of the Lisbon treaty could be linked.

Moreover, the ECJ could directly use the Aarhus Convention: for example, by reviewing any secondary EU legislation which does not follow the international obligations incumbent on the Community as party to the Convention.[129] Moreover, now that the Charter, as it has become primary Community law, has become subject to the jurisdiction of the ECJ (Collins, 2007a), this could also lead to a broadening of the scope of Article 37 (Pedersen, 2010). In fact, the Charter establishes that it should not be interpreted as restricting or adversely affecting rights and freedoms set forth under international law, including the European Convention on Human Rights. The ECJ, hence, could co-ordinate efforts towards environmental rights in Europe by making a direct link with the Aarhus Convention and existing secondary EU legislation implementing the Convention.

---

128   "By linking the body of law surrounding the Aarhus Convention in the EU to Article 37, 42 and 47 of the Charter the ECJ could streamline environmental democracy efforts in the EU legal space", Hectors, 2008, p. 165.

129   Case C-239/03 Commission v. France [2004] ECR I-9325. In the Etang de Berre case, the ECJ holds "that specific implementation of an environmental protection was unnecessary, since the mere accession of the Community to this Convention created Community obligations on the states". Eleftheriadis. 2007. See also ECJ 15 October 2009, In Case C-263/08.

2.2.1.1.3.   Where Can We Find the European Environmental Substantive Rights?
So even if EU law does not expressly provide a right to an adequate environment, a kind of recognition of the right to a healthy environment *per se* at the EU level may be found elsewhere. There are different approaches by scholars.

According to some authors, the sources of this right might be found in the precautionary principle provided in former Article 174 of the Treaty. This principle in brief states that when an activity raises threats of harm to human health or the environment, precautionary measures should be taken even if cause and effect relationships are not fully established scientifically. In fact, Miller writes that this a "powerful and comprehensive principle which, in conjunction with the right to information on discharges and rights conferred by other directives, would appear to endow citizens of the European Union with the fundamental right to an environment adequate for (human) health and well-being" (Miller, 1995, p. 374).

Thus the principle encompasses "a presumption in favour of ordinary citizens' right to protection from environmentally hazardous activities, and places the burden of proof on proponents of a new technology, activity, process, or chemical to show that it does not pose a serious threat" (Hayward, 2000, p. 168). So, although the precautionary principle has undeniable importance in giving substantive meaning to environmental rights, the inherent uncertainties involved in interpreting and applying it mean that the principle cannot in itself be considered a source of rights nor create a fundamental environmental right.

Moreover, following another approach, it has been suggested that the right to environment emerges from the Community's secondary law on procedural environment rights. Indeed, the EU has promulgated an immense body of environmental protection legislation which may constitute an implicit recognition of the right to environment, but this question will be explored later.

Finally, there is the opinion that points out the jurisprudence of the European Court of Human Rights. The silence of the European Convention on Human Rights on the environmental issue, has, however, not stopped the Court, set up under the Convention, from developing jurisprudence in relation to the environment. Indeed, as the European Court of Human Rights has often affirmed "the Convention is a living instrument, which must be interpreted in the light of the present-day condition" (Mularoni, 2008, p. 231).

Space does not permit a discussion of all of the different approaches mentioned above, so it will be interesting to see the development of the jurisprudence of the European Court of Human Rights concerning this right, since the judiciary has already demonstrated a willingness to take a teleological approach to human rights in an environmental friendly manner. Moreover, as already mentioned, the jurisprudence is more important since the entry into force of the Lisbon Treaty, which has recognised that the European Union shall accede to the European Convention on Human Rights.

2.2.1.1.4. ECHR Jurisprudence: Environmental Protection "Par Ricochet"[130]

Following part of the doctrine, one way to develop a right to environmental protection is to interpret existing human rights in an environmentally friendly way. This "greening" (Pasques, 2006, p. 40) process has been an opportunity the ECHR has taken during the last decade (Hectors, 2008, p. 168). Thus, the Court has mobilised existing human rights (Anderson, 1996, p. 4) to recognise the link with environmental protection, *e.g.* to reach indirectly a recognition of an environmental right.[131]

Article 2 of the European Convention provides a right to life which is understood as protection against the arbitrary deprivation of life by the state, but at the same time as a positive duty on states to take the necessary measures to protect human life. The Court has affirmed that the bad conditions of the environment may influence human life; consequently, among the duties of the state there is also the duty to protect the environment.[132]

Moreover, the most frequently invoked human right in the environmental field against environmental degradation affecting individuals is the right to respect for private and family life, and for the home, as guaranteed in Article 8.[133] It has become well-established that serious environmental damage may lead to a violation of this Article. Other substantive human rights which have been "greening" are the right to property[134] and the procedural guarantees enshrined in Article 6 (Schall, 2008, p. 417).

It is interesting to note that the Strasbourg Court does not "attach to environmental protection a significant symbolic value to stand on its own as a fundamental right"; rather, it is a condition for the enjoyment of existing fundamental rights. Unfortunately, as has been remarked, the consequence of this approach entails that the protection of the environment "would 'lose' every time it conflicts with existent fundamental rights" (De Abreu Ferreira, 2007a, p.

---

130   See in particular: Sudre, 2001, p. 275.

131   On the analysis of the ECHR' jurisprudence on human rights and environmental protection see *inter alia* Déjeant-Pons, 2002, p. 23; Frumer, 1998, p. 813; McManus, 2005, p. 575.

132   Oneryildiz v. Turkey (2005) 41 EHRR 20, [65].

133   Article 8 reads: "1. Everyone has the right to respect for his private and family life, his home and his correspondence. 2. There shall be no interference by a public authority with the exercise of this right except such as is in accordance with the law and is necessary in a democratic society in the interests of national security, public safety or the economic well-being of the country, for the prevention of disorder or crime, for the protection of health or morals, or for the protection of the rights and freedoms of others".

134   Athanassoglou v. Switzerland (2001) 31 EHRR 13; Nevertheless the court's jurisprudence on Articles 8 and 10 can sometimes conflict with the right to property enshrined in Article 1 of Protocol 1 to the ECHR.

5). In this situation, the choice when the environment "wins or loses" is taken by the State and so the applicant bears the burden of proof to show that the State has gone beyond its margin of discretion and its choice was wrong (De Abreu Ferreira, 2007a).

2.2.1.1.4.1.   Jurisprudences of ECHR in Environmental matters

The first direction taken by the Court, in 1976, was that no right to preservation of the natural environment as such was included among the Convention's rights.[135] Nevertheless, some time later that view started to change: the Commission noted in 1990 in *S. v. France* that considerable noise and other nuisances could undoubtedly affect the well-being of a person and thereby interfere with the Convention's rights.[136]

This new approach was followed by the Court in *Powell v. United Kingdom* in 1990.[137] Nevertheless, the first real step to align the ECHR with environmental protection was taken in the famous judgement *López Ostra v. Spain*, where

---

135   See X. v. Germany, App. No. 7407/76, 5 Eur. Comm'n H.R. Dec. & Rep. 161, 161 (1976), The case concerns dismissing the applicants' claims that military activities in marshlands violated right to life, prohibitions on torture and inhuman treatment, and rights to liberty and security.

136   See S. v. France, App. No. 13728/88, 65 Eur. Comm'n H.R. Dec. & Rep. 250, 263-64 (1990) (nuisances stemming from construction of a nuclear power plant could not be considered disproportionate to the legitimate interests served by the operation of the plant, especially in light of compensation already received by applicant). See also Arrondelle v. United Kingdom, App. No. 7889/77, 26 Eur. Comm'n H.R. Dec. & Rep. 5, 8-9 (1983).

137   Powell v. United Kingdom, 172 Eur. Ct. H.R. (ser. A) 1 (1990).The case related to the effects of noise levels emanating from Heathrow Airport on citizens living in close proximity. The applicants argued that the noise levels amounted to a violation of Articles 6, 8, and 13 of the ECHR. The court noted that Article 8 was a material provision in assessing the case, as the applicants' lives had been adversely affected by the noise. Article 8 deals with the right to respect for private and family life while also setting out the circumstances under which a possible infringement may be justified. However, the court held, while noting the central role that Heathrow Airport plays in the U.K. economy, that the measures taken by the United Kingdom in relation to noise abatement were within the margin of appreciation and in this light it was not for the court to substitute its own assessment for that of the United Kingdom, concerning what might constitute the best policy. Likewise, the court in Hatton v. United Kingdom (Hatton v. United Kingdom, 2003-VIII Eur. Ct. H.R. 189, 228 (2003)) found that the nuisances from night flights to and from Heathrow Airport did not amount to a violation of Article 8. Although the court noted that "environmental protection should be taken into consideration by States in acting within their margin of appreciation [...] it would not be appropriate for the Court to adopt a special approach in this respect by reference to a special status of environmental human rights". It stressed the positive impact of the airport on the U.K. economy, combined with the relatively slight impact the noise had on house prices and the chances for the applicants to comment on government policy on night flights, in finding that the government had struck a fair balance. By stressing the economic importance of the flights, the court left a rather wide margin of appreciation for the member states as environmental disputes often amount to

the Court identified a violation of Article 8 of the Convention as a result of environmental conditions. Although the court refrained from fashioning a substantive right to the environment under the ECHR, it found Spain violated its positive obligation to ensure López Ostra could live in an environment that did not constitute a serious health threat to her and her family.

Another leading case is *Guerra v. Italy*.[138] The Court affirmed that the Italian authorities had failed in their positive obligation under that provision to secure effective respect for the applicants' right to family life.[139] The Court construed the right to privacy as guaranteeing protection against environmental pollution.[140]

Moreover, the precedent created by the two mentioned cases has subsequently been confirmed in *Taskin v. Turkey*,[141] where the Court held that Turkey, by using sodium cyanide in gold extraction in defiance of domestic court decisions, had violated Article 8. The importance of this judgment is based on two levels.

First, the judgment includes a number of references to the applicants' right to a healthy environment under the Turkish Constitution and then shows that a "domestic guarantee of the right to environment may have substantial legal significance at the supranational level" (Collins, 2007a, p. 120).

Even more significant in this statement is the Court's recognition of the right to environment in international law, referring to the relevant international texts on the right to a healthy environment" and to the procedural environmental rights enshrined in the Rio Declaration[142] and the Aarhus Convention. Furthermore,

---

a balancing act of economic interests on one side and environmental considerations on the other. Pedersen, 2010.

138 In Case of Guerra and Others V. Italy (116/1996/735/932), Judgement ECHR, 19 February 1998. Here, the applicants alleged that the Italian authorities violated Articles 2, 8, and 10 by failing to mitigate the risk of a major accident at a nearby chemical factory and by withholding information from local residents about the risks and about what emergency procedures were in place. The chemical factory was deemed a "high risk" according to Italian law (an explosion at the plant in the 1970s had led to the hospitalisation of 150 people). De Abreu Ferreira, 2007a, p.5.

139 It is also worth noting that however, there are a number of cases where no violation has been found. For instance, in Buckley v. United Kingdom, 1996-IV Eur. Ct. H.R. 1271, 1287, 1996. See also Johannische Kirche v. Germany, App. No. 41754/98 (2001), available at European Court of Human Rights HUDOC Search Portal, available at www.cmiskp.echr. coe.int/tkp197/search.asp?skin=hudoc-en. See Kyrtatos v. Greece, App. No. 41666/98, 40 Eur. H.R. Rep. 390 (2005).

140 See generally Sands, 1999, p. 39.

141 ECHR 10 November 2004, Taskin v. Turkey, 2004-X Eur. Ct. H.R. 145 (2005).

142 Declaration on Environment and Development, Principe 1, Report of the UN Conference on Environment and Development (UNCED). The UNCED was held in Rio de Janeiro (Brazil) from 3 to 14 June 1992 and was attended by 178 States, more than 50 intergovernmental organisations and several hundred non-governmental organisations (NGOs). The European Union also attended the Conference. In addition to the signing by

it is interesting to note that "the Court also unites procedural environmental rights, the right to environment, and the preservation of existing rights through environmental protection all under the rubric of the "right to a healthy environment". It seems that it may be perceiving the right to environment as one "unitary right", encompassing both substantive and procedural aspects (Collins, 2007a, p. 146).

Also interesting in this respect is the case of *Oneryildiz v. Turkey*,[143] where the Court affirmed that an environmental disaster can violate many rights contained in the Convention. Thus, it declared that the Turkish action was in contrast with Articles 2, 8 and 13 concerning the right to an effective remedy for violation of Convention rights, and with Article 1 of Protocol No. 1 relating to the right to peaceful enjoyment of possessions.[144]

The *López Ostra* and *Guerra* precedents were confirmed in *Moreno Gómez v. Spain*,[145] concerning noise pollution. Here, the Court found a breach of Article 8 as a result of the noise generated from an area with a high concentration of nightclubs and bars, after noting that the authorities had lacked a willingness to enforce existing rules which were designed to abate the noise levels. The court made similar findings in *Fadeyeva v. Russia*,[146] involving pollution from the

---

more than 150 States of the United Nations Framework Convention on Climate Change and the Convention on Biological Diversity, the Conference adopted three non-binding instruments: the Rio Declaration, the UNCED Forest Principles and Agenda 21.

143   ECHR 18 June 2002 and 30 November 2004.

144   The applicants claimed that Turkey was responsible for the deaths of their close relatives and the destruction of their property resulting from a methane explosion at a nearby municipal waste dump. See Collins, 2007a, p. 120.

145   ECHR 16 November 2004, Moreno Gómez v. Spain, 2004-X Eur. Ct. H.R. 327, 343 (2005).

146   ECHR 9 June 2005, Fadeyeva v. Russia, Application No 55723/ 00, Reports of Judgments and Decisions 2005-IV. The applicant in Fadeyeva lived in the Russian town of Cherepovets, approximately 450 meters from a steel plant. According to official reports, the Soviet-era plant contributed more air pollution than any other metallurgical plant in Russia, and its emission levels exceeded domestic standards. Throughout the years, the authorities had created a so-called "sanitary security zone" in order to protect people living in the area, but the zone had on a number of occasions been reduced. In addition, the authorities had, without effect, ordered the inhabitants of the "sanitary security zone" to resettle and failed to offer them any effective assistance in their attempt to resettle. Furthermore, the court hinted at the procedural norms enshrined in Article 8 in cases of environmental decisions when noting that "there is no indication that the State designed or applied effective measures which would take into account the interests of the local population affected by the pollution, and which would be capable of reducing the industrial pollution to acceptable levels". Fadeyeva, 2005-IV, Eur.Ct.H.R.at 292-293.

Severstal steel plant, the largest iron smelter in Russia, and also in *Giacomelli v. Italy*,[147] which involved storage and treatment of "special waste".

It is worth noting that the Court has also acknowledged the importance of procedural environmental rights as in the case *Taskin v. Turkey* and other decisions. In fact, procedural rights present a remedy in the European human rights machinery regardless of the court's caution towards recognising a substantive right, and offer adjudication in cases where national authorities pay little attention to the link between human rights and the environment. Thus, the Court has extended the procedural scope of Article 8 to include not only access to certain environmental information but also limited participation and subsequent redress before judicial authorities.

For instance, in *Vides Aizsardzibas Klubs v. Latvia*,[148] a Latvian court affirmed "a defamation suit by a mayor based on public allegations of impropriety made by an environmental NGO and the Court declared that Article 10 of the Convention has been violated by the Latvian Court, because the NGO "acted as an environmental "watch dog" ("chien de garde") and that this function was an essential one in a democratic society" (Collins, 2007a, p. 142).

In summary, it may be concluded that, although the ECHR has refrained from an explicit creation of a substantive right to the environment, the court's jurisprudence represents a significant contribution to the status of environmental rights (Hodkova, 1991, p. 70).

2.2.2. Ecological European Citizens

The creation of an environmental consciousness and a responsibility *vis-à-vis* the environment has started to develop at the European level[149]. If individuals

---

147   ECHR 2 November 2006, Giacomelli v. Italy. The court found an Article 8 violation in this last case, where the decision to issue an operating license to a waste treatment facility had not been accompanied by an environmental impact study in accordance with domestic law.

148   ECHR 27 May 2004 ECHR 27 May 2004.

149   Concerning responsibility *vis-à-vis* the environment Parola (2013) underlines that: "As a counterbalance to the rights-based approach which offers only indirect and limited ecological protection and reinforces the anthropocentric value system that is at the root of ecological degradation, there is an additional view. What is necessary is more emphasis upon the adoption and exercise of responsibilities towards all life, including non-human life (P. Taylor, 2009, p. 89), and a special responsibility to "care for the planet" (Weiss, 1990, p. 199). Increasingly, it is being pointed out that in many cultures individuals have duties and responsibilities towards others and the wider community. Traditionally, the duty-approach offers a subordinated prospective. Nevertheless, during the French Revolution the idea that citizenship is more about duties towards the Republic than rights was dominant. The slogan "no rights without responsibilities" is starting to take a new

are aware that their actions as consumers or direct producers of pollution may have negative effects on the environment, this may motivate individuals to change their action, and ecological duties can be implicitly recognised through participatory rights. Thus, there is a relationship between rights and duties in an environmental approach.[150]

Indeed, public participation is claimed to enhance active ecological citizenship since granting environmental rights leads to taking environmentally responsible private decisions as well (Lee, 2005, p. 125). An example which could explain this link is the access to information: granting this right provides citizens with the necessary information to better judge and evaluate and, finally, to make the environmentally friendly choice.

As pointed out above, in the notion of Environment in Europe the anthropocentric prospective is preeminent, although not exclusive. Hence, there is an implicit rejection of ecological thought. Nevertheless, as will be seen in the next section, the EU has recognised some aspects of the citizens' duty *vis-à-vis* the Earth and not just future generations, as is reflected in several policy instruments in the EU.

It has been stated in the book "*Environmental Democracy at Global Level*" (Parola, 2013) that there are two fundamental characteristics of ecological citizenship: first, ecological citizenship might be recognised as a non-territorial form of citizenship due to the fact that it extends beyond territorial boundaries

---

position in modern green political thought. Indeed, the other face of environmental rights presumes an active attitude on behalf of citizens, and even more, a citizens' duty to protect the environment. Each person has the right to have his or her environment protected, but is also obliged to contribute to the common effort". "Thus, there are two fundamental obligations, one to present and future generations, and another to nature". "Philosophy, religion, green political thought and some legal traditions from diverse cultural traditions have already recognised that man is trustee or steward of the natural environment and from this arises man's duty to conserve the planet for present and future generations. Nevertheless this recognition is not universal and almost all environmental theories note there is a huge lack of inter-generational and intra-generational equity. First, political leaders fail to adequately consider future interests in evaluating policy options. But "this myopia" is not the outcome of a lack of a concern for children or future inhabitants of Earth; instead, it is "the result of institutional constraints that encourage political leaders to prioritise the short-term needs of voters" (Wolfe, 2008, p. 1897)". "The second obligation is the duty to protect the environment, *e.g.* the living and non-living creatures. This duty is reflected in the principle of sustainability and cannot be confused with shallow versions of sustainable development. The indispensable element of the new categorical imperative is responsibility for the community of life (Bosselmann, 2008). If translated to political theory, responsibility for all life requires a total rethinking of law and governance".

150 Moreover, duty-centered approaches can also be found also in some national constitutions of Member States, including duties both of individuals, (The Spanish Constitution) and of government (for example the Dutch Constitution).

of the nation-state, and secondly, these kinds of duties embody both the private and public sphere.

Concerning the non-territorial boundaries it can be noted that this feature characterises the EU vision as well; in fact, it has been decided that more and more issues must be regulated between the 27 States as the boundaries do not exist anymore.

Indeed, the awareness that ecological issues and the protection of the environment surpass political delimitations between the States is already demonstrated by several directives which try to regulate environmental transboundary problems. An example is the Water Framework Directive[151] which promotes a new ecological and transboundary approach to water management. The new WFD rationalises and updates existing water legislation by setting "common" EU-wide objectives for water. The first recital states the importance of water as such and the necessity to adopt legal provisions to protect it. The recital reads as follows: "*Water is not a commercial product like any other but, rather, a heritage which must be protected, defended and treated as such*".

This recital is linked with recital 19 announcing the main purpose of the WFD: "*This directive aims at maintaining and improving the aquatic environment in the Community*". To achieve this aim the Member States have to designate river basin

---

151   Directive 2000/60/EC establishing a framework for Community action in the field of water policy as amended by Decision 2455/2001/EC and Directive 2008/32/EC. The WFD builds the foundation of a modern, holistic and ambitious water policy for the European Union. The decision for establishing a new framework for water management in Europe happened within a changing social and political framework. The increasing internationalisation and complexity of water resource management, the increasing number of actors and institutions involved in this process, the newly vested economic interests in water supply, and the increasing concern and sensitivity towards environmental protection, are amongst these factors. After meetings and consultations the Commission proposed in 1997 the draft of a framework directive that promotes a new ecological and transboundary approach of water management and in 2000 the "Directive 2000/60/EC of the European Parliament and of the Council establishing a framework for the Community action in the field of water policy" was adopted. The WFD establishes a framework for the protection of all water bodies, which prevents further deterioration of water resources, promotes sustainable water use and ensures the progressive reduction of pollution of water bodies. This is because the WFD requires MS to aim to achieve 'good ecological and chemical status' in surface waters and 'good chemical and quantitative status' in groundwaters by 2015. It will do this by establishing a river basin district structure within which demanding environmental objectives will be set, including ecological targets for surface waters. The Directive sets out a timetable for both initial transposition into laws of MS and thereafter for the implementation of requirements. The WFD promotes the integrated management of water resources to support environmentally sound development and reduce problems associated with excessive water abstraction, pollution, floods, ancestry programmes at the river basin scale and, in many cases, transboundary collaboration between European countries.

districts[152] and competent authorities for the river basins.[153] The Member States are under a duty to assign river basins extending to more than one Member State to an international river basin district. In such an international river basin district, the MS shall ensure the coordination of their national measures.[154] Finally, river basins extending into non-member states are subject to a less strict duty to ensure coordination.[155]

Furthermore, the idea of freedom of movement of citizens has grown from the idea of elimination of boundaries and also from the idea of achieving a citizenship arising from a deeper integration of Europe. In environmental matters there are also some attempts in this direction. In fact EU measures to introduce elements of Participatory Democracy in environmental matters have begun to expand notions of citizenship on environmental issues beyond the nation state. Thus, an ecological perspective to citizenship leads a "disruptive challenge to the traditional notion of citizenship", one which looks "outside the city, beyond the public, and further afield than the nation-state" (McGillivray, & Holder, 2001, p. 168).

Another example which demonstrates a movement towards the loosening of the concept of boundaries is the revised Directive on Environmental Impact Assessment which requires public consultation within other member states which may experience significant environmental effects through developments outside of their borders (McGillivray, & Holder, 2001, p. 169).

Thus, from the above-mentioned examples it can be affirmed that at the EU level there is a growing idea to eliminate boundaries between States when the protection of the environment is at stake, as well as the recognition of a common European natural heritage. The idea of a common natural heritage in Europe "ought therefore to elevate the relationship between community and environment to a higher plane, in the process creating a more direct connection between individuals and the environment" (McGillivray, & Holder, 2001, p. 170).

Passing now to the second feature of ecological duties which are embodied both in the private and public sphere, evidence of this character in EU policy and legislation is emerging. For example, the public right to participate can also be read as a public duty to participate even if there is no legal obligation. Granting procedural environmental rights can thus mean giving the possibility to the

---

152   The adoption of the river basin approach means that water protection measures attached to "the area of land from which all surface run-off flows through a sentence of streams, rivers and possibly, lakes into the sea at a single river mouth, estuary or delta". Article 2 of WFD.

153   Article 3 (1) (2) of WFD.

154   Article 3 (4) of WFD.

155   Article 3 (5) of WFD.

citizens to be involved and at the same time also improve their idea that they should feel involved in order to defend their environment.

Of course, the private sphere is more linked to the duties approach. There is, after all, much in the belief that "from an ecological point of view, good citizenship is learnt in private, not in public" (McGillivray, & Holder, 2001). Following this perspective the EU has tried to enforce directly or indirectly this duties approach in the private sphere, for instance, through waste regulation, environmental crimes, environmental liability and eco-labelling (Makuch, 2004, p. 226).

In conclusion, hence, it can be said that some aspects of ecological citizenship already exist and they could also lead to greening of the European citizenry. The following part will focus on finding the legal basis of ecological duties.[156]

2.2.2.1.   Ecological Duties

Concerning this subject there are two questions to answer: are there some sort of statements with regard to ecological duties in EU law? Or are there some principles which can be used to implement those duties?

The first question can be answered by stating that at the moment the EC treaty has not yet recognised explicitly ecological duties. Nevertheless, implicitly such duties are emerging. There are some principles that carry this notion, in particular some which embody the duty to protect the environment and likewise to repair it.

Those principles are the Precautionary Principle, the Preventive Principle, the Sustainable Development Principle and the Polluter Pays Principle, all provided

---

156   It has to note there is in Europe, a corporate social responsibilities movement which are becoming an official government policy in many countries and in July 2001 the Commission issued a Green Paper on a European framework for corporate social responsibilities (COM (2001) 366 final). This policy concerns not the responsibility of the citizen but the citizen as producer. "The Green Paper discusses issues such as what is corporate social responsibility, the internal dimension of CDR, including human resources management, health and safety at work and management of environmental impacts and natural resources, CSR's external dimension, which involves stake-holders such as local communities, business partners, consumers, and activist groups and CSR-integrated management, reporting and auditing". How it has been underlined that "the treatment of these issues in the Green Paper is repetitive and fuzzy, and fails to address the fundamental issues. Unfortunately, this representative of the CSR proponents' thinking". The CSR, as define by the Green Paper, is "a concept whereby companies decide voluntarily to contribute to a better society and a cleaner environment". Thus "although the prime responsibility of a company is generating profits, companies can at the same time contribute to social and environmental objective, through integrating corporate social responsibility as a strategic investment into their core business strategy, their management instruments and their operations". Bergkamp, 2002, p. 136.

for in former Article 174 (2) (now Article 191). It is worth underlining that there are other principles, laid down by that Article, like the high level of Protection Principle, the Source Principle and the Safeguard Clause, but those principles are set out in particular for Community legislation and it is difficult to find a ink with individual and citizens' duties.[157] Space does not permit the analysis in detail of the above-mentioned principles. Nevertheless, a word must be said about how those principles involve ecological duties.

2.2.2.1.1. Preventive Principle and Precautionary Principle
The preventive principle already played a role in European environmental law before it was inserted into the European Treaty through the Single European Act, since it previously had been enshrined in the first three environmental action programmes.[158] From that moment on, secondary environmental legislation of the Community started to reflect this principle as well.[159] The preventive

---

157   For instance Precautionary Principle and preventive action. Both principles have at the basis the idea to act before damage to the environment occurs, thus of course it is linked to the duty to protect. Nevertheless for our purpose those principles are not so fundamental in the view to the citizens' duty. As will be seen later, those principles can also be applied to the citizens' duty to restore and pay for environmental damage. In fact, the Sustainable considerations and the precautionary principle could perhaps be used in connection to environmental crimes. For instance, in cases concerning endangerment crimes, the precautionary principle could lead a judge to be "more severe with defendants who did not bother to explore all the possible consequences of their acts and might thereby have exposed society to clear risks". See Westerlund, 2008, p. 503.

158   First Environmental Action Programme of the European Community of 1973, OJ 1973, C 112/I; Second Environmental Action Programme of the European Community of 1977, OJ 1977, C 139/I; Third Environmental Action Programme of the European Community of 1983, OJ 1983, C 46/I

159   *E.g.* Preambular 34 of Directive 2009/16/EC of the European Parliament and of the Council of 23 April 2009 on Port State Control, OJ 2009, L 131/57; Preambular 2 of Directive 2009/41/EC of the European Parliament and of the Council of 6 May 2009 on the Contained Use of Genetically Modified Micro-Organisms, OJ 2009, L 125/75; Standard A 4.1 (1) (d) of Council Directive 2009/13/EC of 16 February 2009 implementing the Agreement concluded by the European Community Ship owners' Associations (ECSA) and the European Transport Workers' Federation (ETF) on the Maritime Labour Convention, 2006, and amending Directive 1999/63/EC, OJ 2009, 124/30; Preambular 30 of Directive 2008/98/EC of the European Parliament and of the Council of 19 November 2008 on Waste and Repealing Certain Directives, OJ 2008, L 312/3; Article 3(1)(a) of Directive 2008/1/EC of the European Parliament and of the Council of 15 January 2008 Concerning Integrated Pollution Prevention and Control, OJ 2008, L 24/8; Article 1(1)(b) of Council Directive 2006/88/EC of 24 October 2006 on Animal Health Requirements for Aquaculture Animals and Products Thereof, and on the Prevention and Control of Certain Diseases in Aquatic Animals, OJ 2006, L 328/14.

principle is based on the assumption that it is better to prevent environmental harm than to cure it.[160]

Therefore, the principle involves a risk assessment to avoid harm (Kiss, & Shelton, 1993, p. 37). Harm can only be prevented if the possibility of this harm is known. Due to this risk assessment, the principle has been expanded and complemented by the more complex precautionary principle.[161]

Only broadly described, the precautionary principle requires that an action against a potential environmental harm has to be taken even in the absence of scientific certainty that this harm will really occur (Louka, 2004, p. 20). The preventive principle can appear in two forms. It can either anticipate environmental damage in its entirety or it can try to anticipate the spread of already-occurred damage (De Sadeleer, 2002, p. 61).

As it will be shown later, this principle is reflected in the Liability Directive which pushes to enhance the citizens' ecological duties to protect and repair the environment.

2.2.2.1.2. Sustainable Development

Sustainable Development is linked to the recognition of the duty to protect the Environment *vis-à-vis* inter- and intra-generations, inter- and intra-species and Earth. This duty refers mainly to the European Union Institutions and Member States but it can also be used for their citizens. For current purposes, it is not possible to indulge on the theoretical basis of the obligation carried by this principle but it is worth analysing how this principle has been incorporated by the EU.

Sustainable development has a strong legal position among the ultimate objectives of the EU. As early as at the Rhodes Summit of 1988, the heads of government of the European Community, with reference to "environmental problems of increasing magnitude" declared Sustainable Development to be "one of the overriding objectives of all Community policies".[162] This has been followed by several high level policy documents which affirm the significance

---

160   See on the subject: De Sadeleer, 2002, p. 61; Kiss, & Shelton, 1993, p. 37; Krämer, 2003b, p. 25; Louka, 2004, p. 19.

161   See also: Krämer, 2003b, p. 25; Louka, 2004, p. 20.

162   Presidency Conclusions of the European Council, Rhodes, 2–3 December 1988 (DOC/88/10). At the same Summit, the government heads declared that the completion of 'the Single Market cannot be regarded as an end in itself, it pursues a much wider objective' and in the 'wider international context' the Community and the Member States declared their desire to play a leading role in achieving 'a better quality of life for all the peoples of the world' (Annex 1).

of environmental protection, especially when linked to the goal of sustainable development.[163]

This principle is one of the tasks of the European Community under Article 2 EC and remains so under the new Treaty of Lisbon. Article 3(3) of the amended Treaty states the objectives of the EU and defines the principle of sustainable development in Europe with its three elements, namely economic, social and environmental. The wording of the definition has been changed from that in Article 2 of the TEC with regard to the social element of Sustainable Development.

However, the commitments to the environment are maintained through the use of similar words: "*The Union shall establish an internal market. It shall work for the sustainable development of Europe based on balanced economic growth and price stability, a highly competitive social market economy, aiming at full employment and social progress, and a high level of protection and improvement of the quality of the environment. It shall promote scientific and technological advance*". This reference broadens the scope of implementation of the principle beyond the jurisdictional boundaries of Europe to the world.

Another novelty in this Article is the recognition of sustainable development as one of the specific policy goals of the EU in its foreign relations as well, in particular where the Union expresses its will to work to: "*foster the sustainable economic, social and environmental development of developing countries, with the primary aim of eradicating poverty; [...] help develop international measures to preserve and improve the quality of the environment and the sustainable management of global natural resources, in order to ensure sustainable development*".[164]

Moreover, a new ecocentric view may be found in Article 3(5): "*In its relations with the wider world, the Union shall uphold and promote its values and interests and contribute to the protection of its citizens. It shall contribute to peace, security, the sustainable development of the Earth, solidarity and mutual respect among peoples, free and fair trade, eradication of poverty and the protection of human rights, in particular the rights of the child, as well as to the strict observance and the development of international law, including respect for the principles of the United Nations Charter*".[165]

Thus, the duty to protect the environment is a fundamental objective of the EU but it has to be implemented into more concrete legal duties for European citizens.

---

163   *E.g.* Presidency Conclusions of the Brussels European Council 15–16 June 2006 (10633/1/06 REV 1). Sjafjell, 2010.
164   Article 21(2)(d) and (f) TEU.
165   Article 3(5) TEU

2.2.2.1.3.   Polluter Pays Principle

Concerning the duty to repair the environment, the Polluter Pays Principle (PPP) carries the idea that in the case of the environment being damaged by an individual, from this harm arises the duty to repair.[166]

The PPP has existed in Community law since 1973.[167] However, it was not until 1987 that it found its way into the text of the EC Treaty (De Sadelee, 2002, p. 30),[168] following the entry into force of the Single European Act of 1986.[169] It is one of the fundamental principles of European environmental policy and it is enshrined in the new Article 191 of the EC Treaty and in numerous secondary legislation of the Community.[170] It mainly means that the costs resulting from a polluting act should be borne by the person who caused the pollution and not by society as such (Sadeleer, 2002, p. 21).[171] The formulation of the principle leaves some questions open (Grossman, 2006, p. 29), such as: who is actually the polluter who shall bear the costs, (Sadeleer, 2002, p. 38)[172] and which costs exactly must the polluter bear? (Sadeleer, 2002, p. 42; Grossman, 2006, p. 13).

Concerning the question regarding which costs the polluter must pay, the principle has undergone a change. In the beginning, the costs merely comprised the costs of pollution prevention and control and now the principle also extends to costs of restoration (Grossman, 2006, p. 30). Furthermore, the principle is

---

166   See in general about the PPP: A. Bleeker, 2009, p. 289.

167   First Environmental Action Programme of the European Community of 1973, OJ 1973, C 112/I; Second Environmental Action Programme of the European Community of 1977, OJ 1977, C 139/I; Third Environmental Action Programme of the European Community of 1983, OJ 1983, C 46/I; first formal articulation at the European level of the principle had been made already one year earlier in the OECD Guiding Principles Concerning International Economic Aspects of Environmental Policies, OECD Doc. C 72/128 at para. 4.

168   See also: Grossman, 2006, p. 11; Larsson, 1999, p. 90; Thornton, & Beckwith, 2004, p. 84.

169   OJ 1987, L 169/1.

170   See *e.g.* Preambular 2 of the Directive 2008/1/EC of the European Parliament and of the Council of 15 January 2008 concerning integrated pollution prevention and control, OJ 2008, L 24/8; Preambular 14 and Article 15 of the Directive 2006/12/EC of the European Parliament and of the Council of 5 April 2006 on waste, OJ 2006, L 114/9; Preambular 11, 38 and Article 9 of Directive 2000/60/EC of the European Parliament and of the Council of 23 October 2000 Establishing a Framework for Community Action in the Field of Water Policy, OJ 2000, L 327/1; Article 15 of Council Directive 91/156/EEC of 18 March 1991 Amending Directive 75/442/EEC On Waste, OJ 1991, L 78/32.

171   See also: Kiss, & Shelton, 1993, p. 39; in general Larsson, 1993, p. 90; Louka, 2004, p. 16; Thornton, & Beckwith, 2004, p. 84.

172   See also: Grossman, 2006, p. 3; Krämer, 2003b, p. 28; Thornton, & Beckwith, 2004, p. 84; Louka, 2004, p. 16.

seen to have shifted from a merely economic principle to a liability principle (Sadeleer, 2002, p. 33). This will be shown in the following.

Hence, the principle can be enforced by various means, requiring producers or resource users to meet the cost of implementing environmental standards or technical regulations, or by introducing liability regimes that hold producers liable for causing environmental damage. The proposed Sixth Environmental Action Programme provides a clear signal to this effect by proposing the following commitment for the coming decade: "To promote the polluter pays principle, through the use of market based instruments, including the use of emissions trading, environmental taxes, charges and subsidies, to internalize the negative as well as the positive impacts on the environment" (Coffey, & Newcombe, 2001).

All the above instruments can provide incentives for introducing more environmentally sensitive practices, thereby providing clear incentives to alter behaviour; more importantly, this principle can be read in the prospective of a duty to repair.

Conclusion of Chapter 1

It can be said that from a democratic perspective, the EU has tried to find a solution to the democratic deficit by introducing some elements of participatory and deliberatory democracy.

Democracy, recognised at the EU level in particular as confirmed and extended by the Lisbon Treaty, is on the one hand a representative democracy which encompasses elections, political parties, governments by elected officials, and on the other hand, is a participatory and deliberative democracy which involves, for example, citizen initiatives and the recognition of other participatory rights such as access to information. Although an effort exists to shift towards a participatory model, it cannot be viewed as an achieved goal; what's more, the issue of the EU's democratic deficit primarily as a question of the balance of power between the institutions rather than as being concerned with the relationship of the citizens to these institutions should be resolved.

Section I has analysed the relationship between "Europe" and "Environment" and in particular the notion "Environment" which can be found in the European context can be divided into wide and narrow definitions and can be characterised by a mainly anthropocentric approach.

Nevertheless, this strong anthropocentric orientation should eventually be reduced as EU actions in certain fields which entail a more ecocentric approach, for instance, Climate Change, increase; also, some grains of the ecocentric approach have entered into EU environmental law provisions, in particular through ECJ jurisprudence.

The final part of Chapter I has, thus, emphasised that the theoretical model of Environmental Democracy as well as some features of the new citizenship and its environmental rights and ecological duties are starting to be recognised in the European Union. There are, as well, some signs of the EU's efforts to foster the role for citizens and NGOs in environmental fields through explored directives which implement the Aarhus Convention.

CHAPTER 2

Implementation of Environmental Rights and Duties in Europe

"Environmental law is different from other areas of law. The diffuse interests which environmental law often represents cannot easily be captured in the language of individual rights, therefore, the category of environmental rules which may be potentially enforced through the concept of protection of individual right is limited [there is] a need to develop realistic alternatives for the sake of effective environmental protection"

(Prechal, & Hancher, 2002, p. 89).

Over the past decade, there has been a clearly visible shift towards an 'Environmental Democracy in Europe'; in particular, the signature of the Aarhus Convention in 1998, which became an integral part of EC law,[173] contributed substantially to this shift.

Consequently to such signature and ratification, the EU took steps to adjust its existing legislation which was applicable to the Member States to the Convention's requirements. Therefore, in 2003, the EU adopted a revised directive on access to environmental information as well as a new directive on public participation which amended the existing directives on environmental impact assessment and facility licensing.[174] Thus, in order to implement the third pillar, the Commission filed a Proposal for a directive on access to justice in environmental matters which is meant to bind the Member States, but the Proposal until now has not yet been adopted.[175]

---

173   Decision 2005/370, 2005, OJ L 124/1.

174   Directive 2003/4/EEC of 14 February 2003 on public access to environmental information and repealing Council Directive 90/313/ EEC, [2003] OJ L41/2 and Directive 2003/35/EC of 26 May 2003 providing for public participation in respect of the drawing up of certain plans and programmes relating to the environment and amending with regard to public participation and access to justice Council Directives 85/ 337/EEC and 96/61/EC, [2003] OJ L156/17.

175   At least October 2012. Proposal for a Directive of the European parliament and of the Council on access to justice in environmental matters, COM (2003)624 of 23 October 2003.

Moreover, as a signatory to the Aarhus Convention, the European Community is also under the obligation to implement the Convention;[176] in fact, the Community is bound by the Convention's obligations in line with the principles of international law. Consequently, in order to allow for ratification by the Community,[177] pre-existing Community legislation concerning the subject-matter of the Convention had to be changed. Therefore, the Commission prepared a draft regulation which applied the three pillars of the Convention to all EU institutions and bodies (Jendroska, 2006, p. 63), a proposal which was adopted by Regulation 1367/2006: the "Aarhus Regulation".[178]

Although Member States' implementation anticipated implementation at an EU level, the second will be analysed in Section I, and then in Section II at the Member States' level. The reason for this choice is in coherence with the first Chapter of the book. The idea is, in fact, to explore environmental democracy at the local level and the first step is the regional local level; then, little by little descending towards the national local level.

The scope of this part is not to describe in detail the single provisions which were taken in this field, because this has already been done by several authors, but the aim is to try to underline the steps already made towards the construction of an environmental democracy in Europe. Thus, the comments of some Articles of the directives that will be analysed, intend to point out the existence of the environmental rights which could sustain the Environmental Democracy in Europe.

Concerning the implementation of ecological duties, it is worth noting that at the EU level there is not an implementation but just the principles from which, as explained at the end of the first section, such duties emerge. On the contrary, some ways have been found to implement environmental duties at the national level.

---

176   Council Decision in 2005, 2005/370, Official Journal L 124 (2005), p. 1. See also Lee, 2005, p. 181.

177   Decision on ratification by the EU, OJ L 124, 17.5.2005, p. 1. Available at www.ec.europa.eu/environment/aarhus/pdf/dec_2005_370_en.pdf.

178   Regulation 1367/2006 on the application of the provisions of the Aarhus Convention on Access to Information, Public Participation in Decision-making and Access to Justice in Environmental matters to Community institutions and bodies, OJ 2006L 264/13. See Jans, & Vedder, 2008, p. 331, See also for the Proposal Regulation: Dette, 2004, p. 3.

1. Environmental Democracy at the EU Level

1.1. Procedural Rights: Implementation of the Aarhus Convention

It has been remarked that there is not a substantive right to the environment and of course, there is no implementation of it; nevertheless, the path undertaken by the EU which implicitly recognises it has been the implementation of Procedural rights which are, according to some scholars, integral parts of the right to a clean environment.[179]

The Commission set out to implement the Aarhus Convention as one instrument, a single Regulation was meant to impose all three sets of obligations on the Community institutions. The proposal was adopted through the co-decision procedure[180] on 10 October 2003.[181] The European Parliament and the Council had three readings and they proposed numerous amendments. Despite the two institutions disagreeing over the desired content of the measure, they finally adopted the Regulation on 6 September 2006 (Crossen, & Niessen, 2007, p. 332). It took effect in June 2007, a full nine years after the signing of the Convention in 1998 (Jans, & Vedder, 2008, p. 331).

The Aarhus Regulation applies the three pillars of the Aarhus Convention to Community institutions and bodies. First, the regulation contains provisions on public access to environmental information held by European Community institutions and bodies, as well as requiring the European Commission and other Community bodies to actively collect and disseminate such information. Secondly, it organises a new public participation procedure which shall apply whenever Community institutions and bodies prepare, modify or review plans and programs likely to have significant effects on the environment.

Finally, it provides for a special internal review procedure whereby NGOs, meeting certain criteria can request the Commission or any other Community

---

179 According to Avosetta Group, the right to participation, access to courts and access to information are integral part of the Article of the right to a clean environment.

180 The co-decision procedure set out in former Article 251 (now Article 294) of the EC Treaty.

181 Proposal for a Regulation of the European Parliament and of the Council on the application of the provisions of the Aarhus Convention on Access to Information, Participation in Decision- Making and Access to Justice in Environmental Matters to EC Institutions and Bodies, COM (2003) 622; see about the proposal Keessen, 2007, p. 26.

body to reconsider any administrative act it has adopted pursuant to EU environmental law, or to adopt such an act where it was legally required to do so but failed to act (Gourtin, 2006).

Before analysing the listed environmental rights granted to European citizens it is necessary to identify the EC institutions and bodies to which this Regulation must apply.

According to the Regulation the provisions apply to a "*Community institution or body*" which means, following Article 2(1)(c), any public institution, body, office or agency established by, or on the basis of the Treaty except when acting in a judicial or legislative capacity. In its explanatory memorandum to the proposal, the Commission affirms: "*The Aarhus Convention addresses the relationship between individuals and their associations on the one hand, and the public authorities on the other hand. [...] The basic idea is that wherever public authority is exercised – parliaments and courts are exempted to the extent they act in their legislative or judicial capacity – there should be rights under the Convention for individuals and their organisations. [...] It follows from the broad concept used in the remainder of the definition 'public authority' in Article 2(2) of the Convention] that, for the Community [the notion 'institutions' in Article 2(2)(d)] has to be interpreted in a broad sense, and cannot be limited to the Community institutions mentioned in Article 7 of the EC Treaty*".[182]

Moreover, the above exceptions are the same that the Aarhus Convention provides in the exact same wording. The category of institutions or bodies acting in a judicial capacity includes at least the ECJ, the Court of First Instance and the Civil Service Tribunal (Crossen, & Niessen, 2007, p. 332). More issues arise from the wording "*institution*" and "*body*" acting in legislative capacity. In fact, in EU law there is no distinction between the words executive and legislative. The ECJ has affirmed that regulations and directives are "considered to be legislative in nature",[183] but classically, the Court has to decide the legislative nature of the act, and the criteria for general application (Crossen, & Niessen, 2007).

Moreover, the regulation includes other exceptions in Article 2(2): it excludes the application of the legislation to Community institutions and bodies from internal review when "*acting as an administrative review body*" and it lists four

---

182   Proposal for a Regulation of the European Parliament and of the Council on the application of the provisions of the Aarhus Convention on Access to Information, Public Participation in Decision-making and Access to Justice in Environmental Matters to EC institutions and bodies, COM (2003) 622 final, 24 October 2003, p. 8. See Pallemaerts, 2009, p. 11.

183   On regulations, see ECJ 17 June 1980, Joined Cases 789 and 790/79, Calpak SpA and Società Emiliana Lavorazione Frutta SpA v. Commission, [1980] ECR 1949, at paras 7–8; and on directives, see ECJ 29 June 1993, Case C-298/89, Gibraltar v. Council, [1993] ECR I-3605, at para. 16.

cases: the Commission when taking decisions in competition proceedings; the Commission when adopting decisions in infringement proceedings; the Ombudsman when reporting on an inquiry; and the European Anti-Fraud Office when making decisions related to fraud investigations.

1.1.1.　First Pillar: Access to Environmental Information

The right of access to environmental information is now officially an integral part of the *acquis communautaire*, although it was a long time coming, and some doubts still rest about the correct implementation of these rights.

1.1.1.1.　Background on Public Access to Information in Europe

As was already pointed out, the right of access to information is an essential vehicle to improve Environmental Democracy at the EU Level, because the existence of such a right is a tool to democratisation and it is also the first step towards reducing the democratic deficit. Indeed, only informed citizens are able to control the management of environmental issues, and then take part in environmental decision-making.

So granting this right allows the public the role of "watch-dog" of polluters and public regulators, who in turn are aware that their actions are under public scrutiny. This situation is referred to as the passive access to information,[184] as opposed to the active access to information[185] through active dissemination

---

184　Passive access to information is related to the right of the public to *receive* information from public authorities, as well as the obligation of the public authorities to give information after a submission. This right is covered by Article 4 of Aarhus Convention: "Each Party shall ensure that, subject to the following paragraphs of this Article, public authorities, in response to a request for environmental information, make such information available to the public, within the framework of national legislation, including, where requested and subject to subparagraph (b) below, copies of the actual documentation containing or comprising such information: (a) Without an interest having to be stated; (b) In the form requested unless: (i) It is reasonable for the public authority to make it available in another form, in which case reasons shall be given for making it available in that form; or (ii) The information is already publicly available in another form. 2. The environmental information referred to in paragraph 1 above shall be made available as soon as possible and at the latest within one month after the request has been submitted, unless the volume and the complexity of the information justify an extension of this period up to two months after the request. The applicant shall be informed of any extension and of the reasons justifying it"

185　Active access to information involves the right of the public to *obtain* information and the obligation of authorities to collect and disseminate information of public interest without the necessity of a precise request. The recognition of this right reflects the deliberative and participatory theories in which the *informed* citizen is seen as a step closer to awareness and participation than the uninformed. Article 5 of Aarhus Convention *covers*

of information. Such rights tend to be seen as tools to enhance environmental awareness, improving the likelihood of positive environmental decisions by individuals.

Furthermore, such rights contribute to awareness-raising and the creation of an environmental citizen who is willing to acknowledge and act upon her/his responsibilities towards the environment.

We have already seen that the traditional approach to access to information in the EU was linked to the "culture of secrecy" (Lee, 2005), justified by the diplomatic nature of international decision-making. But thanks to a growing perception that openness is the way to regain public confidence in government actions, the approach of the EU has moved towards legislation of access to Community documents.

The idea of instituting a specific right of access to environmental information at the EU level was introduced in the early nineties when such rights were provided at a Member State level; this will be examined later. At the EU level the development of such a legal regime arises largely as a result of the clear political will expressed within the text of TEU 1992 to improve a legal culture of transparent decision making at the EU level, specifically in relation to the administrative and legislative process employed by the legislative institution of the Union.[186]

The EU took several steps in 1993-1994 intending to bind its political institutions to a code of conduct on disclosure of documents. Thus the first step towards the recognition of a right to information in Europe was taken in 1993.[187] The Council adopted a Code of Conduct on access to Council documents; the

---

active access to information and establishes the obligation of the government to collect and disseminate information and it includes an extensive variety of different categories of information that Parties should supply to members of the public. Usually, it comprises information such as emergency information, product information, pollutant release and transfer information, information about laws, policies and strategies, and information concerning methods of receipt of information. The Aarhus Convention obliges the States to establish internal processes to ensure the ample flow of all significant environmental information and in addition concentrates on the real implementation of procedures for collecting and distributing information related to any threat to human health or the environment.

186   See Declaration n. 17 on the right of access to information incorporated in the TEU 1992.

187   Council Decision 93/731/EC on public access to Council documents (20 December 1993), Consolidated version of the Decision of the Council of the European Union of 20 December 1993 on public access to its documents, incorporating the amendments introduced by the Council Decision of 6 December 1996.

Commission followed suit in 1994[188] and the same measures were then taken in relation to the European Parliament.[189]

It was not until the Treaty of Amsterdam in 1997 that the EC Treaty was amended to include a specific set of provisions concerning access to information (Hedemann-Robinson, 2007, p. 378); notably, former Article 255 which provided that legal basis for the enactment of Regulation 1049 in May 30 2001 in Public Access to European Parliament, Council and Commission Documents, also known as the "Transparency Regulation".[190]

Although this could have been the opportunity to apply the Aarhus Convention's requirements to EU institutions and bodies, this Regulation is an instrument of general application and does not specifically concern environmental information. Hence, the implementation of the first pillar was deferred to Aarhus Regulation[191] which represents a partial repair of the shortcomings of the general rules of Regulation 1049/2001.

Although the Aarhus Regulation should be viewed as a normative landmark for its affirmation of the specific right of access to environmental information, this piece of legislation is "not revolutionary" (De Abreu Ferreira, 2008, p. 187) because the Aarhus Regulation does not contain a new access regime but makes the most of the provisions of the Regulation on Access to EU Documents applicable to environmental information.

The Transparency Regulation does not deal specifically with environmental information, but it was and in some ways still is the vehicle through which it is possible to gain access to environmental information. Thus, in the examination of this right's legal regime, the Transparency Regulation remains in great measure

---

188   Commission Decision 94/90/ECSC, Euratom of 8 February 1994.

189   Decision 97/632, OJ 1997 L263/27.

190   Regulation (EC) N° 1049/2001 of the European Parliament and of the Council of 30 May 2001 regarding public access to European Parliament, Council and Commission documents, OJ L 145, 31.5.2001, p. 43, available at www.eur-lex.europa.eu/LexUriServ/ LexUriServ.do?uri=CELEX:32001R1049:EN:HTML. See Von Unger, 2007, p. 440.

191   How Hallo (2007, p. 38) has well remarked "As originally proposed in 2000, Regulation 1049/2001 was roundly criticized by journalists, legal transparency experts and others, including EEB. This last focused on the proposed Regulation's failure to take account of the Convention's requirements. Parliament responded to criticism of the original proposal with amendments reinforcing the proposal in important ways. The Regulation ultimately incorporated many of them. But the effort to strengthen the Regulation's general rules left little room for attention to the Convention's specific requirements. Instead, the Regulation said it was "without prejudice to rights of public access to documents held by the institutions which might follow from instruments of international law or acts of the institutions implementing them" (Article 2.6)".

applicable. It is also worth noting that there is a Commissions Proposal to amend this Regulation[192] but as of the date of writing it is still only a proposal.

1.1.1.2. Passive Access to Environmental Information

1.1.1.2.1. General Rules

The legal regime of access to environmental information results today from the combined application of the Transparency Regulation and the Aarhus Regulation, because, although they differ on some points, they are complementary. In this part, the Regulations will not be analysed comprehensively, but only so far as is necessary to explain the prevailing rules on access to environmental information and focus on the extent to which the Aarhus Convention is compatible with the Regulations. In some respects, EU law goes beyond what is required by the Convention.

The first question to answer is: who has such a right? In the new Aarhus Regulation, in line with the Convention, there is no distinction between EU and non-EU natural or legal persons and the access to information is available to the public in general. This point is very important for the conceptualisation of environmental citizenship because this broad subject matter represents an innovation compared to the older regulation. However, it has been suggested that "this provision entails an opportunity to materialise a *de minimis*, transitional concept of eco-citizenship whereby any (foreign) citizens can assess the sustainability footprint of the EU's public authorities" (De Abreu Ferreira, 2008, p. 188).

It is worth noting that Article 2(2) of the Transparency Regulation has already opened the door providing that the institutions "*may grant*" access to documents to any natural or legal person not residing or not having its registered office in a Member State under the same conditions. Moreover, the Commission's proposal to amend the Transparency Regulation also provides for ending the present discrimination between citizens and non-citizens (Harden, 2009, p. 239).

The Aarhus Regulation does not provide that the holders of the corresponding duty grant access only regarding the European Parliament, Council and Commission, as provided by regulation 1049/2001, but address this obligation to all Community institutions and bodies[193] "*except when acting in a judicial or legislative capacity*". But concerning access to environmental information, the above-mentioned exception applies only to bodies when acting in a judicial capacity (Article 2(1)(c)). The Aarhus Convention is not applicable to the "*public*

---

192   COM(2008) 229 final. Harden, 2009, p. 239.
193   Article 2 (c) and Article 3, Aarhus Regulation. See De Abreu Ferreira, 2007b, p. 399.

authorities for the Parties except of bodies or institutions acting in a judicial or legislative capacity". In that respect, both Regulations go beyond the Aarhus Convention, in that its legislative activity is in principle also covered.[194]

The second question is related to the object of access. The Aarhus Regulation grants a right of access to "information" instead of a right of access to documents and introduces a concept of environmental information that is the same as the one used in the 2003 Access to Environmental Information Directive (De Abreu Ferreira, 2008, p. 187). It is interesting to note the opinion of Advocate General Léger who underlines that the distinction between documents and information is purely formal: "the right of access to a document concerns the content of the document and not its physical form. No one can claim that when making a request for access to documents he is seeking the document itself and not the information it contains. [...] It is necessary, therefore, to interpret the concept of the right of access to 'documents' as meaning a right of access to the information contained in the documents".[195]

Moreover, the Transparency Regulation refers to the information received or produced and held in alternative to information only produced and held by European institutions and bodies. One important change is that the "authorship rule", existing under the Decision 94/90EC, was not incorporated in the new system. In fact, the old regime provided that the institutions rely on the "authorship rule" in order to deny access to documents which were in their possession but had been authored by third States or Member States of the EU". Nevertheless, a similar rule had been reintroduced by Article 4(5) of the Transparency Regulation.: "*A Member State may request the institution not to disclose a document from that Member State without its prior agreement*". Moreover, this provision has also been supported by the Court of First Instance (CFI) which on several occasions interpreted this rule as one of the exceptions to

---

194   Schram has noted that "the Aarhus Convention also tempers the exclusion of bodies and institutions acting in a legislative capacity by recognising the desirability of transparency in all branches of government and inviting legislative bodies to implement the principles of this convention in their proceeding", see recital 11 of the Preamble of the Convention. See Schram, 2005, p. 52

195   Opinion of 10 July 2001 in Case C-353/99P, n. 37 above, para. 92- 94. The sensitive documents provided by Article 9 Transparency Regulation. Such documents are defined as sensitive directly by the Institution through internal rules which can be very arbitrary. But according to the CFI's jurisprudence this document is not categorised as such but following the nature of the interest under protection; that is, those to which Article 4 (1) makes reference. The risk of such regime is nuanced by the duty to provide reasons for a refusal or by the publicity requirement applicable to internal institutional rules governing this type of documents.

the right of access to documents of the institutions,[196] despite it being expressly left out by the Transparency Regulation. This interpretation was overruled in 2007 by ECJ in *Sweden v. Commission*.[197] So the ambiguity seems to have been finally cast out of this legal regime.[198]

1.1.1.2.2. Exceptions of the Access to Information

The right of access to information is not an absolute right, so there are some cases where this right can be refused.[199] These exceptions in the Aarhus Regulation follow some of the general rules of Regulation 1049/2001 despite not coinciding with the exceptions provided by the Aarhus Convention[200].

---

196   See Case T-76/02, Mara Messina v. Commission of the European Communities, 17 September 2003; Case T-168/02, IFAW Internationaler Tierschutz-Fonds gGmbH v. Commission of the European Communities, 30 November 2004; Case T-187/03, Isabella Scippacercola v. Commission of the European Communities, 17 March 2005.

197   The Court was of the opinion that a clause in the EC legislation which entitled a member state to veto access to environmental information which the member state had sent to the Commission prevailed over the citizens' right to know. ECJ, Case C-64/05P, Kingdom of Sweden v. Commission of the European Communities, 18 December 2007. See in particular Harden, 2009, p. 239.

198   With regard to documents originating in Member States that are held by the institutions, the Commission's proposal replaces Article 4(5) of the Transparency Regulation by a new Article 5(2). This would provide, in relevant part, that: "The institution holding the document shall discuss it unless the Member State gives reasons for withholding it, based on the exceptions referred to in Article 4 or on specific provisions in its own legislation preventing discussion of the document concerned. The institution shall appreciate the adequacy of reasons given by the Member States insofar as they are based on exceptions laid down in this Regulation". The use of the conjunction 'or' and the limited scope of the 'appreciation', "envisaged in the second sentence could together imply that a Member State may rely on its own legislation as an alternative to the exceptions laid down in Article 4(1)-(3) of the Regulation. This proposal seems to be based on a misreading of the judgement of the ECJ in the Sweden v. Commission". See Harden, 2009, p. 239

199   It is worth tnoting that another proposed change by the Proposal would significantly narrow the scope of the Transparency Regulation. The most far-reaching is to amend the definition of document so that no application for access to a document drawn up by an institution could be made unless that document had been 'formally transmitted to one or more recipients or otherwise registered. This would mean that a document that had not been formally transmitted outside the institution would not even be a document for purposes of the regulation, unless it had been registered. The commission's proposal would therefore give it, in practice, wide discretion to decide which documents would be covered by the Regulation". Article 3(a). Harden, 2009, p. 239.

200   The Aarhus Convention includes exceptions, as do all international agreements, created *via* political negotiation. There are eight specific cases that any authority may use as justification to refute an applicant's request. These exceptions include matters of national defence, the protection of trade secrets, and the protection of personal data and judicial or law enforcement matters in progress (Cramer, 2009, p. 100). The employment of an exemption is controlled by the words of the Convention, in particular by the final paragraph of Article 4: "The aforementioned grounds for refusal shall be interpreted in a

Indeed, all exceptions in the Convention are discretionary, "*may be refused*"; consequently, parties of the agreement have the choice to make the exceptions either mandatory or discretionary. The Transparency Regulation, instead, contains only mandatory exceptions, "*shall refuse*" as in Article 4 (1), (2) and (3), despite the Aarhus Regulation introducing a discretionary exception in Article 6(2).

The first category of exception is employed when there is a real possibility that one of the listed interests of Article 4(1) of the Transparency Regulation can be damaged by their release of the requested information.[201] The burden of proof falls to the Institution. Regulation 1049/2001 contains first an exception for the "*financial, monetary or economic policy of the Community or a Member State*", which is absent in the Convention; second, the legislation protects commercial interests more broadly than does the Convention.

The Article 4(2) provides that an Institution shall refuse access where certain private or public interests are likely to be undermined. However, it has been noted that the Commission "has kept secret the letters of formal notice and

---

restrictive way, taking into account the public interest served by disclosure and taking into account whether the information requested relates to emissions into the environment". It has been underlined that a "blanket approach" to exceptions would be beyond the "spirit" of the Convention, and there is an obligation to engage in some sort of "consideration of the pros and cons of disclosure and confidentially: exceptions to access are provided not for convenience, but to protect genuinely competing public interest" (Holder, & Lee, 2007, p. 104).

In the case of refusals the reasons for them are to be issued in writing where requested. A time limit applies as for the supply of information: one month from the date of the request, with a provision for extending this by a further month where the complexity of the information justifies this. Where a public authority does not hold the information requested, it should either direct the requester to another public authority which it believes might have the information, or transfer the request to that public authority and notify the requester of this. Nevertheless, there is a limitation in this Article centred on public authorities, providing no right of access in respect of information held by private parties. Article 4 applies only to information held by public authorities, very important information held by industry or subject to the convention's commercial and industrial exception is not covered, although a Protocol on Pollutant Release and Transfer Registers adopted in 2003 will require the industry to collect and report information about pollution emissions which parties must then make publicly available. The convention requires its members to encourage those operators to keep the public informed. The limitation is however compounded by the changing nature of public responsibilities because in recent years, in some states formerly public functions and activities have passed out of "government hands" (Lee, 2005, p. 153).

201 It worth noting that the Commission proposes to add "a new exception" to Article 4(1) which is for the protection of the 'environment, such as breeding sites of rare species', with no possibility of an overriding public interest in disclosure (Article 4(1)e). Furthermore the Commission also proposes to separate the protection of (1) ' commercial interests of a natural or legal person' from that of ' (2) intellectual property' and with regard to (1) deem that an overriding public interest exists 'where the information requested relates to emissions into the environment'. See Harden, 2009, p. 239.

the reasoned opinions to Member States in infringement proceedings". There is no real reason for keeping these letters confidential since they are part of the infringement procedure prior to any action before the Courts and their disclosure does not undermine the protection of any court proceedings (as required by Article 4(2) of Regulation 1049/2001).[202]

In addition, these letters only present the legal basis for a potential Commission decision to act on specific cases, which would be decided and does not undermine any legal advice or investigations as required by Article 4(2) of Regulation 1049/2001. One critic (Krämer, 2007, p. 460) has observed that this policy of secrecy "*is neither comprehensible nor justified*" (Ballesteros, 2009, p. 54).

Then, according to Article 4(3) there is the exception related to protecting internal use during a decision-making process that is not yet complete, or even after completion of that process, where that release "would seriously undermine the institution's decision making process, unless there is an overriding public interest in disclosure" (Schram, 2005, p. 41). The adjective "*seriously*" underlines that this exception is the highest of all three, so the Institution has to prove that risk is beyond doubt to undermine the institutions' proceedings. Moreover, this Article distinguishes the internal and/or preliminary document or documents received by an institution where on one hand a decision has not yet been made and on the other hand the decision has already been made.[203]

Article 6 of the Aarhus Regulation adds three new cases into the regime established under Article 4 of the Transparency Regulation. Indeed, Article 6 (1) provides an "exception to the exception" of Article 4 (2) of the Transparency Regulation by stating that in the case of emissions into the environment a public interest in disclosure will always be deemed to exist.[204]

---

202   The other new exception to be added to Article 4(2) by the Commission's proposal is "to protect 'the objectivity and impartiality of selection procedures' subject to the possibility of an overriding public interest in disclosure. According to the Commission, this exception would apply to procedures for the award of contracts and for the section of staff", see Harden, 2009, p. 239.

203   Finally Article 4 provides three rules concerning the exceptions: first a duty of consultation with third parties (4(4)) to assess if an exception under Article 4(1) or (2) is applicable to requested documents which were authored by them; a partial access rule when possible (4(6)) and a time limit on the refusal of access to document (4(7)). The delay is thirty years for the application of the above exceptions, despite the starting date the delay starts counting. The most available interpretation of this Article is that the delay stat counting from the date of the official publication of the document. Concerning the exceptions protecting privacy and commercial interests they may, if necessary, continue to apply to requested documents.

204   Relative to the information concerning emissions into the environment: this was the subject of the European Pollutant Emission register Decision (Decision 2000/479,

The second case concerns the general public interest test, in other words the possibility for the public authorities to ponder when (or if) to release the relevant information.

Finally, Article 6 adds an environmental exception to the list of exceptions, in the view of compliance with the requirements of the Aarhus Convention. This latter case provides a discretionary exception, "*may refuse*", "*where disclosure of the information would adversely affect the protection of the environment to which the information relates*" in its Article 6 (2).

Furthermore, the Aarhus Regulation, according to the Convention, adds in its Article 6, that all the exceptions are to be interpreted restrictively, taking into account the public interest in disclosure, and also adds that consideration should be given to whether the information sought relates to information on emissions (Hallo, 2007, p. 38).

The procedure for requesting access to a document held by an Institution is established in Articles 6 to 8, and Articles 10 and 11 of the Transparency Regulation. Article 6 (1) stipulates that an application has to be made in written form plus it has to be sufficiently precise and does not need to state reasons.

In summary, it may be said that concerning the passive approach to the access to environmental information, the Aarhus Regulation satisfies the requirements of the Aarhus Convention.

1.1.1.3. Active Access to Environmental Information

The active access to environmental information is provided by Article 4 of the Aarhus Regulation. This new Regulation extends and concretises the duty of the Institution to collect and disseminate environmental information to the public according to Article 5 of the Aarhus Convention.

The Transparency Regulation does not establish explicit provisions on the collection, dissemination and the accessibility of environmental information. Nevertheless, it contains general provisions concerning information that has to be made available (Schram, 2005, p. 63). The regime of the active access to environmental information has to be read in accordance with the Transparency Regulation.

The Aarhus Regulation states that Community Institutions and bodies must organise the environmental information which is relevant to their functions, and which is held by or for them, with a view to its active and systematic

---

OJ 2000 L 192/36). The European Community had to implement the UNECE Protocol on Pollutant Release and transfer registers to the Aarhus Convention. The implementation has been realised by Regulation 166/2006, the pollutant Release and Transfer Register Regulation. OJ 2006 L 33/1. See Jans, & Vedder, 2008, p. 331.

dissemination to the public. This is to be achieved, in particular, by means of computer telecommunication and/or electronic technology in accordance with Article 11 (1-2)[205] and 12[206] of the Transparency Regulation.

The institutions and bodies must make this environmental information progressively available in electronic databases that are easily accessible to the public through public telecommunication networks. To this end, they must place the environmental information that they hold on databases and accompany these with search aids and other forms of software designed to assist the public in locating the information they require.

Article 4(2) states that the information shall be updated, and lists the documents which shall be included in databases or registers. This list includes the documents in Article 12(2) and (3), concerning special registers of all documents of the institutions, and in Article 13(1) and (2), concerning the publication of the documents in the official Journal of Transparency Regulation and adds some new documents, such as "*texts of international treaties, Conventions or agreements, and of Community legislation on the environment or relating to it, and of polices, plans and programmes relating to the environment*" and also "*reports on the state of the environment*".

Finally, where EU institutions or bodies do not hold the information requested, they shall "*as promptly as possible*" and "*within 15 days*" tell the applicant which body they believe holds the information or make an onward transfer themselves (Hallo, 2007, p. 38). This provision tracks a Convention requirement and is not expressly found in Regulation 1049/2001. Indeed, it has been highlighted that under Regulation 1049 no sanction can be taken if an Institution does not respect the 15 working days requirement, making it almost impossible to enforce this provision (Gourtin, 2006).

---

205   Article 11 Registers: "Sensitive documents are documents originating from the 1. Each institution shall provide public access to a register of documents. Access to the register should be provided in electronic form. References to documents shall be recorded in the register without delay. 2. For each document the register shall contain a reference number (including, where applicable, the inter institutional reference), the subject matter and/or a short description of the content of the document and the date on which it was received or drawn up and recorded in the register. References shall be made in a manner which does not undermine protection of the interests in Article 4".

206   Direct access in electronic form or through a register 1. The institutions shall as far as possible make documents directly accessible to the public in electronic form or through a register in accordance with the rules of the institution concerned. 2. In particular, legislative documents, that is to say, documents drawn up or received in the course of procedures for the adoption of acts which are legally binding in or for the Member States, should, subject to Articles 4 and 9, be made directly accessible. 3. Where possible, other documents, notably documents relating to the development of policy or strategy, should be made directly accessible. 4. Where direct access is not given through the register, the register shall as far as possible indicate where the document is located.

Thus, as concerns the active and passive approaches to the access to environmental information, it can be said that the Aarhus Regulation satisfies the requirements of the Aarhus Convention.

1.1.2. Second Pillar: Environmental Participation

As pointed out at the very beginning, European institutions believe that public participation enhances political or civil awareness, encourages active citizenship and could be a solution to the democratic deficit, as pointed out by the Commission's White Paper on European Governance which invokes the "democratising *potential of public participation*". Nevertheless, this instrumental view of participation contains a gap between the rhetoric of the political declaration and the effective mechanisms which have been provided by the EU.

A clear example of this situation is the Aarhus Regulation, which, despite seeking a "new form of supranational participatory democracy", remains at the moment a "wild goose chase" (Harlow, 1993, p. 179). This legislation, indeed, states how important public participation is, but then it does not state how the participation could take place.

The Aarhus Regulation merely implements Article 7[207] of the Aarhus Convention through Article 9. The reason for the exclusion of the implementation

---

[207] This Article requires parties to make "appropriate practical and/or other provisions for the public to participate during the preparation of plans and programmes relating to the environment". Commentators have noted that the term "relating to the environment" is wide, "covering not just plans or programmes prepared by an environment ministry, but also sectoral plans such as transport, tourism, etc, where these have significant environmental implications" (Wates, 2005a, p. 6).

Participation requirements related to plans and programs are not specified in similar detail as in the case of Article 6, because the strength of the participatory requirements diminishes as we move from plans and programmes, which are often regional, to policies and executive regulations, which can also be national. Public participation should take place in a transparent and fair framework and also follow numerous principles which are provided under Article 6, as well as realistic timeframes, early participation, and due attention to the result of the participation.

Article 7 devotes only one sentence to policies: "To the extent appropriate, each Party shall endeavour to provide opportunities for the public participation in the preparation of policies relating to the environment". The institution of representative democracy is required to be consulted only "to the extent appropriate" and one has no obligation to take "due account" of any public comments (Bell, 2004, p. 99). Article 7 differentiates between plans and programs on the one hand, and policies on the other. As far as the former are concerned, the provision includes elements of Article 6, especially relating to the time-frames and occasions for public participation, as well as the commitment to guarantee that public participation is taken into consideration. With respect to the regulation of policies, there is no express incorporation of any of the principles of Article 6.

The Implementation Guide of the Convention has suggested cohesion with strategic environmental assessment (SEA) as a method of implementing Article 7 through public

of Article 6[208] of the Convention can be found in the Commission's proposal for the regulation and its explanatory memorandum.[209]

The Commission has affirmed that decision-making covered by Article 6 of the Convention was not relevant for the purposes of the regulation, since decisions to authorise the listed activities are not taken at a Community level but by Member States.[210] In fact, Article 6(a) of the Convention requires public participation with respect to decisions to permit certain activities listed in Annex 1, which covers a wide range of activities, *inter alia*, in the energy sector, production and processing of metals, mineral industry, chemical industry, waste and different sorts of heavy industry.

Secondly, Article 6 (b) states that public participation shall be provided also in respect to decisions on proposed activities not listed in Annex 1 that may have a significant effect on the environment. The Commission considered whether this might require public participation in respect to its decisions to list specific substances under the various directives on marketing of products containing dangerous substances, but decided against it since the administrative decisions on the authorisation of chemicals, pesticides and biocides are, as a rule, also taken at the level of Member states. In other words, it seems that the Commission referred to the general procedure in most of these directives where it authorises dangerous substances, whilst it is still for Member States to authorise products containing these substances.[211]

---

participation procedures (Stec, & Casey-Lefkowitz, 2000, p. 113-114). The obligation that States guarantee that "due account is taken of the outcome of public participation" means that "there must be a legal basis to take environmental considerations into account, in plans, programmers and policies" (Stec, & Casey-Lefkowitz, 2000, p. 113-114).

208   Article 6 concerns participation in decisions permitting certain activities listed in Annex I of the Convention; for example, activities within chemical installations and waste management, or other activities which may have a significant effect on the environment. The emphasis here is not only specific and local but also 'reactive' and 'defensive'. The public has the opportunity to react to and defend themselves against proposals for activities with significant environment impacts. Activities under Article 6 generally include activities subjected to the environmental impact assessment (EIA) procedure under the UNECE Espoo Convention on environmental Impact Assessment in a Trans-boundary Context.

209   COM(2003) 622, 12.

210   This idea was explained in the Proposal for a Regulation of the European Parliament and of the Council on the application of the provisions of the Aarhus Convention on Access to Information, Participation in Decision- Making and Access to Justice in Environmental Matters to EC Institutions and Bodies, COM (2003) 622 ('the Commission Proposal').

211   However, it has been underlined that this distinction is not necessarily relevant under Article 6(b) because Article 6(a) "refers to decisions 'whether to permit the proposed activities – which on a narrow reading could refer to the actual permitting of products on the national level – Article 6(1) libra b refers to 'decision [...] which may have a significant effect on the environment". "This broader phrasing would in my opinion cover Commission

Also the vagueness of Article 9 implementing Article 7 of the Aarhus Convention in substance breaches the agreement. This provision deals with public participation in plans and programmes relating to the environment, but is "silent on policies" (Hallo, 2007, p. 38). Examining the provision in detail, the first paragraph establishes that public participation is open to natural or legal persons as well as associations of these and concerns the preparation, modification or review of plans or programmes related to the environment.

The definition of plans and programmes relating to the environment is broad in Article 2 (1) but is significantly restrained by the last paragraph of that provision which provides: *"This definition shall not include financial or budget plans and programmes, namely those laying down how particular projects or activities should be financed or those related to the proposed annual budgets, internal work programmes of a Community institution or body, or emergency plans and programmes designed for the sole purpose of civil protection"*.

It then identified three obligations of the European institutions and bodies: first, to inform the public of the proposals and the possibility of public participation; second, said institutions and bodies have a duty to take due account of the results of the public participation; and, finally, the public must be informed of the final decision and of public participation.

It has been remarked that the last obligation is formulated differently for the Member States and the EU. Only the Member States are obliged to inform the public of the public participation process, whereas the EU Institutions must inform the public of public participation. According to Jans, this could mean that "Member States must only inform the public of the procedure followed (time-limit, etc.) and not of the actual impact on the public consultation" (Jans, & Vedder, 2008, p. 331; Jans, 2006, p. 447).

In conclusion, it could be affirmed therefore that Regulation 1367/2006 is in breach of Article 6 and 7 of the Aarhus Conversation by failing to provide for public participation in such decision-making.

1.1.3. Third Pillar: Access to Justice in Environmental Matters

Within the EU, access to justice for individuals and NGOs has been elusive for a long time, and in many respects it still is. In fact, the *locus standi* requirements in the Treaty, as interpreted by the ECJ, are strict, with little opportunities for

decisions listing dangerous substances in particular bearing in mind that Member States recently have begun to challenge such Commission decisions". See Wenneras, 2007, p. 224.

individuals and NGOs to bring cases. Nevertheless, some changes shall be seen in this matter after the signature of the Aarhus Convention and its implementation, because the EU committed itself to providing its citizens access to justice in matters of environmental law.

Thus, in this section, access to justice at the European Level, the difficulties of recognising these rights, what kind of implementation has been achieved, developments following the signing the Aarhus Convention[212], and the entering into the force of the Aarhus Regulation will be analysed.

1.1.3.1. Background on Former Article 230 EC

The EC Treaty does not contain specific provisions on the access to justice in environmental matters. The treaty-based access follows the general rules of access to the ECJ and the CFI according to former Article 230 of the EC Treaty (now Article 263). There are other provisions which regulate the judicial review procedure; nevertheless, for the current purpose, former Article 230 EC is the most important Article concerning environmental access to justice.[213]

---

212   Article 9 of Aarhus Convention contains two categories of provisions. First, access to justice means that members of the public have legal mechanisms, that could be used against potential violations of the two other pillars, – access to information and public participation. Second, access to justice means that the public is equipped with legal mechanisms which they can use to gain review of potential violations of domestic environmental law and thus, the public's ability to help enforce environmental law is acknowledged. This third part of Article 9 is not linked with the other pillars of the Convention, but it should be considered a new right recognised by the Convention. Hence, paragraphs 1 and 2 are directly related to the internal provisions of the Convention while paragraph 3 reinforces external domestic standards. The specificity of this form of "external review" (Redgwell, 2007, p. 168) has led to it being considered a fourth pillar (Jóhannsdóttir, 2008, p. 221) of the Convention. This is also due to the fact that it has no connection with either of the first two pillars of the Convention. See on this topic: Parola 2013.

213   The Court of Justice is competent to decide actions brought by the European Commission against Member States under Article 226/228 EC, and according to Article 234 to provide rulings on questions of EC law and on the validity of EC measures referred to it by national courts.

The Court of First Instance (CFI) has jurisdiction to hear cases brought by private persons against acts or omissions of the European Community's institutions, and appeals from the CFI may be made to the ECJ on points of law (Article 225). The EC treaty provisions include the rights of private persons to take specific types of legal proceeding before the CFI, namely a right under Article 232 CE to bring an action before the CFI in respect of failure to act by the European Parliament, European Commission or Council of the EU. For instance relative to the action provided by art 232 EC the private persons legal standing to sue is subject to fulfilment of certain conditions, thus they have standing when the institution has "failed to address to that person any act other than a recommendation or an opinion" Article 232(3) EC. Furthermore the individual has several times sought unsuccessfully to use that Article as a basis for overturning decisions on the part of the European Commission

This provision establishes a judicial review procedure in respect to acts, recommendations or opinions taken by the European Institution and its purpose to avoid acts which are in violation of EU law. The citizen has to fulfil specific conditions in order to have legal standing to sue.

Before the Treaty of Lisbon came into force, Article 230 (4) granted the possibility for natural or legal persons to be able to bring proceedings only against a decision specifically addressed to them or against a decision which, although in the form of a regulation or decision addressed to another person, is of "*direct and individual concern*" to them.

The problem is that these kinds of situations are rare in environmental cases since damages are done to the environment and not to individuals. One reason for this wording was to avoid the legislative system of the Community being encumbered by litigation sponsored by interest groups or individuals and to ensure that it could "be able to pass general legislation in the public interest without fear of the possibility of minority interest litigation placing legal certainty of these measures into question" (Hedemann-Robinson, 2007, p. 356).

---

not to begin infringement proceedings against a Member State under Article 226 EC. This last Article is also linked to the enforcement of EC environmental law because Member States may be held to account for failures to implement EC environmental legislation correctly. And the Court of Justice has confirmed several times that this provision involves an exclusively bilateral relationship between the Commission and the respective Member State (Case 4/69 Lutticke, Case 559/93 Bernardi and T-201/96 Smanor, confirmed on appeal in Case C-317/97P Smanor), although it has been remarked that Individuals and NGOs play an important role in providing information about implementation by Member States, so that the Commission can properly fulfil its watchdog function, concerning Article 226 EC. The complaint procedure started as an initiative in internal market and the free circulation of goods. When the Treaty was re- formed by the Single European Act in 1986 and the environmental policy recognised as a Community policy, the European Commission established a service, which, on the insistence of the EP, included a unit in charge of monitoring implementation of environmental law. The Commission services took the lead and announced the possibility for any person or body to send complaints to DG Environment whenever a breach of environmental legislation was identified. See Ballesteros, 2009, p. 54.

According to Articles 235 and 288(2) EC the individual has the right to seek compensation in respect of acts or omissions caused by EC institutions, the European Central Bank or their servants in the performance of their duties. Nevertheless 235 and 288(2) EC do not offer appropriate judicial remedies to secure rectification of environmental damage caused by illegal EC institutional in/action. Moreover under Article 234 EC there is a procedure by which national courts may and under certain circumstances are obliged, to refer to the ECJ for a preliminary ruling on question for correct interpretation of EC law and the validity of EC measure and this mechanism can be used by private individuals to seek judicial review by the ECJ of measure taken by EU Institutions.

All mentioned procedures give little opportunity in general for the citizen to access to justice, and moreover the narrow interpretation made by the ECJ and CFI has worsened the situation, in particular concerning the jurisprudence concerning the Article 230(4) now 263. Hedemann-Robinson, 2007, p. 352.

Nevertheless, with this excuse the ECJ has given a very narrow interpretation of the standing requirements in the former Article 230(4).

The first time that the ECJ interpreted the phrase "*individual concern*" was in the leading case of *Plaumann*: "Persons other than those to whom a decision is addressed may only claim to be individually concerned if that decision affects them by reason of circumstances in which they are differentiated from all other persons and by virtue of these factors distinguishes them individually just as in the case of the person addressed".[214] This interpretation is now known as the "*Plaumann* test",[215] and it has, since then, been referred to by the Courts in order to examine whether natural and legal persons are individually concerned by acts of EU institutions.

This interpretation of the criterion of the "*individual concern*" is, therefore, excessively restrictive and provides a very narrow standing to the persons who are not the addressees of the contested decision. It, however, has invariably been relied on by the CFI and the ECJ to determine whether natural or legal persons, other than those to whom community acts are addressed, have *locus standi*.

The *Plaumann* jurisprudence was used for the first time in environmental matters in the *Stichting Greenpeace Council* case.[216] It is interesting to note that in the environmental field the Court had, before this decision, a very innovative approach.[217] In 1991 in the *Commission v. Germany* case the Court ruled that environmental standards are also aimed at the protection of human health. Persons therefore had the right to access courts in order to ensure that environmental standards were respected. This decision, hence, opened the door

---

214   The leading case remains ECJ 15 July 1963, Case 25/62, Plaumann & Co. v. Commission, [1964] ECR 95. See paragraph 107 of judgement.

215   Plaumann and Co, a German corporation, sought the annulment of a decision of the European Commission refusing to authorise the Federal Republic of Germany to suspend, in part, customs duties applicable to fresh mandarins and clementines imported from third countries.

216   Stichting Greenpeace Council and Others v. Commission, T-585/93, 9 August 1995. De Lange, 2003, p. 227.

217   In a judgement of 1991 (Case 131/88, Commission v. Germany (1991) ECR I-825), it ruled that environmental standards also aimed at the protection of human health. Persons therefore had the right to access courts in order to ensure that the environmental standards were respected. This decision, in theory, opened the door wide for access to justice for persons, local citizens' groups and environmental ONGs, though it was hardly ever made use of in subsequent years. And the administration of the member states and the Community institutions was intelligent enough to draft environmental standards in such a way that their enforcement by private persons or bodies became impossible. Krämer recalls for instance the standards such as "Best available technique" for installation (Directive 96/61EC on industrial installation (1996) OJ L 257/26), "good environmental quality" for water (Directive 2000/60/EC). See in particular, Krämer, 2009, p.195.

for access to justice for individuals, NGOs and citizens' groups (Krämer, 2009, p. 208). Nevertheless, the Member States and the Community Institutions were intelligent enough to draft environmental standards in such a way that their enforcement by individuals became impossible.[218]

The Court followed the aforementioned States and Community Institutions' intentions and in the *Greenpeace* decision, the CFI excluded the possibility of access to justice to this environmental NGO. In that judgement, Greenpeace International together with local associations and residents in Gran Canaria, were seeking the annulment of a decision adopted by the Commission to disburse to the Kingdom of Spain a certain sum by way of financial assistance provided by the European Regional Development Fund for the construction of two power stations in the Canary Islands without first requiring or carrying out an environmental impact assessment. However, the CFI reasserted the *Plaumann* jurisprudence and did not set up an exception for environmental NGOs, interpreting the "*individual concern*" criterion in the same way.

On appeal,[219] the ECJ confirmed this decision applying again the *Plaumann* test. So the Court insisted that standing only existed where the matter was of direct and individual concern and argued that any change of this interpretation would need an amendment of the EU Treaty. This landmark case was maintained in following years. Indeed, as it will be seen in this section, there is not one single case where an environmental NGO has ever been granted standing before the Court of Justice.

One example is the *Danielsson* case.[220] In this sentence, three inhabitants of Tahiti sought the annulment of a decision of the European Commission according to which Member States did not have to take additional measures when the French nuclear weapon tests were carried out in the region. The Court again made clear that even where the applicants would suffer harm they still have no right to judicial review since they do not distinguish themselves from other people who might suffer equal harm.

The *UPA case*[221] did not implicate NGOs or bear on environmental matters. However, it is central for the purpose of this section because it illustrates the reasoning of the CFI and the ECJ as regards standing at the European

---

218   For instance there are standards such as "good environmental quality" for waters in WFD (Directive 2000/30/EC); or as "best available technique for installations" in the Directive 96/61 EC on installation.

219   Stichting Greenpeace Council and Others v. Commission, C-321/95 P, 2 April 1998.

220   Marie-Thérèse Danielsson, Pierre Largenteau, Edwin Haoa v. Commission of the European Communities, T-219/95 R, 22 December 1995.

221   Union de Pequenos Agricultores v. Commission, Case T-173/98, 23 November 1999.

level. On appeal, *UPA* claimed essentially that the dismissal of its application as inadmissible infringed on its right to effective judicial protection for the defence of its own interests and those of its members. In addition to reasserting the *Plaumann* jurisprudence to deny standing to *UPA*, the Court rejected *UPA's* argument on the lack of effective remedies against EC institutions' decisions.

It held that it was for the Member States to establish a system of legal remedies and procedures which ensured respect for the right to effective judicial protection and that the only way to relax the standing rules at the European level would be to reform the current system, that is, to amend the EC Treaty. The Court applied the finding of this decision in two subsequent judgments which bear on environmental matters, the *European Environmental Bureau (EEB)* and *WWF-UK* cases, discussed later on.

In the *Jégo-Quéré et Cie SA* case,[222] the CFI showed that another interpretation of the old Article 230(4) of the EC Treaty and particularly of the "*individual concern*" criteria was possible. The CFI held that the standard interpretation of individual concern in Article 230(4) EC had the effect of denying in practice effective judicial protection of rights of private persons. On appeal, however, the CFI's judgment was quashed by the ECJ[223] which reasserted the *Plaumann* case.

The ECJ reaffirmed that such reinterpretation of that Article is not possible within the current framework of the EC Treaty, and a specific amendment is required to be made to the treaty provision by agreement of the Member States. However, this position of the Court has been criticized as ill-founded, given that the current wording of that Article is open enough to be interpreted along the lines suggested by CFI (Hedemann-Robinson, 2007, p. 364).

Moreover, the Court confirmed its position in the *EEB and Stichting Natuur en Milieu* case.[224] This case is crucial for two reasons. The first one is that when the Court adopted its judgment, the Aarhus Convention was already in force in the European Community.

---

222   Jégo-Quéré et Cie SA v. Commission, T-177/01, 3 May 2002. The CFI then reversed the Plaumann test and considered that "there is no compelling reason to read into the notion of individual concern a requirement that an individual applicant seeking to challenge a general measure must be differentiated from all others affected by it in the same way as an addressee". As a result, the Court decided that "a natural or legal person is to be regarded as individually concerned by a Community measure of general application that concerns him directly if the measure in question affects his legal position, in a manner which is both definite and immediate, by restricting his rights or by imposing obligations on him. The number and position of other persons who are likewise affected by the measure, or who may be so, are of no relevance in that regard".

223   Commission v. Jégo-Quéré & Cie SA, C-263/02P, 1 April 2004. Dodeller, & Pallemaerts, 2005, p. 287.

224   EEB and Stichting Natuur en Milieu v. Commission, T-236/04, 28 November 2005.

The second reason is that the CFI stressed its refusal to grant NGOs access to justice since it considered that the proposal for the Aarhus Regulation that applies the provisions of the Aarhus Convention to the EC institutions and bodies did not grant standing to environmental NGOs unless the latter meet the "*individual concern*" criterion as set out in Article 230 paragraph 4 of the EC Treaty. Consequently, the applicants were not considered as individually concerned by the contested decisions and their action was dismissed.

The CFI, hence, reasserted the *Plaumann* interpretation and considered that the European Commission's decisions affected the applicant in the same manner as any other person in the same situation and that the fact that their purpose was the protection of the environment and the conservation of nature did not establish that they were individually concerned by the decisions.

The above interpretation, which will be explored below, has been criticised by several scholars and by the NGOs which have started a communication to the Aarhus Compliance Committee[225], because, according to them, the ECJ has contributed to narrow individual action under Article 230 and particularly in the context of environmental law enforcement, and prevents NGOs from using judicial remedies to compel Community institutions to comply with Community environmental law.[226]

---

225   Aarhus Convention establishes a non-compliance procedure before a committee of independent experts marks a positive step toward "the setting up of a review mechanism for possible violations by States parties for their obligation to guarantee appropriate remedial action to all persons subject to their jurisdiction who may lament environmental injuries or abuses" (Francioni, 2008, p. 25).

Thus, the innovative element of the Convention's institutional mechanism is the Compliance Committee (Pallemaerts, & Moreau, 2004), established by Article 15, because it "represents an important and inventive approach to the supervision of international agreements" (Pedersen, 2010). Furthermore, his Article is especially important in the light of the absence of supranational forums for the direct enforcement of international environmental law. Review of compliance is such an important tool not only because it is a way to assure access to justice—and not just at the domestic level—but also because the role of the public is stressed. Such provisions granting to individual citizens and NGOs the right to actually participate in the monitoring, by an international body, of state compliance with legal obligations is "unprecedented in international environmental law" (Pallemaerts, 2004, p. 20).In fact, for the first time in international environmental law, provisions contained in a Convention open up the possibility of the establishment of a review mechanism accessible not only to states, but also to individuals. The most innovative part of Article 15 provides for the establishment of "arrangements of a non-confrontational, non-judicial and consultative nature", and for reviewing compliance of parties which "shall allow for appropriate public involvement and may include the option of consideration of communications from members of the public on matters related to this Convention". See Parola 2013.

226   In fact private persons have faced great difficulties in seeking to challenge the legality of Community decision making affecting environmental protection issues in contexts other than Article 226/228EC. Crossen, & Niessen, 2007, p. 332.

After this overview of the Court jurisprudence, how this situation has changed after the ratification of the Aarhus Convention and the entry into force of the Aarhus Regulation will be examined.

In the following section, the implementation that has been made by the Aarhus Regulation concerning the three modes of access to justice provided in the Convention corresponding to Article 9 paragraph 1, 2, and 3 shall be discussed in depth.

1.1.3.2. Implementation of Article 9(1) of the Aarhus Convention

The Convention requires in Article 9(1) that a person being denied access to information must have the possibility to review this denial.[227] A kind of judicial implementation of this provision was partly met by Regulation 1049/2001/EC (Crossen, & Niessen, 2007, p. 332); in particular Article 7 and 8 of Regulation 1049/2001 provided for a *"two-stage administrative procedure"* and *"access to the European Ombudsman or a Court"*.

Moreover, this legal procedure was completed by Article 10 to 12 of Regulation 1367/2006, as we shall see in part below, concerning the review of decisions refusing access to environmental information. If, within fifteen working days from the registration of a request to access, the institution does not reply or refuses access, the applicant has a right to an administrative review procedure

---

227   Article 9(1) acknowledges that any person, who believes that his or her request for information was ignored, wrongfully refused, or inadequately answered, has, in accordance with national law, access to a judicial or non-judicial review procedure. Article 9 (1) provides "Each Party shall, within the framework of its national legislation, ensure that any person who considers that his or her request for information under Article 4 has been ignored, wrongfully refused, whether in part or in full, inadequately answered, or otherwise not dealt with in accordance with the provisions of that Article, has access to a review procedure before a court of law or another independent and impartial body established by law. In the circumstances where a Party provides for such a review by a court of law, it shall ensure that such a person also has access to an expeditious procedure established by law that is free of charge or inexpensive for reconsideration by a public authority or review by an independent and impartial body other than a court of law". Under this provision, any person has a right to exercise the review procedures and has standing to challenge decisions made under Article 4. Moreover, Article 9(1) is in conformity with Article 4's language, which grants any member of the public the right to request information. In addition, this paragraph provides that the review procedure must be before a court of law or any other "independent and impartial body established by law". See Parola, 2013. The significance of "independent and impartial body" can be explained by the Convention for the Protection of Human Rights and Fundamental Freedoms: independent and impartial bodies do not have to be courts, but must be "quasi-judicial, with safeguards to guarantee due process, independent of influence by any branch of government and unconnected to any private entity". States have the obligation to guarantee that the public has access to faster and less expensive review procedures than reviews in courts (Stec, & Casey-Lefkowitz, 2000, p. 127). Moreover, the public authority has to be bound by final decisions.

by a higher official within the same Institution. Failure by the institution to reply within the prescribed time limit shall be considered as a negative reply and entitle the applicant to institute court proceedings against the institution and/ or make a complaint to the Ombudsman, under the relevant provisions of the EC Treaty.

At the end, the ECJ has confirmed that a reply refusing access to information constitutes a decision for the purposes of former Article 230 (4), which addressed to private parties grants standing under that provision.[228] This procedure will be analysed in detail in the following.

1.1.3.3. Implementation of Article 9(2) of the Aarhus Convention

When an EC institution or body refuses to organise a public consultation about a plan or a programme relating to the environment it has "prepared, modified or reviewed, (or fails to conduct such a consultation in a proper manner further to the criteria set out in Article 6 of the Aarhus Convention), the members of the public concerned should have the right to institute proceedings before the Courts to challenge this refusal, further to requirements laid down by Article 9(2) and 9(3) of the Convention".[229]

Unfortunately this possibility is not provided by EU law and this is evidence of an omission in implementation of the Aarhus Convention. Indeed, as shown before, Regulation 1367/2006 is incompatible with Article 6 of the Aarhus Convention. The consequence is that the Regulation does not implement Article 9(2)[230] of the Aarhus Convention, which provides access to justice to challenge

---

228 See Case T-76/02 Messina (2003) ECRI-3203.

229 Communication ACCC/C/2008/32, submitted on 1 December 2008 by ClientEarth and others, available at www.unece.org/env/pp/compliance/C2008-32/DatasheetC-2008-32v2009.01.19.doc.

230 Article 9(2) provides that members of the public and any NGOs which have *sufficient interest* or who maintain "impairment of a right where the administrative procedural law of a Party requires this as a precondition" are able to "challenge the substantive or procedural legality of any decision, act or omission" under Article 6, and also any decision under other relevant provisions of the Convention (Kravchenko, Skrylnikov, & Bonine, 2003, p. 27). The general provisions of Article 3 and the provisions concerning the collection and dissemination of information in Article 5 could be provisions that would fall under the expression "other relevant provisions". In determining the standing of the public concerned, the Convention defers to national law, but emphasis is given to the objective of giving the public concerned wide access to justice. Furthermore, bodies that fulfil the Convention's definition of the public concerned, which includes NGOs, are automatically considered to have a sufficient interest, or rights capable of being impaired (Lee, & Abbot, 2003, p. 101). Art. 9's "sufficient interest" is not defined by the Aarhus Convention; however, it appears for some commentators to be narrower than the "public concerned" employed in Article 6, and the parties could not agree on how far it provides

the procedural and substantive legality of decisions falling under Article 6 (Wenneras, 2007, p. 226).

In the explanatory proposal the Commission declares that the procedure in the Aarhus Regulation to implement the requirements of Article 9(3) of the Convention "is sufficient to provide for access to justice as participation in environmental decision making can be part of environmental law" (Crossen, & Niessen, 2007, p. 332). However, legal provisions on participation in environmental decision-making can be part of "environmental law", in which case "access to justice would be possible under the general procedure established to implement Article 9(3) of the Convention".

Moreover, it is interesting to note the finding of the decision of 5th May 2009.[231] The ECJ affirms that even if an individual or entity enjoying a procedural right can show individual concern, they will not have standing to bring proceedings contesting the legality of a Community act in terms of its substantive content.

In particular the Court held: "the fact remains that a person or entity enjoying such a procedural right will not, as a rule, where there is any type of procedural guarantee, have standing to bring proceedings contesting the legality of a Community act in terms of its substantive content". Thus, "the mere fact of relying on the existence of a procedural guarantee before the Community judicature does not mean that an action will be admissible where it is based on pleas alleging the infringement of substantive rules of law. Even assuming the appellant did enjoy such procedural guarantees in its own right, that would not mean that it was entitled to challenge the substance of the contested regulation".[232]

This is clearly not what the Aarhus Convention intended. In fact, its Implementation Guide states that in relation to Article 9(2) "The public concerned within the meaning of this paragraph can challenge decisions, acts or omissions

---

for public-interest litigation by NGOs (Birnie, Boyle, & Redgwell, 2009, p. 295). Aarhus "creates a fiction concerning standing requirements, as the necessary 'sufficient interest' to institute proceedings is already constituted by the interest of any NGO acknowledged by national law. Therefore, there is a general objective of Aarhus to give the public concerned wide access to justice" (Schall, 2008, p. 417). Hence, persons or groups who meet these conditions will still need to satisfy the requirements of national law, but with the provision "that any such requirements must be consistent with the objective of giving the public concerned wide access to justice within the scope of Convention" (Redgwell, 2007, p. 169). See Parola 2013.

231   Order of the ECJ in Case C-355/08 dated 5th May 2009.

232   Paragraph 44, 47 and 48.

if the substance of the law has been violated (substantive legality) or if the public authority has violated procedures set out in law (procedural legality)".[233]

Despite the lack of implementation of this second paragraph of Article 9, action to challenge improper consultation or the refusal to organise one could therefore be brought under Articles 10 and 12 of the Aarhus Regulation which transposes Article 9(3) of the Convention. Notwithstanding, it is not clear whether the rights granted by Article 9(3) of the Convention are provided for by Article 12 of the Aarhus Regulation since only administrative acts and administrative omissions can be contested under that provision. Indeed, both apply only to adoption or omission to adopt an "administrative act" as defined.

1.1.4. Fourth Pillar: Implementation of Article 9(3) of the Aarhus Convention

Article 9(3) has been considered the fourth pillar of the Aarhus Convention, because it provides access to administrative or judicial procedures to challenge acts and omissions by private persons and public authorities which breach environmental law (Marshall, 2006, p. 126). Article 9(1) and (2) is directly related to the internal provisions of the Convention while paragraph 3 reinforces external domestic standards. The specificity of this form of "external review" (Redgwell, 2007, p. 168) has led to it being considered a fourth pillar (Jóhannsdóttir, 2008, p. 221) of the Convention. This is also due to the fact that it has no connection with either of the first two pillars of the Convention.[234]

---

233 This Communication is submitted by way of an Amicus intervention in respect of Complaint ACCC/C/2008/32, which is due to be considered by the Aarhus Convention Committee in September 2009.

234 Article 9(3) creates an additional category of cases, where citizens have access to administrative or judicial procedures to challenge acts and omissions, whether or not these are related to the information and public participation rights, by private persons and public authorities which contravene national law relating to the environment. The eighteenth preamble paragraph as well as the Sofia Guidelines already provided standing to certain members of the public to enforce environmental law in a direct or indirect manner. Concerning direct citizen enforcement, citizens are given standing to go to court or other review bodies to implement the law rather than just to redress personal damage. Indirect citizen enforcement means that citizens can contribute to the enforcement process through, for instance, citizen complaints (Stec, & Casey-Lefkowitz, 2000, p. 130). Moreover, the Convention allows a person to challenge acts and omissions by private persons and public authorities which contravene provisions of national law relating to the environment. This wording includes on the one hand, failures to take action provided by law, and on the other, actions that themselves infringe the law (Bonine, 2003, p. 31). This provision obliges States to guarantee standing to enforce environmental law for those citizens who meet criteria provided for by national law (Stec, & Casey-Lefkowitz, 2000, p. 130). Standing under Article 9(3) is even more restrictive than under Article 9(2). The reason therefore is "the price paid for the right to challenge violations of national laws"

The Aarhus Regulation implements Article 9(3) in two stages: first, Article 10 of the Regulation provides a right for certain members of the public to request Community institutions and bodies to conduct an internal review of their acts and omissions.[235] In other words, the Regulation provides a right for NGOs that meet entitlement criteria under the Regulation to make a request for an 'internal review' to the Community institution or body that adopted an administrative act under environmental law, or should have adopted such an act ('administrative omission').

Secondly, Article 12 allows for judicial review of the outcome of that procedure before Community courts. Thus, any NGO that makes a request for an internal review may institute proceedings before the ECJ in accordance with the relevant provisions of the EC Treaty (Crossen, & Niessen, 2007, p. 332). It should be noted that Article 9(3) of the Aarhus Convention provides that access to justice can be possible to the administrative and procedural process. As this book is concerned primarily with the internal review procedure under the Aarhus Regulation, an analysis of the different administrative procedures will not be explored here.[236]

---

relating to the environment or omissions by public authorities (Redgwell, 2007, p. 169). National law must make the decision whether redress is administrative or judicial, and establish standing requirements in order to challenge acts or omissions in connection with national environmental law (Redgwell, 2007, p. 169). It should be remarked that judicial interpretation could play a significant role in the enforcement of the Aarhus Convention (Savoia, 2003, p. 39). See Parola 2013.

235   Acts and omissions by private persons that contravene environmental law are not covered by any instrument applicable to Community institutions. The Commission considers it is a task of the Member States to ensure private persons abide by the law and accordingly it is proposed to cover this requirement of the Aarhus Convention in the proposed directive on access to justice. See Commission Proposal, ibid.

236   Concerning the other Administrative review procedures there is the Review by the European Ombudsman and Special review procedures for acts of Community agencies. The first is comes from the former Article 195 which empowered the European Ombudsman to receive complaints from any citizen of the Union or any natural or legal person residing or having its registered office in a member state concerning instances of maladministration in the activities of the Community institutions or bodies". The Ombudsman's power to "conduct inquiries for which he finds grounds, either on his own initiative or on the basis of complaints submitted to him "does not apply "where the alleged facts are or have been the subject of legal proceedings"". Therefore administrative review by the Ombusman does not satisfy the requirements of Article 9(4) of the Aarhus Convention, since it cannot provide an effective remedy in the event of a violation of EC environmental law by a Community institution or body". It is the review procedures by the Community agencies which are bodies governed by European public law, with their own legal personality distinct from the institutions established by the ECT Treaty itself. In the Environmental field there are many examples (Some examples are: the Community Fisheries Control Agency (CFCA)(Council Regulation (EC) No 768/2005 of 26 April 2005 establishing a Community Fisheries Control Agency and amending Regulation (EEC) No 2847/93; the European Agency for Safety and Health at Work (EU-OSHA)(Council Regulation (EC) No 2062/94 of 18 July 1994 establishing a European Agency for Safety and Health at Work, OJ L 216, 20.08.1994, p. 1.), 23 the

1.1.4.1. Internal Review Process by a Community Institution or Body

The preliminary internal review procedure was introduced as a means of ensuring access to judicial review. In fact, the lack of individual concerns to challenge Community acts directly under former Article 230 (4) EC, push the Commission to construe a procedure so that certain members of the public can

---

European Food Safety Authority (EFSA)(Regulation (EC) No 178/2002 of the European Parliament and of the Council of 28 January 2002 laying down the general principles and requirements of food law, establishing the European Food Safety Authority and laying down procedures in matters of food safety, OJ L 31, 01.02.2002, p. 1.), the European Maritime Safety Agency (EMSA) Regulation (EC) No 1406/2002 of the European Parliament and of the Council of 27 June 2002 establishing a European Maritime Safety Agency, OJ L 208, 05.08.2002, p. 1.) and in particular the most important is the European Environment Agency (EEA) (Council Regulation (EEC) No 1210/90 of 7 May 1990 on the establishment of the European Environment Agency and the European environment information and observation network, OJ L 120, 11.05.1990, p. 1). All these agencies, which are "legal persons having public responsibilities or function, of providing public service in relation to the environment", according to Aarhus Convention, Article2(2)(c), "are to be regarded as public authorities whose acts and omissions fall within the scope of Article 9 (3) of the Aarhus Convention. Those agencies work under the control of the Commission and the Commission decision taken in 2003 (Council Regulation (EC) No 58/2003 of 19 December 2002 laying down the statute for executive agencies to be entrusted with certain tasks in the management of Community programmes, OJ L 11, 16.01.2003, p. 1) establishes a special administrative procedure for the review of the legality or their acts. In particular the Commission acts as an administrative review body and it to take a decision on such administrative proceedings within two months of the date on which they were instituted and reply in writing to the complaint, giving grounds for its decision (See in particular Article 22 of Council Regulation (EC) No 58/2003). Of course the Commission's decision is itself subject to judicial review by the ECJ, as an action for annulment of an "explicit or implicit decision to reject the administrative appeal may be brought before the Court of Justice, in accordance with Article 230 of the Treaty". The most relevant agency according to the Article9(3) of the Aarhus Convention is for authoritative author the European Chemicals Agency (ECHA), the new agency which was established under the REACH Regulation and is playing a key role in the implementation of this new and unprecedented regulatory system for chemicals (Regulation (EC) No 1907/2006 of the European Parliament and of the Council of 18 December 2006 concerning the Registration, Evaluation, Authorisation and Restriction of Chemicals (REACH), establishing a European Chemicals Agency, amending Directive 1999/45/EC and repealing Council Regulation (EEC) No 793/93 and Commission Regulation (EC) No 1488/94 as well as Council Directive 76/769/EEC and Commission Directives 91/155/EEC, 93/67/EEC, 93/105/EC and 2000/21/EC, OJ L 136, 29.05.2007, p. 3). This is not the place for a detailed analysis of those powers but it has to be noted that this agency exercises autonomous decision-making in technical matters of considerable importance for the protection of human health and the environment. The REACH Regulation established an appeal procedure for the benefit of any natural or legal person affected by decisions taken by the Agency. Article 92(1) of REACH lays down the following conditions for the exercise of the right of appeal: "Any natural or legal person may appeal against a decision addressed to that person. Any natural or legal person may also appeal against a decision which, although addressed to another person, is of direct and individual concern to the appellant". See in particular, Pallemaerts, 2009, p. 11.

petition the Community institutions, and by virtue of being the addressee of the internal review decision secure standing under former Article 230 (4) EC (Wenneras, 2007, p. 227).

1.1.4.1.1. Article 10 Request for Internal Review of Administrative Act

Under Article 10 of the Aarhus Regulation, any NGO that meets the specified criteria is entitled to make a request for internal review of an "*administrative act under environmental law*" or an "*alleged administrative omission*" to adopt such act. The request must be made to the Community institution or body that has (or should have) adopted the act, it must be in writing and it must state the grounds for the review. The institution or body concerned must consider any request for review "*unless it is clearly unsubstantiated*" and must respond with a "*written reply*" no later than 12 weeks after receipt of the request (Crossen, & Niessen, 2007, p. 332).

Moreover, this norm provides that a request for internal review must be made in writing within six weeks after the contested act was adopted, notified, or published, whichever is the latest. The same applies to omissions to act, where the time limit refers to the point in time when the act was required.

1.1.4.1.1.1. The Meaning of "Administrative Acts and Omissions"

To understand Article 10, it is necessary to analyse the questionable meaning of "*Administrative Acts and Omissions*". The Regulation does not allow NGOs to have recourse to challenge any acts or omissions of Community institutions and bodies, but only to "*administrative acts*" and "*administrative omissions*" under "*environmental law*".

This legislation defines an administrative act as "*any measure of individual scope under environmental law, taken by a Community institution or body, and having legally binding and external effects*". The key issue with the above definition is the requirement of 'individual scope' because it is not found in the EC Treaty. This is a term sometimes used by the ECJ and CFI to distinguish Community acts of an administrative nature from those of a legislative or regulatory nature.[237] Keesen suggests that the expression "*individual scope*" could refer to a distinction between measures of "general application" and measures "binding upon those to whom it is addressed". Under former Article 249 of the EC Treaty the term individual scope is used to distinguish between regulations and decisions, which are already excluded from the scope of internal review as a consequence of the exception of Community institutions acting

---

237 ECJ Judgment of 24 October 1989, Case 16/88, Commission v. Council, ECR [1989] 3457, par. 16.

in a legislative capacity. Nevertheless, Keesen's interpretation of 'individual scope' seems to be the correct one, because a "narrower definition of the term would effectively make the internal review procedure redundant, if there are no potential decisions that can realistically become the subject of review" (Crossen, & Niessen, 2007, p. 332).[238]

Indeed "it would appear that the improper conduct of a public consultation by an EC institution would not fall within the definition of an "*administrative act*" in Article 2(1)(g) of the Regulation, as such an act would not be of "*individual scope*". Similarly, it would appear that an omission to organise a public consultation could not be interpreted as an "*omission to adopt an administrative act*" further to the definition in Article 2(1)(h) of the Regulation, unless the organisation of a public consultation could be construed as a "measure of individual scope under environmental law".[239]

The second qualification of the act "*legally binding and external effect*" is according to the doctrine "apparently derived from the established case-law interpreting the provisions of Article 230 EC to determine which acts of the institutions can be challenged through an action for annulment" (Pallemaerts, 2009, p. 22). However, the approach chosen in Regulation 1367 is logical considering that non-binding acts in any event fall outside the scope of review under Article 230 (4) EC.[240]

The requirement that the act be legally binding excludes recommendations and opinions, as under Article 249 of the EC Treaty, that have no binding force (Crossen, & Niessen, 2007, p. 332). This expression also excludes decisions taken under Article 226 EC, which the ECJ has found to be administrative preliminary acts which are non-binding.[241] The same applies for other preparatory acts, *e.g,.* environmental action programmes and plans drawn up under the auspices of such programmes.[242]

---

238 "Narrowing the types of challengeable acts and omissions this way prevents the review of acts and omissions in relation to the conduct of public consultation on plans and programmes relating to the environment and in the lack of transposition of Article 9(2) of the Aarhus Convention into the community legal order and in the incorrect transposition of Article 9(3)". See Communication ACCC/C/2008/32, submitted on 1 December 2008 by ClientEarth and others: available at www.unece.org/env/pp/compliance/C2008-32/DatasheetC-2008-32v2009.01.19.doc.

239 Communication ACCC/C/2008/32, submitted on 1 December 2008 by ClientEarth and others, available at www.unece.org/env/pp/compliance/C2008-32/DatasheetC-2008-32v2009.01.19.doc.

240 Case C-301/03 Italy v. Commission (2005) ECR I-10217.

241 Case T-126/95 Dumez v. Commission (1996) ECR II- 2863.

242 Case C- 142/95 P Rovigo v. Commission (1996) ECR I-6669.

It is noteworthy that Article 9(3) of the Aarhus Convention does not contain the condition that the acts must be legally binding to be amenable to administrative or judicial review. This restriction also runs counter to the ECJ's case law under former Article 234 EC, in which it has accepted judicial review of non-binding Community acts since they may have legal effects, in other words, those that "the national course are bound to take [...] into consideration in order to decide disputes submitted to them, in particular where they cast light on the interpretation of national measures adopted in order to implement them or where they are designed to supplement binding Community provisions".[243]

Having "*external effects*" appears to mean that the act does not only bind the institution itself, but also binds another party. The EC Treaty poses the same requirement for reviewable acts in the context of proceedings before the ECJ: "having legal effects vis-à-vis third parties" (Crossen, & Niessen, 2007, p. 332). The requirement of external effect rules out acts which only have relevance for "the internal workings of Community institutions",[244] "procedures governing the relationship between different Community institutions", or "specific Community practice".[245] However, under certain circumstances, such rules "may have legal effects for third parties, and thus be subject to review".[246]

It can be noted that there is one more element laid down in Article 2(2) of the Regulation which provides that "*administrative acts and administrative omissions shall not include measures taken or omissions by a Community institution or body in its capacity as an administrative review body*". So the internal review does not apply if Community institutions or bodies act in a judicial or legislative capacity and when they act in their capacity as an administrative review body. This point is unclear, as numerous authors have remarked, and in particular it does not conform to the Convention (Jans, 2008, p. 215-216; Pallemaerts, 2009, p. 22).

The right of internal review applies also to administrative omissions. The term "*administrative omission*" is defined in Article 2(1)(g) as "*any failure of a Community institution or body to adopt an administrative act as defined in (g)*". These terms seem to refer "to the moment when the act should have been adopted. The omission concerns failure to adopt an act that must be published, the start of the time limit should be when the Community institution was obliged to act, corrected for the additional time which publication usually takes. The six-

---

243   C- 322/88 Salvatore Grimaldi v. Fonds des maladies professionnelles (1989) ECR 4407. P. Wenneras: The Enforcement of EC Environmental law, p. 233.

244   Case T-17/00 Will Rothley v. Parliament (2002) ECR II- 579.

245   Case C-159/96 Portugal v. Commission (1998) ECR I- 7379.

246   Case T-17/00 Will Rothley v. Parliament (2002) ECR II- 579. See p. 233.

week time limit is in any event very short [...] and it is difficult to understand the justification for a stricter regime" (Wenneras, 2007, p. 230).

In conclusion, there are two possible interpretations of acts subject to internal review. According to a narrow interpretation, only administrative acts which are of individual scope fall within its field. Consequently, it has to exclude practically all Community acts. However, if the above provision is interpreted in conformity with the Aarhus Convention, acts that by nature are administrative, even if not of an individual scope, are subject to internal review (Wenneras. 2007).

1.1.4.1.1.2.   The Meaning of "Environmental Law"
The Aarhus Regulation, rather than providing a right to challenge any administrative act or omission that potentially contravenes environmental law as required by the Aarhus Convention, only allows NGOs to challenge acts and omissions of EU institutions and bodies "*under environmental law*".

This wording, for some scholars, may narrow the scope of the Regulation. A Community institution or body could adopt an act having an effect on the environment, yet not under environmental law, without risk of receiving any applications for internal review or being challenged before the ECJ by a concerned NGO (Crossen, & Niessen, 2007, p. 335).

Nevertheless, other opinions point out the definition of the term of Environmental law, made by Article 2(1) f) where Environmental law means: "*Community legislation, which irrespective of its legal base, contributes to the pursuit of the objectives of Community policy on the environment according to the Treaty established by the European Community: preserving, protecting and improving the quality of the environment, protecting human health, the prudent and rational utilisation of natural resources and promoting measures at international level to deal with regional or worldwide environmental problems*".

This is a wide definition of environmental law and notably shows that it is the objective and not the legal basis which determines whether the legislative act should properly be considered as part of environmental law. The consequence of this definition is that it includes not only measures adopted under former Article 175, but also acts adopted under other Articles in the EC Treaty to the extent that they pursue environmental objectives: acts adopted under Article 95 (now 114 internal market) 37 (now 43 agriculture and fisheries), 71 (now 91 transport), 152 (now 168, public health); and 153 EC (now 169, Consumer protection). One reason for this broad definition could be the "logical consequence of the integration principle of Article 6 EC according to which environmental protection shall be taken into account when drafting legislation and policy in other areas of EC Law" (Wenneras, 2007, p. 237).

1.1.4.1.1.3.   The Meaning of "Written Reply"

Another question is linked to the meanings of *"written reply"* which is the answer addressed to the applicants' request. The second paragraph of Article 10 provides: *"The Community institution or body referred to in paragraph 1 shall consider any such request, unless it is clearly unsubstantiated. The Community institution or body shall state its reasons in a written reply as soon as possible, but no later than 12 weeks after receipt of the request".*

It has to be noted that in the original proposal the Commission used the term *"decision"* instead of *"written reply".*[247] The purpose was to grant NGOs standing under Article 230(4) EC by way of an internal review, making the requirement of individual and direct concern superfluous, but the Council changed the term of Article 10.

The amendment was contested by several NGOs, who argued that the new wording was designed to "exclude them from standing under Article 230 (4) EC, which reserves standing to decisions addressed to the plaintiffs" (Wenneras, 2007, p. 239). Nevertheless, some doctrines have held that this "criticism is misguided" because, according to the jurisprudence, it is the "substance of an act, not its form, which determines its classification".[248]

Finally, the reason for this change was to align the text of Regulation 1367 with Article 7 and 8 of 1049/2001 which uses the expression *"written reply".*[249] In addition, it is worth noting that the ECJ has interpreted the notion of written reply to be a decision addressed to the plaintiff for the purposes of Article 230(4) EC, which is capable of granting standing to challenge that decision.[250]

The Aarhus Regulation does not utilise the word "decision", despite the fact that a written reply is clearly in substance a *"decision".* According to other opinions, some problems could arise when this expression *"written reply"* is interpreted as a decision addressed to an NGO, because a reply is necessarily addressed to a person, as it is a reaction to a question posed. Nevertheless, a solution could be to read this Article in accordance with the Preamble of the Regulation and Article 1.

---

247   Article 249 of the EC Treaty describes a 'decision' as a measure 'binding in its entirety upon those to whom it is addressed'. The ECJ recognises that a measure may be a decision in substance although it is cast in a different form or carries a different label(ECJ 15 March 1967, Joined Cases 8–11/66, Société Anonyme Cimenteries C.B.R. Cementsbedrijven N.V. and Others v. Commission (Noordwijks Cement Accord), [1967] ECR 75, at 91).

248   See C-147/96 Netherlands v. Commission (2000) ECR I-4723; Case T-84/01 Association contre l'heure d'été v. Parliament and Council (2002) ECH II-99.

249   ECJ 25 April 2007, Case T-264/04, WWF European Policy Programme v. Council of the European Communities, [2007] ECR. See T. Crossen and V. Niessen: "NGO Standing in the European Court of Justice – Does the Aarhus Regulation Open the Door?", p. 332.

250   Case T-76/02 Messina (2004) ECR I-3203.

The first provision establishes that "*where previous requests for internal review have been unsuccessful, the non-governmental organisation concerned should be able to institute proceedings before the Court of Justice in accordance with the relevant provisions of the Treaty*". Moreover, Article 1 states the objective of the Regulation, which is to contribute to the implementation of the obligations arising under the Aarhus Convention. The consequence of those provisions is that Article 10 enables NGOs access to the European courts (Crossen, & Niessen, 2007, p. 332).

1.1.4.1.2.   Article 11 Criteria for Entitlement at Community Level
Article 9(3) does not require Aarhus contracting Parties to provide access to justice to any and all members of the public without distinction, in other words an *actio popularis* (Parola, 2013). It requires such access to be provided to members of the public who "*meet the criteria, if any, laid down in [...] national law*". As regards the EC, this provision should be interpreted as referring to criteria laid down in Community law.

Thus the Aarhus Regulation provides different criteria: Article 11 contains four cumulative requirements that must be met by NGOs which, according to Ebbesson, should not be too difficult to meet.

The first criterion is that the NGO must be an independent, non-profit legal person according to a Member State's national law or practice. The reference to national law or practice is probably only relevant in respect to the status as a legal person, whilst the notions of independence and non-profit making are likely to be interpreted as autonomous Community law nations. The notion of independence is difficult to establish and also the requirement of non-profit has to be examined on the basis of the statutes of an organisation (Wenneras, 2007, p. 228).

According to the second criteria NGOs have to have as their primary stated objective to promote environmental protection in the context of environmental law. This means that this objective has to be the primary goal, and it is met when, for instance, the statutes of the environmental organisations provide for such.

Then, the NGO must have been in existence for longer than two years, pursuing actively, during that time, the objective of environmental protection. This requirement has been interpreted by the doctrine that "the use of present form suggests that the NGO must not necessarily have been actively pursuing that objective during the whole of that past period, as long as it does so when the question arises" (Wenneras, 2007, p. 228).

The last criteria relates to the subject matter of the internal review, which must concern an issue which is covered by the NGO's objectives and activities. This has to be interpreted as merely excluding specialised organisations from requesting an internal review of issues which clearly fall outside their objectives, otherwise "if it would be interpreted that the mere requirement of the primary objective of the NGO to be environmental protection would be meaningless". This requirement should therefore be understood differently; an NGO cannot request an internal review of environmental acts that do not concern the protection of birds, if it is not specialised in this field, but general organisations, such as Greenpeace, can challenge decisions concerning specific issues, including bird protection (Wenneras, 2007, p. 229).

It is worth noting that in the original Commission proposal, access to the internal review procedure would have been reserved to qualified entities, such as environmental NGOs "*active at Community level*", recognised by the Commission in accordance with criteria laid down in the regulation. Moreover, according to the proposal, the NGOs would have had to submit to a prior recognition procedure through the rules which would have been laid down by the Commission. But the Council decided to "relax the criteria" (Pallemaerts, 2009, p. 20), and decided to give the Commission the power to decide whether or not to grant to NGOs the status of qualified entities. In fact, it is the Community Institution whose acts and omissions are most likely to be the subject of requests for internal review. This is evidently an improvement (Ebbesson, 2006).

Moreover, Regulation 1367 does not say anything about how the authorisation of NGOs will function in practice. Article 11(2) indicates that these issues will be decided by the Commission through the adoption of guidelines, but it seems unsatisfactory to allow such important issues to be decided by the Commission. Also in the new prospective, the question rests whether it is satisfactory to delegate the crucial task of determination of the requirements of the authorisation procedure of Article 11(1). This has been considered "dubious" considering that the large majority of acts subject to review are likely to be Commission decisions (Wenneras, 2007, p. 229).

1.1.4.2. Proceeding Before the Court of Justice

As has been analysed, the Aarhus Regulation provides a right for NGOs that meet entitlement criteria to make a request for an internal review to the Community institution or body that adopted an administrative act under environmental law, or should have adopted such an act (Crossen, & Niessen, 2007, p. 332).

Thus, if the NGO is dissatisfied with the internal review response from the EU institution or body concerned, it has the opportunity to invoke the second stage of the review process, according to Article 12 of the Regulation which institutes proceedings before the Court. In this section, it will be considered, on one hand, whether the judicial review procedures available to members of the public before the ECJ and CFI are adequate to ensure compliance with the obligations under Article 9(3) of the Aarhus Convention and, on the other hand, what has happened vis-à-vis the "*individual concern*" after the signing of the Aarhus Convention and the coming into force of the Aarhus Regulation.

1.1.4.3. Limits of Aarhus Regulation Compared to the Aarhus Convention

The Aarhus Regulation appears not to provide a complete implementation of the Aarhus Convention provision for the right of access to justice for NGOs for three fundamental reasons.

The first is related to the subjective element; indeed, the Regulation fails to provide any means for individuals to challenge Community acts or omissions. Thus, it remains almost impossible for individuals to challenge a decision which is not directly addressed to them. Without meeting the criteria laid down under the regulation they do not have access to internal review.

In fact, Articles 10 to 12 of the Regulation only provide access to the internal review procedure and to court proceedings to NGOs. Individuals and other applicants may not therefore refer to the provisions of the Aarhus Convention to challenge EC institutions' decisions before the Courts. They are only subject to the Treaty conditions laid down in former Article 230(4) (Ebbesson, 2006).

Thus, the lack of any possibility of access to the internal review procedure for individuals is in breach of the requirements of Article 9(3). In fact, the Commission did not consider it "*reasonable*" to extend access to justice to members of the public other than selected NGOs.[251]

Despite Article 9(3) of the Aarhus Convention which recognises discretion of parties to the Convention to set the criteria under which members of the public have access to administrative and judicial review "it seems that the Community has exceeded its margin of discretion by completely excluding individuals". Indeed, the Community would follow the literal meaning of the Article 2(4), 2(5) and 9(3) of the Aarhus Convention.

The first provides that since "*members of the public are natural persons as well as legal persons, including NGOs*", it "*can thus not exclude altogether one of the major classes of the public*" (Wenneras, 2007, p. 228). The "*public concerned*" is defined by Article 2 paragraph 5 of the Aarhus Convention as "*the public affected or likely to be affected by, or having an interest in, environmental decision-making; for the purposes of this definition, non-governmental organisations promoting*

---

251   COM (2003) 662 final. p. 16. The Council agreed, but the European Parliament initially proposed an amendment to open up the internal review procedure to natural persons meeting certain criteria. This amendment was not maintained at second reading. See Position of the European Parliament adopted at second reading on 18 January 2006 with a view to the adoption of Regulation of the European Parliament and of the Council on the application of the provisions of the Aarhus Convention on Access to Information, Public Participation in Decision-making and Access to Justice in Environmental Matters to Community institutions and bodies. See Pallemaerts, 2009, p. 21.

environmental protection and meeting any requirements under national law shall be deemed to have an interest".

And finally Article 9 paragraph 3 which provides that *"members of the public"* *"where they meet the criteria, if any, laid down in [the parties'] national law"* shall have access to courts. Hence, for NGOs the Regulation can be considered as resulting in some progress, but only if the NGOs will be given standing to challenge the replies for requests before the ECJ. For individuals, "the regulation does not make any change whatsoever" (Ebbesson, 2006).

The second problem relates to the possibility recognised by the Aarhus Regulation of NGOs to challenge *"administrative acts"* and *"administrative omissions"* of EC institutions and bodies in contrast to the Aarhus Convention which does not reduce the right of access to justice to administrative acts and omissions, but refers only to acts and omissions.[252]

Originally the Commission's proposal was in line with the Aarhus Convention on this point, stating: *"Any qualified entity who has legal standing according to Article 10 and who considers that an administrative act or an omission is in breach of environmental law is entitled to make a request for internal review to the Community institution or body that has adopted the act or, in case of an alleged omission, should have acted"*.

But in the final version the Article rather than providing a right to challenge any administrative *"act or omission that potentially contravenes environmental law"*, NGOs can only challenge acts and omissions of EU institutions and bodies under environmental law. The reason for this change from the Convention is not *"entirely clear"*, and as analysed before, *"it may limit the scope of the Regulation"*.[253]

It is interesting also to note the way in which acts and omissions were defined. Indeed, an administrative act was defined as *"any administrative measure taken under environmental law by a Community institution or body having legally binding and external effect"*. An omission was defined as *"any failure of a Community institution or body to take administrative action under environmental law, where it is legally required to do so"*.

---

252   Under Article 2(1)(g) of the Aarhus Regulation, an administrative act is defined as "any measure of individual scope under environmental law taken by a Community institution or body, and having legally binding and external effects". An omission is defined as "any failure of a Community institution or body to adopt an administrative act as defined in (g)" (Article 2(1)(h)).

253   "For example, a Community institution or body could adopt an act having an effect on the environment, yet not under environmental law without risk of receiving any applications for internal review or being challenged before the ECJ by a concerned NGO. This may not eventuate, however, as under Article 6 of the EC Treaty, measures in such areas as agriculture, energy and transport may be considered to be environmental law". See Crossen, & Niessen, 2007, p. 332.

Under the Aarhus Regulation Proposal, an omission was established as such when an institution or a body failed to take administrative action under environmental law in general. Under the present Regulation, an omission is characterised by the failure to adopt an administrative act. Moreover, an administrative act is defined as a measure of "*individual scope*" which restricts the type of acts and omissions that may be contested yet further.

Hence, under these definitions set out in the Regulation, as said before, "legislative" acts, directives and regulations, but also certain decisions of the Commission and other EC institutions and bodies will not be subject to the review provisions of the Aarhus Regulation, contrary to what Article 9(3) of the Convention provides. According to this Article, members of the public should be allowed to challenge acts and omissions which contravene provisions of national law relating to the environment. It hence refers to any acts or omissions, giving members of the public a very wide access to justice.

The final problem not dealt with by the Convention is the fact that the procedures before the ECJ are very costly, which makes it impossible for some NGOs to use the procedures provided for by the Regulation. The Aarhus Convention, on the other side, expressly states that the remedies should not be prohibitively expensive. Nevertheless, a part of the doctrine, on the contrary, affirms in many member states, the cost of proceedings is not a major obstacle to access to justice at the EU level, because the actual proceedings "are free of charge and the costs that a losing plaintiff may have to bear are relatively limited and rather predictable" (Pallemaerts, 2009).

1.1.4.4. "Individual Concern" After the Entry into Force of the Aarhus Regulation

The Court has continued to apply the *Plaumann* test notwithstanding the approval of the Aarhus Convention by the European Community and the adoption of the Aarhus Regulation. As stated before, according to the *Plaumann* test a person is individually and directly concerned if affected by the decision in a manner which distinguishes that person from others. However, environmental matters do not usually concern private and specific interests of one individual but rather public interest that affects more than one person in particular. Thus, according to this understanding of the requirement, direct and individual concern will usually not be fulfilled in environmental matters.

This has led to the paradoxical result that the greater the harm to the environment is and the more people are affected by it, the less likely *locus standi* under Article 230 (4) EC Treaty will be. The CFI reasserted the mentioned jurisprudence in the *WWF-UK* case[254] despite the fact that the action was brought by the applicant after the entry into force of the Aarhus Convention in the European Community, and the Aarhus Regulation had been adopted though it was not yet in force. The CFI once again concluded that the *WWF-UK* was not individually concerned by the contested regulation in reasserting the *Plaumann* jurisprudence and dismissed the action.

But most importantly, it further stated that: "Any entitlements which the applicant may derive from the Aarhus Convention and from Regulation No 1367/2006 are granted in its capacity as a member of the public. Such entitlements therefore cannot be such as to differentiate the applicant from all other persons within the meaning of [the *Plaumann* jurisprudence]".

In addition, the CFI reasserted this position in the *Autonomous Region of the Azores* case,[255] in which the Autonomous Region sought the annulment in part of a regulation on the management of the fishing effort relating to Community fishing areas and resources. The environmental associations asked that Article 230(4) EC should be interpreted by the Courts in such a way as to render it compatible with Article 9(3) of the Aarhus Convention.

But the Court held that the Convention had not been approved by the Community when the present action was brought. Then, it recalled that Article 9(3) of the Aarhus Convention refers expressly to "*the criteria, if any, laid down in [the] national law*" of the contracting parties, and that those criteria were laid down, with regard to actions brought before the Community judicature, in Article 230 EC. The Court once again dismissed the action as it considered the applicant not to be individually concerned by the contested act under Article 230 paragraph 4 of EC Treaty.[256]

It can be said that the interpretation of the criterion of the "*individual concern*" is doubtful: to be individually concerned does not mean to be exclusively concerned as the Court has held. An environmental NGO should be considered individually concerned by an act impacting on the environment and be allowed to challenge such an act before the Courts. Moreover, numerous NGOs may each be individually concerned by the same act.

Consequently, the interpretation by the Court of First Instance of the Aarhus Convention and of the Aarhus Regulation in the two above-mentioned cases does not comply with the requirements of Article 9 paragraphs 2 to 5 of the Aarhus

---

254   WWF-UK Ltd v. Council of the European Union (T-91/07), 2 June 2008. It is an annulment action brought by WWF-UK against certain provisions of Council Regulation (EC) n. 41/2007 fixing the total allowable catches (TACs) of cod for the year 2007 in certain Community waters.

255   Regiao autonoma dos Açores v. Council, T-37/04, 1 July 2008.

256   CFI Order of 2 June 2008, Case T-91/07, WWF-UK Ltd v. Council, paras. 72-73.

Convention. The Courts indeed interpreted the criteria laid down in former Article 230 EC so strictly that they prevent all environmental organisations and individuals from challenging acts relating to the environment which are not in compliance with European law.[257]

In conclusion, it is clear that none of the texts provide a satisfactory implementation of the Convention and the ECJ contribute to narrowing the interpretation of the provisions on access to justice, breaching the Aarhus Convention.

Concerning the above-mentioned breaches, a number of the environmental NGOs have sent a communication to the Aarhus Convention's Compliance Committee, for the failure of the EU to meet its obligations to provide access to justice in terms of Article 9(3) of the Aarhus Convention.

Thus, we shall briefly talk about this Communication, still pending at the moment of this writing in front of the Committee. The reason is that it highlights the lack of effective remedies at a European level for NGOs and individuals in environmental matters.

1.1.4.5. Communication to the Aarhus Convention's Compliance Committee

It has been mentioned that several environmental NGOs have submitted a communication to the Aarhus Committee, in accordance with Article 15 of the Convention and section VI of Decision I/7 on Review of Compliance of the First Meeting of the Parties,[258] alleging that the EU fails to comply with its obligations under Article 9(2)-(5) of the Convention.[259] The applicants have pointed out to the Committee that if the jurisprudence of the European Courts and the legislation of EU are not altered, the European Community "will continue to fail to comply with Article 9 paragraphs 2 to 5 of the Aarhus Convention by preventing NGOs and individuals from having access to justice with respect to EC institutions' and bodies' decisions in environmental matters".[260]

---

257   Communication to the Aarhus Convention's Compliance Committee by ClientEarth, available at www.unece.org/env/pp/compliance/Compliance%20Committee/32TableEC. htm. Levi, 2006.

258   The above provisions were analysed in Parola 2013.

259   Communication ACCC/C/2008/32, submitted on 1 December 2008 by ClientEarth and others, available at www.unece.org/env/pp/compliance/C2008-32/DatasheetC-2008-32v2009.01.19.doc.

260   Communication ACCC/C/2008/32, submitted on 1 December 2008 by ClientEarth and others, available at www.unece.org/env/pp/compliance/C2008-32/DatasheetC-2008-32v2009.01.19.doc

In particular ClientEarth has accused the fact that the jurisprudence of the European Courts has blocked all access to justice for individuals and NGOs in environmental matters, due to "an erroneous reading" of the EC Treaty, in particular as seen in the Article 230 paragraph 4.

This NGO has suggested another interpretation of the criteria laid down in this provision in accordance to Article 9 of the Aarhus Convention.

First, the Aarhus Convention and the Aarhus Regulation are now EU law; there is thus a need for the ECJ to acknowledge that they cannot simply reassert their old jurisprudence on standing in environmental matters. Moreover, the refusal of the ECJ to grant individuals and NGOs access to justice results in a real non-equilibrium between the different actors who may challenge EC institutions' and bodies' decisions. Indeed, Corporations and trade associations have a much wider access to the European Courts than individuals and NGOs do.

The Courts' jurisprudence clearly favours the protection of private economic interests over public interests, including the protection of the environment. The Court has also, in commercial matters such as the field of competition, state aids, anti-dumping and concentrations, progressively established a jurisprudence that automatically grants standing to applicants who challenge decisions taken pursuant to EU Regulations which entitle them to some specific procedural guarantees.[261]

To underpin its arguments the ENGOs refer to the findings and recommendations the Compliance Committee has adopted regarding the jurisprudence of the Belgian Conseil d'Etat. The issue is that there is a serious chance that it may actually find the EU in breach of its obligations under the Convention if the Committee will follow in a similar case involving the lack of effective NGO access to the Belgian administrative. Findings and recommendations of the Compliance Committee with regard to compliance by Belgium with its obligations under the Aarhus Convention in relation to the rights of environmental organisations to have access to justice, ECE/MP.PP/C.1/2006/4/Add.2, 28 July 2006. According to the complainant, Bond Beter Leefmilieu, the recommendations of the Committee had a tremendous impact since the Conseil d'Etat modified its jurisprudence and granted access to NGOs.

261   In Comité Central d'Entreprise de la Société Générale des Grandes Sources and others (Order of the President of the Court of First Instance of 15 December 1992, CCE Grandes Sources, T- 96/92), the President of the Court of First Instance summarised the position of the Court on the granting of *locus standi* to applicants who are entitled to specific procedural guarantees in commercial matters: "In its case-law on the *locus standi* of third parties in relation both to competition and State aid and to dumping and grants, the Court of Justice has held that where a regulation confers on undertakings procedural rights entitling them to request the Commission to find an infringement of the Community rules or to submit observations in an administrative procedure, those undertakings may be able to institute proceedings in order to protect their legitimate interests (see the judgments of the Court of Justice in Case 26/76 Metro v. Commission I [1977] ECR 1875, Case 191/82 FEDIOL v. Commission [1983] ECR 2913, and Case 169/84 COFAZ v. Commission [1986] ECR 391). The need to protect legitimate interests may also be a decisive criterion in

Secondly, the NGOs suggest that the Courts consider the environmental NGOs, "which fulfil criteria for entitlement provided by Article 11 of the Aarhus Regulation, as individually concerned by the reply of the EC institution or body to the internal review request and by the contested decision, act or omission of the EC institution or body" in such a way as to give NGOs procedural rights. They, thus, ask the Committee to make a recommendation clearly setting out the Courts' obligation to interpret Articles 10, 11 and 12 of the Aarhus Regulation in compliance with the requirements of Article 9(3)(4) and (5) of the Aarhus Convention.

One more word must be said about the effect that the entry into force of the Treaty of Lisbon has had on the necessity of the NGO's communication made beforehand. In fact the question is: is there still motivation for this recourse?

There are various potential ways in which the Lisbon Treaty, in particular Articles 6 and 263, and the EU Charter of Fundamental Rights, could improve access to environmental justice as administered by the EU institutions.

The new wording of Article 263 may be helpful in future cases because applicants seeking to challenge a decision in the form of an EU Regulation will not be required to show "*individual concern*". The Lisbon Treaty would appear on the face of it to have improved matters in respect of one element; the change that would result from the new wording would not constitute a major step forward to the broadening of access to justice. Indeed, the change would only apply to a limited sub-category of acts of Community institutions (Pallemaerts, 2009, p. 30).

Moreover, the position is also not clear regarding the future development of the test of "*direct concern*" by the ECJ.[262] Indeed, the text of Article 263 retains the requirement for an applicant to show that a decision addressed to another

deciding whether a natural or legal person may be regarded as directly or individually concerned by a decision in the same way as an addressee".

Moreover this jurisprudence was upheld in Vittel and CE Pierval (CFI, Comité Central d'Entreprise de la Société Anonyme Vittel and Comité d'Etablissement de Pierval and federation Générale Agroalimentaire v. Commission, T-12/93, 27 April 1995, paragraph 47). In this case, the CFI was even more flexible in its interpretation of the notion of individual concern since it did not require the applicant to effectively trigger the specific consulting procedure. The fact that the applicant had procedural guarantees under the contested regulation was sufficient to consider that it was individually concerned by it. See also Metropole Télévision SA and Reti Televisive Italiane SpA and Gestevisión Telecinco SA and Antena 3 de Televisión v. Commission, 11 July 1996, joined cases T-528/93, T-542/93, T-543/93 and T-546/93, where the ECJ confirmed its jurisprudence.

262 Comments regarding the impact of the entry into force of the Lisbon Treaty on the above Communication by WWF, available at www.unece.org/env/pp/compliance/Compliance%20Committee/32TableEC.htm

person, or a regulatory act, is of "direct concern" to it.[263] On all past occasions the question about direct concern was not addressed by the Court because the judgements did not progress beyond a finding that the individual concern threshold was not met.[264]

So the Communication to the Committee is still useful because after the amendment of the above provision, the Courts could replace a strict interpretation of individual concern with a strict interpretation of direct concern. The communication's applicant has concerns that there remains ample scope for the Courts to interpret the direct concern test and/or the sufficient interest test in such a way as to continue to prevent access to environmental justice.[265]

Another point to take into account is the modification by the new Treaty of Article 6 which now establishes the legal basis for the EU's accession to the European Convention on Human Rights. As has already been underlined, submitting the EU's legal system to independent external control would have the potential to strengthen the protection of human rights in Europe as well as giving EU citizens the same protection vis-à-vis acts of the Union that they presently enjoy from Member States. Accession would give the right to challenge an act of an EU institution before the ECHR in Strasbourg, whereas previously, the normal EU remedies were all that was available.

As such, for the first time the EU would have to put into effect Article 13 of the European Convention on Human Rights – which requires it to give individuals (and NGOs) whose rights and freedoms as set out in the European Convention on Human Rights have been violated, an effective remedy before a national authority, in this instance the ECJ. Indeed, a challenge on the basis of Article 13 (for failure to provide an effective remedy for a breach of environmental rights sufficient to fall within Article 8 of the Convention) could be envisaged as potentially providing a safety net if standing were refused by the ECJ.

263 According to the Courts' jurisprudence for an applicant to be directly concerned by a measure: (1) that measure must directly affect the legal situation of the applicant; and (2) its implementation must be purely automatic and result from Community rules alone without the need for any intermediate measures.

264 See the WWF's Case (T-91/07 and C-355/08). Also in the Case C-321/95 P Stichting Greenpeace and Others v. Commission, in which the Commission argued that Greenpeace was not directly affected by the contested decision. Once again, the Court held that it did not need to address whether Greenpeace was directly concerned by the contested decision because it failed to satisfy the test of individual concern.

265 In Case C-321/95, P Stichting Greenpeace and Others v. Commission, the Courts accepted that interests may, in theory, be economic or otherwise, and thus measures affecting an applicant's legal situation could apply to environmental interests, just as to economic interests. However, once again, the question of legal interest was not addressed by the Courts in WWF's case.

A final issue is related to the EU Charter of Fundamental Rights which by Article 6 of the Lisbon Treaty shall have the same legal value as the Treaties. EU institutions are bound to observe the rights laid down in the Charter, which include the Article 47 Right to an effective remedy and to a fair trial.[266] Furthermore, it shall be noted that the Explanations by the Convention which accompany the Charter affirm that Article 47 is not "*intended to change the appeal system laid down in the Treaties, particularly the rules relating to admissibility, and that the principle of the right to an effective remedy is to be implemented according to the procedures laid down in the Treaties*". Whilst the Explanation is not legally binding, nevertheless it gives a strong indication that the Charter is not likely to alter the status quo as far as access to the EU Courts is concerned.

For all the above-mentioned reasons, despite the changes made by the Lisbon Treaty, it can be affirmed that there are still several reasons to maintain the communication admissible, to achieve a statement about the level of EU implementation of the Aarhus Convention

2. Environmental Democracy at National Level

Section II will focus on implementation of environmental rights and duties in European Community Law at a national level. In particular it will begin with the analysis of the main difference between EU law and the Aarhus Convention without repeating where the legislations and the Convention overlap. It will show how EU law is, in some ways, more effective at a national level compared to the EU level, and, as it has been argued, "EC legislation is capable of providing a very hard edge to the sometimes vague international commitments contained in the Convention" (Lee, 2005, p. 152).

This part gives an overview of the origins of the Community law concerning public rights to environmental information and participation and access to justice. The first two are milestones in the development of the relevant pieces of legislation and of the role of the Aarhus Convention in this respect. It will be remarked that there is a significant interplay between the Aarhus Convention

---

266 "Everyone whose rights and freedoms guaranteed by the law of the Union are violated has the right to an effective remedy before a tribunal in compliance with the conditions laid down in this Article.

Everyone is entitled to a fair and public hearing within a reasonable time by an independent and impartial tribunal previously established by law. Everyone shall have the possibility of being advised, defended and represented. Legal aid shall be made available to those who lack sufficient resources in so far as such aid is necessary to ensure effective access to justice".

and Community law and they both provide stimulus to further development of each other.

Then, the implementation will be scrutinised, especially some examples of implementation, e.g., concerning the ecological duties to protect and repair the Environment. As in the analysis in Section I, it will not attempt to provide a comprehensive coverage of all issues related to EU legislation, because this has already been done by important scholars and it would be just a simple repetition of well-known questions. On the contrary, the aim of this part intends to put forward where the EU legislation at a National level moves towards recognition of an Environmental Democracy.

2.1. Procedural Environmental Rights

2.1.1. First Pillar: Access of Environmental Information

Historically, one of the first initiatives for access to environmental information was the Directive on Environmental Impact Assessment.[267] Article 6 already established in 1985 that information concerning activities covered by the directive should be made available to the public. Prior to the cited Directive, a 1975 directive on bathing water quality pointed out that "*public interest in the environment and in the improvement of its quality is increasing*" and "*the public should therefore receive objective information on the quality of bathing water*".[268]

The striving towards environmental rights on the EU level took a further step forward in 1987 with the Fourth Action Programme, which declared that the "Commission will study the need for, and desirability of, a Community Freedom of Environmental Information Act and will make appropriate proposals".[269]

The response to this goal was, in particular, Directive 90/313 concerning access to information on the environment.[270] It is worth noting that in Article 4 of

---

267   The first EIA Directive was implemented in 1985 and since then several amendments have followed. The EIA Directive (EU legislation) on Environmental Impact Assessment of the effects of projects on the environment was introduced in 1985 and was amended in 1997. Following the signature of the Aarhus Convention by the Community on 25 June 1998, the Community adopted in May 2003 Directive 2003/35/EC.

268   Council Directive Concerning the Quality of Bathing Water 76/160, 1975 O.J. (L 31) 1 (EEC).

269   Fourth Programme of Action, 1987 O.J. (C 328) 2.6.2.

270   Council Directive 90/313, 1990 O.J. (L 158) 56 (EEC). On this Directive see See Hallo, 1996; Montanaro, 2002, p. 114. Indeed access to environmental information plays central role in other directives as, for example, the 1996 directive on integrated pollution

the Aarhus Convention so-called passive disclosure of information is designed in a similar way to the EC Directive 90/313. It provides freedom of access for any natural or legal person, even without having to prove an interest, to information on the environment held by any public authority, also in a transboundary respect – given the non-discrimination principle and the fact that the Directive aims to guarantee free access to any person "*throughout the Community*".

In 2003 this Directive was repealed and replaced by a new Directive on Public Access to Environmental Information. This replacement was considered necessary "in the order to clarify and explain the definitions of environmental information and public authorities, and also to emphasise that the directive purports to establish a right to information and that a refusal to disclose information only exists in specific and clearly defined cases" (Heldeweg, 2005, p. 2).

However, the old directive focused merely on passive dissemination of information and insufficiently addressed the issue of active dissemination of information by public authorities. In addition, Directive 2003/4 adds the specific access to justice provisions from the Aarhus Convention that relate to refusal of access to information, which were not present in the 1990 directive.

2.1.1.1. Directive 2003/4/EC on Public Access to Environmental Information

This Directive implements the Articles 2, 4, 5 and 9 (1) of the Convention in respect of the rights to information held by public authorities in the Member States. Although the word "*right*", was not mentioned the Directive establishes a "*right*" and not a simple "freedom", because, as underlined by the scholar (Krämer, 2004, p. 1) and also by the jurisprudence,[271] all provisions reflect the existence of a right, not merely an obligation for administrations.

Concerning all requirements mentioned in Articles 4 and 5 of Aarhus, both active and passive aspects of access to information were incorporated into the new directive (Jendroska, 2006, p. 63). Indeed, this legislation follows the Convention very closely and almost all provisions are similar to or coincide with this agreement, in order to regulate on one hand the passive access to

---

prevention and control.(Council Directive 96/61, 1996 O.J. (L 271) 26 (EC).) For instance, the directive states that "the public must have access, before any decision is taken, to information relating to applications for permits for new installations or substantial changes and to the permits themselves" and that authorities shall ensure that the public can comment on applications for permits for new installations or amendments to existing ones. (Recital 24, Article15). See Pedersen, 2010.

271   The ECJ affirms "the purpose of the Directive is to confer a right on individuals which assures the freedom of access to information on the environment". Case C-217/97, Commission v. Germany (1999) ECR I-5087.

information,[272] exceptions,[273] modalities[274] and charges[275] of that right and on the other hand active access to information.[276]

Thus, the interesting point here is to indicate where the EU legislation has taken steps to further the Convention and where the Directive has used even slightly more expansive language.

Directive 2003/4/EC, indeed, in some aspects goes beyond the provisions of the Aarhus Convention (Jendroska, 2005, p. 12). For instance, Article 2(1)(a) of the Directive adds a non-exhaustive list containing three examples of "*natural sites*" "*wetlands, coastlands and marine areas*" whereas Article 3(a) of the Convention simply mentions "*natural sites*". The Directive also adds (Article 2(1)(d)) "*reports on the implementation of environmental legislation*" to the list of matters falling under the general heading of "*environmental information*" (Roy, 2006, p. 51).

Article 2 (1) contains a very wide definition of environmental information, encompassing all aspects of the environment. The public authority is similarly widely defined in Article 2(2), to also include bodies without a specific environmental function or objective at all levels of government as well as private entities having public functions or responsibilities.

Moreover, the Directive adds specific pieces of information to the definition of "*environmental information*" that are not included in the Aarhus Convention,

---

272   Directive imposes positive obligations on public authorities, requiting active and systematic dissemination of environmental information and data, underlining the importance of computer telecommunication and or electronic technology. Reports on the state of the environment are to be published at least every four years, including information on the quality of, and pressures on, the environment. See for a attentive analysis of all similar disposition Roy, 2006, p. 51.

273   The access to environmental information is subject to exceptions listed in Article 4 of the directive. It follows closely the exceptions to rights of access of Aarhus, all subject to a public interest proviso, and all to be interpreted restrictively. Moreover the directive similarly to the Convention provides both that the act or omission can be reconsidered by a public authority, and reviewed administratively by an independent and impartial body established by law.

274   "Article 3 of the Directive organises the modalities of granting access to environmental information. See Krämer, 2004, p. 16-18; Jans, & Vedder, 2008, p. 327.

275   The question of administrative charges is provided by Article 5 of Directive and follows the line made by Article 4(8) of the Convention. See in detail Krämer, 2004, p. 18-19.

276   "Article 7 of the Directive deals with the dissemination of information, and is comparatively brief, omitting any reference to the encouraging of 'operators whose activities have a significant impact on the environment to inform the public regularly of the environmental impact of their activities and products' (Article 5(6) of the Convention). Article 8 of the Directive is concerned with the quality of environmental information, including the duty to update such information (Article 5(1)(a) of the Convention). The Directive largely remains faithful to the text of the Convention". See for an attentive analysis of all similar dispositions Roy, 2006, p. 51; Krämer, 2004, p. 21-23.

such as information on the "*contamination of the food chain*". This means that information on food contamination caused by pesticides, heavy metals or other contaminants is covered by the Directive.

Furthermore, it effectively broadens the scope of available information by requiring accessibility not only as regards information "held by" the authorities but also as regards information "held for" the authorities. Also worth noting is the attempt to include authorities acting in a judicial and legislative capacity within "the ambit of the directive indeed these are excluded from the scope of both directive 90/313 and the Convention" (Jendroska, 2006, p. 63).

Another important step to the Convention provisions concerns the exemption clause (Jendroska, 2005, p. 16). In general, the directive has similar categories of exceptions; nevertheless, it goes a little further than Aarhus which prohibits refusal of a request for information relating to emissions into the environment.

Indeed, the Convention requires in most cases only that the information requested concerning emissions into the environment be taken into account; only in respect of commercial or industrial confidentiality does the Aarhus Convention state that information on emissions "shall be disclosed" (Lee, 2005, p. 155).

Thus, there is no doubt that full application of the Access to Information Directive according to its words and its scope, constitutes an important achievement on the long and difficult way towards an open European society (Krämer, 2003a, p. 27). Nevertheless, it is interesting to note that the ECJ jurisprudence with regard to citizens' right to know is unfortunately "rather disappointing" (Krämer, 2009, p. 202).[277] It has not succeeded in inserting

---

277   Concerning the ECJ Jurisprudence related to the access to information Lavrysen affirms that "The Court of Justice has had the opportunity on several occasions to pronounce itself on interpretation problems in connection with this Directive. The term 'information relating to the environment' should be broadly interpreted, namely as also covering a statement of views given but a countrywide protection authority in development consent proceedings if that statement is capable of influencing the outcome of those proceedings as regards interests pertaining to the protection of the environment (ECJ, 12 June 1988 (C.321/96), Mecklenburg, Jur., 1988, I-3809.). According to this case law, the grounds for exception should be interpreted restrictively. The court considered that the term "preliminary investigation proceedings" should be given a restrictive interpretation." The term "preliminary investigation proceedings" is to be interpreted as including an administrative procedure which takes place prior to a judicial procedure and the outcome of which is capable of forming the subject-matter of judicial review by the administrative courts, only if it immediately precedes a contentious or quasi-contentious procedure and arises from the need to obtain proof or to investigate a matter prior to the opening of the actual procedure (ECJ, 9 September 1999 (C-217/97), Commission of the EC v. Federal Republic of Germany, T.M.R., 2000, p. 65) where there are admissible grounds for refusal of access to information on the environment, the Directive provides that the Member States must examine whether the information that does have to be made available can be detached from the information that requires confidential treatment. This provision

the Article into the European Treaty, and it could have interpreted access to information in a broader way, limiting the numerous attempts by administrations to keep access to environmental information restricted.

2.1.2. Second Pillar: Participation in Environmental Matters

Historically, EU law started quite early to require Member States to provide for the involvement of the public and impose procedural rather than substantive requirements in directives. Moreover, the Aarhus Convention has added an obligation to change and improve the existing legislation on public participation. This led also to the adoption of Directive 2003/35/EC, providing for Public Participation in Respect of the Drawing up of Certain Plan and Programmes Relating to the Environment.[278]

The directive changes the existing public participation provisions in the EIA Directive 85/337[279] and the IPPC Directive 96/61, as well as six other directives adopted prior to the Aarhus Convention. The modification includes the addition of environmental NGOs to the definition of the "public" and access to review procedures in relation to public participation decisions taken under the directives.

---

imposes on the Member States an obligation which is precise as regards the result to be obtained and directly affects the legal situation of individuals. Such a provision must be transposed into national law in a clear and precise manner. According to the Directive, a reasonable charge may be levied when access is granted to information relating to the environment. Member states, however, must not make a charge in cases where requests for information are refused", Lavrysen, 2008, p. 77.

278   Directive 2003/35 providing for public participation in respect of the drawing up of certain plans and programmes relating to the environment, OJ 2003 L 156/17.

279   The 1985 Directive was the first piece of Community environmental legislation to focus almost exclusively on the imposition of processes and procedures. By virtue of Article 2, in particular, Member States are obliged to ensure that all proposed projects likely to have a significant impact on the environment by virtue of their nature, size or location, be assessed with regard to their environmental effects. Article 7 provided that: "Where a Member State is aware that a project is likely to have significant effects on the environment in another Member State or where a Member State likely to be significantly affected so requests, the Member State in whose territory the project is intended to be carried out shall forward the information gathered pursuant to Article 5 [the information gathered by the developer] to the other Member State at the same time as it makes it available to its own nationals. Such information shall serve as a basis for consultations necessary in the framework of the bilateral relationship between the two Member States on a reciprocal and equivalent basis".

Article 6 contains detailed rights of information and consultation for citizens prior to consent being given. Member States shall therefore ensure that a concerned public is given the opportunity to express an opinion before the project is initiated. It is up to Member State law to make detailed arrangements for such information and consultation by determining who forms a part of the 'concerned' public. See Reich, 1997, p. 155.

2.1.2.1.   Directive 2003/35/EC

In implementing the second pillar, the decision was made to change the Directives EIA and IPPC and the changes are included in Directive 2003/35. Article 1 of the directive affirms that the objective "*is to contribute to the implementation of the obligations arising under the Aarhus Convention*" and then introduces two tools: first "*providing for public participation in respect of the drawing up of certain plans and programmes relating to the environment*" and secondly "*improving the public participation and providing for provisions on access to justice within Council Directives 85/337/ EEC and 96/61/EC*".

As to the first measure, Article 2 establishes provisions for a general public participation procedure.[280] The actual obligation to allow for public participation applies to natural and legal persons, but the first stage of public participation involves informing the public about the proposals and the possibility of participation. After this, there must be the possibility for effective participation. This refers to the stage in the decision-making process when the options are still open.

The central obligation under Article 2(2)c is to take due account of the views of the public consultation. Moreover, the public must be informed of the final decision and public participation process. The scope of the general public participation procedure is defined primarily by Annex I.[281] However, the list only includes six directives; and the reasons for their selection are "far from being clear" (Jendroska, 2006, p. 63).

Indeed it has been noted "on the one hand, the list includes plans and programmes which all may well be subject to the requirement of strategic assessment together with the requirement for public participation under the SEA Directive, Directive on the Assessment of the Effects of Certain Plans and Programs on the environment".[282] On the other hand, "it does not include plans related to the management of Nature 2000 sites which seem to be meeting the criteria of Article 7 of the Aarhus Convention (plans relation to the environment)

---

280   See in general: Jans, & Vedder, 2008, p. 331.

281   The following plans and programmes are subject to the public participation requirement: waste management plans pursuant to the waste framework Directive; plans to reduce the environmental impact of batteries and accumulators pursuant to Article 6 of the batteries Directive 91/157; programs for vulnerable zones pursuant to Article 5 (1) the Nitrates Directive 91/676; hazardous Waste Directive 91/689 – Packaging waste management plans pursuant to Article 14 of the Packaging Waste Directive 94/62; Plans for zones where air quality exceeds the limits pursuant to Article 8(3) of the Ambient Air Quality Directive 96/62. See also Jans, & Vedder, 2008, p. 331.

282   See Commission, Implementation of directive 2001/ 42, 2003, p. 48.

but which are not subject to strategic assessment under the SEA Directive" (Jendroska, 2006, p. 63). [283]

The principal measures for implementing the relevant Aarhus obligations are considered to be the SEA Directive[284] and the Water Framework Directive, as will be explained better in the following. Both Directives were singled out as performing such functions by the Article 2(5) of the directive.[285] This exclusion means "to supplement the scheme with providing for a set of public participation requirements in relation to plans and programmes considered to be 'relating to the environment' and envisaged by environmental directive adopted before the Aarhus Convention" (Jendroska, 2006, p. 63).

Relating to the second measure to achieve the objective of the directive, Articles 3 and 4 respectively amend the EIA and IPPC Directive in order to improve public participation as part of those directives.

2.1.2.2. Implementation of Article 6 of Aarhus Convention: EIA Directive and IPPC Directive

The eleventh recital confirms that Directive 2003/35/EC purports to bring Community EIA law into line with obligations arising under the Aarhus Convention.

The EIA Directive, defined as the "first milestone" (Jendroska, 2006, p. 63), was the first piece of EU environmental legislation which established a clear and relatively elaborated requirement for providing public participation, and in particular, public participation in the "decision-making".

For the most part, the provisions of the Convention were literally transposed in the amended EIA Directive.[286] About these we shall not go into detail here. Nevertheless, some authors have remarked on certain differences between

---

283   Implementation of Directive 2001/ 42, 2003, p. 12.

284   Directive 2001/42 on the Assessment of the effects of certain plans and programmes on the environment (2001) OJ L 197, p. 30. See Sheate, 2003, p. 331; See also Morrow, 2004, p. 49.

285   "This Article shall not apply to plans and programmes set out in Annex I for which a public participation procedure is carried out under Directive 2001/42/EC of the European Parliament and of the Council of 27 June 2001 on the assessment of the effects of certain plans and programmes on the environment or under Directive 2000/60/EC of the European Parliament and of the Council of 23 October 2000 establishing a framework for Community action in the field of water policy".

286   For example Article 6(2) of the EIA Directive obliges Member States to ensure that 'the public concerned' is given the opportunity to express its opinion on the proposed project before development consent is granted. In line with the principle of subsidiary, Article 6(3) provides that the 'detailed arrangements' for informing and consulting the public are left to be determined by the Member States. Article 8 provides that the results

the texts which were "probably not an accidental mistake, because almost all provisions of the Convention were meticulously copied".[287]

First, there is a fundamental difference between the concepts of "*public*" and "*public concerned*" which in the Directive have been used in a confusing way. The EU legislation grants the right to participate in the decision-making process to a more restricted group of people (only people who are affected by or have an interest in the decision) than the Aarhus Convention. So only the public concerned is given the right to engage in the participation process, whereas the Convention enables the public to participate. The same provision is present in Article 15 of the IPPC Directive, which is also the only one provided for public participation.

An important addition made by the EIA Directive in Article 6(3) has been to state that the authorities have to make accessible to the public any information that becomes available even after the time the public concerned was originally informed. This has been seen as an important addition that is "especially necessary for participation in decision-making on large projects for which an EIA has to be undertaken. Because they are so complex, it can take considerable time before a final decision on such projects is reached" (Verschuuren, 2004, p. 36). Furthermore, the Articles on public participation in the EIA and IPPC Directive have a broader scope in that they also provide for cross-border public participation[288] and provisions on access to justice.[289]

Although the projects subject to public participation listed in Annex I of the Aarhus Convention are mainly IPPC Installations, the Public Participation in Plans and Programmes Directive introduces the additional duty to initiate a public participation procedure for all projects that are subject to an EIA according to the EIA Directive (Ryal, 2007, p. 247).

An aspect that was not explicitly transposed in the Directive is Article 6(5) of the Aarhus Convention, which requires "*the parties to encourage prospective applicants to identify the public concerned, enter into discussions, and to provide information regarding the objectives of their application before applying for a permit*" (Verschuuren, 2004, p. 39). It was a missed opportunity to not include this important provision.

Finally, a change may be noted in Article 7 of the EIA. The provision is very interesting for our purpose because it recognises the special importance of the

---

of consultations and the information gathered during the EIA process must be taken into consideration in the development consent procedure.

287   See for more detail analysis: Verschuuren, 2004, p. 35.

288   Article 7 of the EIA Directive and Article 17 of the IPPC Directive.

289   Article 10 of the EIA Directive and Article 15 of the IPPC Directive. Jans, &Vedder, 2008, p. 331.

citizens of the other States. So the provision states that the information that is made available to the public on the proposed project and the decision that may be taken also must be sent to another Member State if significant environmental effects take place in that Member State.[290] Indeed, the public affected in the other Member State has the opportunity to actively participate in the decision-making process in the neighbouring state. This provision goes further than the Convention because the latter does not necessarily impose a duty to involve citizens from neighbouring states.[291]

2.1.2.3.   Implementation of Article 7 of Aarhus Convention

As pointed out at the beginning, the general rules about the implementation of Article 7 of the Aarhus Convention "*public participation in the preparation of plans and programs*", are found in Article 2 of the directive 2003/35.[292] Nevertheless, the basic assumption within the EU is that any environmental directive adopted since 2000 which regards provisions on the elaboration for plans or programmes also establishes for provisions concerning public participation aiming to implement the Convention (Jendroska, 2006, p. 63). It has already been seen that the main tool for implementing the relevant Aarhus obligations are considered to be the SEA Directive [293] and the Water Framework Directive.

The SEA Directive plays a role in enhancing the integration of environmental considerations in policy and planning processes because it is directed at strategic decision making. The general benefits of SEA are that it can help decision makers

---

290   "The other Member State can then decide, according to Article 7(2) whether it wishes to participate in the decision-making process, and whether it will enable the public concerned in this Member State to participate in the decision-making process as well. When the other member state indicates that it will participate, then all other relevant information that is made available to the public also has to be sent to the other Member State". See Verschuuren, 2004, p. 37.

291   Nevertheless this obligation is provided by other international convention as UN Convention on Environmental Impact Assessment in a Transbouday Context in it article 3 (8, also called Espoo Convention, 25 February 1991.

292   Some authors have criticised it for a failure to comply with Article 7 of the Aarhus Convention. See Mathiesen, 2003, p. 46. According to Article 7 of the Aarhus, each party must introduce probate practical and /or other provisions for the public to participate during the preparation of plans and programmes relating to the environment, within a transparent and fair framework, having provided the necessary information to the public. The relevant public authority must designate the public, taking into account the objectives of the Convention, before it is able to participate. To the extent approbate, each party must also endeavour to provide opportunities for public participation in the preparation of policies relating to the environment. See also Marsden, & De Mulder, 2005, p. 50.

293   See Sheate, 2003, p. 331; See also Morrow, 2004, p. 49; see also Ming-Zhi Gao, 2008, p. 341; Ming-Zhi Gao, 2006, p. 129.

by first achieving environmentally sound and sustainable development, and furthermore by "strengthening policy, plan and programme-making processes; saving time and money by avoiding costly mistakes; improving good governance and building public trust and confidence in decision making" (Marsden, & De Mulder, 2005, p. 50).

The purpose of the directive is to identify and assess environmental consequences of certain plans and programs before their adoption, in order to secure the integration of environmental considerations. According to Article 6, the draft plans and programs drawn up in accordance with the directive must be made available to the public before they are adopted, and the public must be given an opportunity to comment on the plans and programs.

The directive, hence, enhances early consultation during the SEA process, which incorporates the Aarhus provisions encouraging participation at the earliest opportunities (Sheate, 2003, p. 334). The public must also be consulted on the draft plan or programme and environmental report if the public is affected by or has an interest in the decision-making. Finally, the directive states that the final plan or program shall take into account the consultations made by the public (Sheate, 2003, p. 334).

The Water Framework Directive, aimed at regulation of inland surface waters, transitional waters, coastal waters, and groundwater recognises, similarly to the SEA Directive, the importance of public participation in European Environmental Law. According to Article 14, the WFD encourages Member States to involve all interested parties in the implementation of the directive as well as to facilitate public participation in the creation of river basin management plans.

In conclusion, it is worth noting that the jurisprudence of the ECJ is ambiguous in the area of citizens' participation in environmental decision-making. On the one hand there are attempts to increase citizens' participation,[294] and on the other hand, there have been spurious attempts to consider the participation rights of citizens as a fundamental right.[295]

---

294 For instance in 1993 the Court decided that member states had to inform other member states of measures which they intended to take with the purpose of combating air pollution, in order to allow the participation of citizens in consultation and deliberation of such measures. See Case C-186(91, Commission v. Belgium, (1993) ECH I-185. It is also crystal clear from the case law that the ECJ acknowledges the important role played by the public in the EIA process See, *e.g.* Case C-332/04 Commission v. Spain [2006] ECR I-0000 at para 58.

295 For instance in the Case C-216/05, Commission v. Ireland of 9 November 2006, the ECF was of the opinion that member states were entitled to raise fees for citizens' participation in the environmental impact assessment procedure. See Krämer, 2009, p. 202.

2.1.3. Third Pillar: Access to Justice in Environmental Matters

Although the legislation in place relating to access to environmental information and public participation is substantial, the attempts made by the European Community to introduce conformity on the Member State level with the Aarhus Convention's provisions on access to justice have thus far failed. The Commission proposed a directive on access to justice in environmental matters in 2003, which is still in the drafting stage.[296] Nevertheless, some possibilities of access to justice related to the implementation of Article 9 (1) and (2) still exist.

2.1.3.1. Implementation of Article 9 (1)

In the case of access to information a rule for a judicial remedy was already available under Directive 90/313. Now the regime follows Article 6 of the Directive 2003/4, which provides for this right in connection with requests for access to information. This provision followed very closely the provisions of the Aarhus Convention because the Commission, when making its proposal, had not yet drafted a proposal for a directive on access to justice, but had thought that it could satisfy the basic requirements of the Convention (Krämer, 2004, p. 1). It can be said that this was a fortunate turn of events as even now, after seven years, the proposal on access to justice is still a proposal!

Article 6 of the Directive 2003/04 so states: "*A person who considers that his request for information has been unreasonably refused or ignored, was inadequately answered, or otherwise not dealt with in accordance with Article 3, 4 or 5 by a public authority, may seek a judicial or administrative review of the decision in accordance with the relevant national legal system*". Compared   to the similar provision in Directive 90/313 the current wording is significantly wider. This has been interpreted by some authors as "judicial review is not limited to the statement of reasons alone and could also involve a review of the reasons invoked" (Jans, & Vedder, 2008, p. 327). Nevertheless, by comparison to the "more-or-less verbatim manner" in which the Directive has transposed other Articles of the Convention, Article 6 is a rather more cursory transposition of Article 9 (Roy, 2006, p. 52-53; Ziehm, 2005, p. 287).

Indeed, the Directive does not specify that all review procedures should be "*equitable, timely and not prohibitively expensive*", and that injunctive relief should be among the remedies available in respect of a refusal to grant access

---

296   Commission Proposal for a Directive of the European Parliament and of the Council on Access to Justice in Environmental Matters, COM (2003) 624 final (Oct. 24, 2003).

to information (Article 9(4) of the Convention). There is also no requirement for Community Member States to consider *"the establishment of appropriate assistance mechanisms to remove or reduce financial and other barriers to justice"* (Article 9(5) of the Convention). Only the administrative review procedure required by Article 9(1) of the Convention is specifically required to be *"expeditious and either free of charge or inexpensive"*.

2.1.3.2. Implementation of Article 9 (2)

In respect to the second pillar of the Aarhus Convention on public participation in decision-making, Directive 2003/35/EC provides in Article 3(7) for the EIA Directive and in Article 4(4) for the IPPC Directive that, in accordance with the relevant national legal system, the public concerned as well as NGOs have access to a review procedure before a court of law or another independent and impartial body established by law to challenge the substantive or procedural legality of decisions, acts or omissions subject to the public participation provisions on this directive.

These amendments were made through the Public Participation Directive as recital 11 of the Directive recalls: *"Council Directive 85/337/EEC of 27 June 1985 on the assessment of the effects of certain public and private projects on the environment (1), and Council Directive 96/61/EC of 24 September 1996 concerning integrated pollution prevention and control (2) should be amended to ensure that they are fully compatible with the provisions of the Aarhus Convention, in particular Article 6 and Article 9(2) and (4) thereof'.*

It has been remarked that these amendments do not provide any indication of a requirement to enable access to justice in cases where rights to participate in the preparation of plans and programmes, let alone policies and legislations, are impaired. In fact the decision to accept this restrictive interpretation did not "cause any significant debate at all within Community" (Jendroska, 2005, p. 19).

According to Article 2(3) of Directive 2003/35/EC, Member States shall identify the public entitled to participate, including relevant NGOs meeting any requirements imposed under national law, such as those promoting environmental protection.

However, the almost verbatim use of the provisions of the Aarhus Convention in Article 10 of the EIA Directive and Article 15 of the IPPC Directive place Member States under even greater obligation to implement the Aarhus Convention as an international agreement (Ziehm, 2005, p. 287).

Nevertheless, despite the changes introduced through Directive 2003/35EC granting access to justice for NGOs with regard to a broad range of administrative decisions, it has been noted that this access remains limited because the access to justice is connected to a participation right under the EIA or IPPC Directive (Sadeleer, 2005, p. 205). As a consequence, any impairment to the environment that falls outside the scope of these Directives will not be covered by the Articles providing for access to the courts. For instance, any violation of the Habitats or Wild Birds Directive that is not caused by an EIA or IPPC project would not be covered. A further shortcoming is that all product linked impacts on the environment as well as those related to chemicals or CMOs are not covered (Sadeleer, 2005, p. 205).

Finally, it is worth noting that EU legislation does not provide specifically for access to justice in respect of decisions subject to Article 7; for example under the SEA Directive. The main justification is that this is not clearly required by the Convention.

2.1.4. Fourth Pillar: Implementation of Article 9 (3)

2.1.4.1. The Proposal on Access to Justice in Environmental Matters

The implementation of Article 9(3) is still outstanding; indeed, the Proposal for a Directive of the European Parliament of Council on Access to Justice in environmental matters has yet to be adopted.[297] In 2003 the Commission proposed this directive, which contains the general provisions on access to justice in addition to the specific rules on access to justice resulting from public participation in the EIA and IPPC directive and the rules on access to environmental information. The draft is still pending[298] before the Council, although it has already received a first reading by the Parliament, which in March 2004 was critical and required a number of amendments within the framework of a co-decision procedure. Since then the process appears to have stopped.[299]

The main reason for this halt is that the Directive is not greatly welcomed. Indeed, most Member States had already well-established traditions in this regard (De Sadeleer, 2005), in certain cases much more liberal than that envisaged by the proposal (Jendroska, 2004, p. 68). Hence, the chance for the directive to be adopted is "rather limited" (Jendroska, 2006, p. 80).

The draft covers a double objective: first, it contributes to full implementation of Article 9, encompassing also the fourth pillar; and secondly, it will fulfil some

---

297 Proposal for a Directive of the European Parliament and of the Council on access to justice in environmental matters, COM (2003) 624 final.

298 Still pending also today that is 25 October 2012.

299 Or so suggests the relevant OEIL entry, Ref. COD/2003/0246.

shortcomings in controlling the application of environmental law.[300] Both objectives are very interesting for this book's purpose because they put the attention on the role of citizens.

In fact, as the Proposal explains, "*these shortcomings (of implementation of EC Environmental law) are due to, among other things, the lack of a financial private interest in enforcing environmental law, in contrast to other areas of Community law where economic operators require the correct application of legislation, such as internal markets and competition. Moreover, the failure to fully enforce environmental laws can distort the functioning of the internal market by creating unequal terms of economic competition for the economic operators. Thus, depending on the Member State concerned, the economic operators in non-compliance with their environmental obligations may receive an economic advantage over those that respect environmental law. Moreover, "practical experience gained from granting legal standing to environmental non-governmental organisations indicates that this can enhance the implementation of environmental law*".[301]

It is also interesting to note that the core principles of the proposal for a Directive came from a deliberative consultation process. Member States, NGOs, associations of companies, regional and local authorities, and the candidate countries, during spring and autumn 2002, were able to meet for the purpose of finalising a draft proposal for a Directive on access to justice in environmental matters.

Indeed, the text of the proposal takes into account their comments and observations. For instance, the NGOs wanted a more forward-looking proposal since, from their point of view, it constrains the field of application of the Aarhus Convention, mainly as far as the legal standing issue is concerned. They expected a much broader provision and asked for a general legal standing without restrictions, known as "*actio popularis*". The Commission did not share this point of view since the "*actio popularis*" is not explicitly required by the Aarhus Convention and must be therefore left to Member States.

These organisations also disagreed with the fact that the second working document only took up acts and omissions by public authorities and not by private persons. They also regretted that the acts and omissions to be challenged do not include criminal matters. Further comments touched upon the point referred to as the "*qualified entities*". For most of them, these groups will have

---

300   See for the analysis of this Article, Parola, 2013.

301   See the Proposal for a Directive of the European Parliament and of the Council on access to justice in environmental matters, COM (2003) 624 final.

to fulfil very severe requirements to be recognised under the future proposal as one of these entities.[302]

2.1.4.2. The Main Novelties of the Proposal on Access to Justice

The proposal complies with the requirements arising from the objective and mechanisms of Article 9(3) of the Convention.[303] The main focus of the proposed Directive is to provide for access to justice in the Member States when public authorities fail to apply laws relating to the environment by an act or an omission.

The Proposal sets out a judicial and an administrative review procedure in its Articles 6 and 7. The first Article introduces a preliminary procedure, which allows members of the public and qualified entities who have access to justice against an act or an omission to be able to submit a request for internal review. This request is a preliminary procedure under which the person or entity concerned can contact the public authority designated by the Member State before initiating legal or administrative proceedings. If the authority does not respond to the request within the period fixed for this purpose or if its decision does not enable compliance with environmental law, the party submitting the request may initiate an administrative or judicial procedure (Eleftheriadis, 2007).

Under Article 7, access to justice is available only if the natural or legal person or the qualified entity has first submitted a request for internal review. Only when this request for internal review proceedings is not taken within 12 to 18 weeks or when the decision is insufficient to ensure compliance with environmental law is there a right to start "*environmental proceedings*".

It is worth noting that Article 9(3) of the draft directive does not define "*environmental proceedings*", but it is defined by Article 2(1) f) as the administrative or judicial review proceedings in environmental matters, other than proceedings in criminal matters, before a court or other independent body established by law which is concluded by a binding decision.

The proposal distinguishes between standing for members of the public and standing for associations, called qualified entity. Members of the public, defined as one or more natural or legal persons by Article 2 (1) (b) of the draft, are granted access to environmental proceedings if they either have sufficient interest or maintain the infringement of a right, where the administrative procedural law requires this as a precondition (Article 4). This will not bring about a change in the Member States' situation of standing as the national rules on standing are

---

302   See the Proposal Directive. Ziehm, 2005, p. 287.

303   For a detailed analysis of this point see in particular: Hedemann-Robinson, 2007, p. 304-345; Wenneras, 2007, p. 75.

still decisive. It is incumbent on Member States to determine what constitutes a sufficient interest or a relevant impairment of a right. In other words, it does not demand that Member States expand the rights of the public in terms of an *actio popularis* if they do not wish to do so (Von Unger, 2007, p. 205).

Concerning the standing of environmental interest groups the Commission introduces the concept of "*qualified entities*". It worth noting that the term "*qualified entities*" is a concept that does not appear in the Aarhus Convention; it was also included in the proposal of the Aarhus Regulation but in the final version it was modified. The Member States should lay down a procedure for recognising qualified entities, but there are some restrictions: one is linked to the definition of qualified entities according to Article 2. A "*qualified entity*" must meet certain criteria, including operating on a non-profit basis and pursuing the objective of protecting the environment, being legally constituted and having experience in environmental protection and having its annual accounts certified by a registered auditor (Article 8) (Eleftheriadis, 2007; Dross, 2005, p. 22). Moreover, qualified entities recognised in a Member State may have recourse to such proceedings in another Member State.

Under Article 5 of the draft directive, qualified entities shall have standing without having to show a sufficient interest or maintaining the impairment of a right, if the subject of the procedure is within the scope of their statutory and geographically relevant activities.

It is interesting to note that the European Parliament proposed an important change in its first reading, namely to broaden the definition of qualified entity to include any association which "*at a given moment is involved in a specific situation requiring protection of the environment in which it is located*". This amendment is an explicit attempt to include citizens' groups (Dette, 2004, p. 3; Von Unger, 2007, p. 205).

Despite the Parliament's suggestion to include the Convention's definition of public authority, the proposal's definition is limited to the public administration of the Member States and it does not include natural or legal persons performing public administrative functions in relation to the environment, as in Article 2(2) of the Aarhus Convention.

In conclusion, the draft directive could open the door to a wide access to justice in environmental matters and bring into coherence, albeit imperfectly, Community legislation with the obligations of the Aarhus Convention (Von Unger, 2007, p. 205). Nevertheless, the failure to adopt would mean that the issue of access to justice in environmental matters remains firmly in the hands of Member States' national law.

After this overview, it may be said that notwithstanding the lack of consensus at the Member State level to coordinate common policies in relation to access to justice in environmental matters, the procedural environmental rights enshrined in EU legislation remain significant and represent a noteworthy indication of the importance attached to such rights in Europe (Pedersen, 2010).

2.2. Ecological Duties

The notion of ecological duty is emerging also from EU Environmental Law at a national level. As pointed out at the very beginning, ecological duties oblige citizens to protect and act in a responsible and sustainable way for the sake of the Earth and its inhabitants. Consequently, it can therefore be argued that this obligation as such can be violated. In other words, the breach of an obligation to protect entails the obligation to repair whatever has achieved unsustainability.

There are a range of possible responses by regulators to implement the ecological duties to protect and repair, and the following section will explore some examples of tools used by EU environmental law to push the citizens to respect their ecological duties (Fedrigo, & Tukker, 2009).

2.2.1. Implementation by Waste Legislation

The EU waste law may be considered as a step to implement the duty to protect the environment. Lack of time and space prevents a full exploration of the body of waste directives and of regulations dealing with waste issues; nevertheless, some points should be briefly underlined (Gallego, 2002, p. 8).

Our societies are consuming more and more products and as a result, discarding more waste into the environment. The treatment of industrial, household and agricultural waste has become a huge business as well as a serious political problem. Needless to say, discarding waste in landfills and burning residues in incinerators amounts to a sheer waste of resources.

With regard to waste reduction,[304] when individuals are able to recycle waste and other substances, they prevent the production of further waste, because special companies are recycling large quantities of waste. Among the actions to be undertaken with the aim to achieve this objective, EU law has stressed the establishment of a strategy on the one hand of recycling waste and on the other hand influencing the behaviour of individuals as well as producer responsibility by market means.[305] Such an approach appears to be entirely consistent with

---

304 The specific target was to reduce the quantity going to final disposal by 20 per cent by 2010 and 50 per cent by 2050.

305 Producer responsibility requires the producer to take responsibility for waste production. The idea of such legislation is to extend their responsibility further through the life cycle of a product, to the post waste phase. The Directive imposes responsibility

the EU Principle of Sustainable Development, the purpose of which is to save resources and so to implement the duty to protect the Environment vis-à-vis present and future generations.

2.2.2. Implementation by Environmental Criminal Law

Another very interesting example of EU implementation of ecological duties is the attempt to introduce environmental crimes.[306] The subject of this book,

---

for the costs of waste management (recycling or recovery) since the producer has to meet "all or a significant part of, the costs". This measure attempts to harness market forces to encourage the minimisation of a product's environmental impact. Just as it is consistent with a 'market' approach to environmental regulation, producer responsibility also falls within a broad understanding of the reflexive approach to law. "Reflexive law does not determine the outcome of a process, but develops mechanisms to encourage reflexion within social structure, including firms forcing those structures to adapt in response to their environmental effects. The doctrine, in fact, has hold that to influence the behaviour of individuals and producers is probably more "readily accessible via the market". However, producer responsibility is not itself a legal tool or mechanism, but must be applied through legal tools. It is not therefore necessarily removed from traditional command and control mechanisms, and neither the recycling and recovery targets, nor the producer's financial obligations are within the parts of the Directive that can be implemented by agreement with industry" (Lee, 2002a, p. 114). An example is The WEEE Directive, which entered into force in 2003, outlines the principle of Individual Producer Responsibility (IPR) for financing the waste management of electric and electronic equipment (WEEE). IPR is an individualisation of the idea of Extended Producer Responsibility (EPR), which tends to internalize the environmental burden of products by asking producers to cover the costs of waste management linked to their products. This IPR principle means that producers should only be responsible for the end of life costs of their own products. This principle is seen as a major lever which offers incentives to producers to integrate end of life thinking into the design of their product (e.g. for recycling and for dismantling). In fact, "producers are more likely to use end of life thinking if they can minimise the costs of end of life processing with better design, and would therefore benefit themselves from such initiatives" (Arditi, 2010). The Directives 2006/12/EC of 5 April 2006 on Waste (revised by directive 2008/98/EC of 19 November 2008 on waste and repealing certain Directives For a analysis of the new Directive see Nash, 2009, p. 140. The directive 2006/12 will be repealed with effect from 12 December 2010) encompasses the obligation to prevent waste being discarded applies to a broad range of socio and economic activities. Hence, a more sustainable approach has to be applied to every sector producing waste, as they are being called upon, first, to prevent waste, second to recover waste by means of four operations. Among the various recovery operations, recycling is of utmost importance. Article 1 defines the word 'holder' which shall mean the producer of the waste or the natural or legal person who is in possession of it; and Article 8 establishes that "Member States shall take the necessary measures to ensure that any holder of waste: (a) has it handled by a private or public waste collector or by an undertaking which carries out the operations listed in Annex II A or II B; or b) recovers or disposes of it himself in accordance with the provisions of this Directive". See generally Teubner, 1994; see also De Sadeleer, 2008, p. 399.

306   For this topic, see: Hedemann-Robinson, 2008, p. 279; Comte, 2003, p. 147; Faure, 2008, p. 69.

mainly in public law, does not permit the entrance into a theoretical discussion of the necessity of environmental crimes as a response to ecological duties; nevertheless it shall mention at least some aspects. Indeed, there is an important link and similarity between environmental law and criminal law: both are concerned with how to regulate potentially dangerous behaviour.

There are two situations where criminal law is used in the protection of the environment. The first is in the protection of the administrative system. For instance, a fundamental tool of environmental law is the requirement to apply for a license before beginning certain activities. Secondly, criminal law comes into play whenever the atmosphere, water, ecosystems or other parts of the Environment as such are damaged.

There are rules that concern different types of violations against Nature in itself and the corresponding crimes "against Nature" are more complicated to sanction than crimes against the administrative system (Westerlund, 2008, p. 503). Thus, both kinds of criminal provisions seem to fulfil important functions in connection with environmental protection and in the implementation of the duty to protect.

The main reason to introduce and use criminal sanction in the environmental field is that criminal sanctions demonstrate a social disapproval of a qualitatively different nature compared to administrative sanctions or a compensation mechanism under civil law.[307] Criminal law protects the Environment in a more direct way, because control and regulation of the actions of citizens protect society's most important values (Westerlund, 2008, p. 503). Hence, in the view of duty perspective, the role of criminal sanctions is a deterrent to enforce behaviour that promotes the achievement of sustainability objectives (Pereira, 2007, p. 254) and consequently for "the future of the planet" (Comte, 2003, p. 190).

Nevertheless, from a criminal point of view, there are limits to how far one can go in the use of it to protect the Environment. It is not possible to write a rule which explicitly requires that everyone who breaches the duty to protect the environment behaves in an unsustainable way. So a rule that prohibits damaging the environment, and which requires the subject to exercise caution could perhaps be seen as less problematic.

According to Pereira "if one knows there is a legal requirement to exercise caution, one would have to act according to that requirement. Therefore it ought to be possible to use the precautionary principle in an argument about whether or not a person pursuing an activity has taken an unlawful risk and if

---

307 Explanatory memorandum to the Proposal for a directive of the European Parliament and of the environment through criminal law 2007/0022.

the behaviour therefore can be considered to be negligent and unsustainable. If precaution in order to achieve sustainability is explicitly required in a legal text then it will be possible for everyone to anticipate a reaction if precautionary measures are not taken. This leads to the conclusion that it is not enough to criminalise acts that cause damages if we want to induce people to act in a sustainable and precautionary way. To be less careful than is needed to prevent accidents must to some extent be criminalised" (Pereira, 2007, p. 254).

There must be endangerment criminalisation. Such criminalisation can prohibit the endangerment of human life or the life of specific species, but in order to be sustainable the endangerment law ought to prohibit acts that endanger ecological balance. For criminal law to play a major role as one of several legal instruments implementing the duty to protect and repair, it is necessary for criminal law to adhere to the principles of sustainable development and precaution.

Going beyond the above theoretical discussion, it is interesting to note that the developments in criminal environmental law at the EU level seek also to ensure that national regulators are fully equipped to assure that such obligations are respected. The Commission and the Council are of the view that the availability of criminal sanctions is vital to the enforcement of EU environmental law: "the use of criminal sanctions by Member States could improve the level of enforcement of environmental regulations implementing EC environmental legislation" (Pereira, 2007, p. 254).

Consequently the Commission organised a conference in Brussels in November 2003 entitled "*Environmental Crime in Europe: rules of sanctions*" aimed primarily at examining what kind of sanctioning systems exist in Europe to tackle environmental crime, and particularly whether criminal law is indeed necessary to secure an effective protection of the environment.

In light of this, in 2003 the Commission proposed a directive and a Council Framework-decision on the protection of the Environment through criminal law, which envisages the creation of minimum standards on the use of the criminal law protecting the environment in the EU.[308]

---

308 This approach has been defined naïve because according to Faure (2004, p. 18) "today, in many Member States administrative sanctions are used and have often proven to be at least as effective in the 'war on environmental crime' as criminal sanctions". There have also been some episodes where ECJ has required Members States to introduce "effective, dissuasive and proportionate" sanctions to enforce community law, which some have read as giving a green light for the EU to force member states to introduce criminal sanctions.

The recent adoption of EC Directive 2008/99/EC on the protection of the environment through criminal law[309] has proved the will to establish that all countries introduce criminal sanctions for certain environmentally harmful activities. In these cases there should be effective, proportionate and dissuasive criminal sanctions in place. Here criminal law is not used to sanction violations against the administrative system but concerns different types of violation against the environment in a broad definition of this term with some ecocentric elements.

Indeed, the protected objects of the directive 2008/99/EC are human health, flora or fauna. An interpretation in accordance with the principle of sustainable development could include not just humans and plants but the whole ecosystem, "as sustainable development requires not only protection of species but also the relations between them; a stable ecosystem is important for future generations. Furthermore, a sustainable interpretation of the 'damage' could include not just total extinction of a species, but also such changes of the ecosystem that endanger the living conditions of the species" (Westerlund, 2008, p. 503).

After the brief overview above concerning the mentioned measures to attempt to implement ecological duties through EU Law, the following part will pay special attention to the Environmental Liability Directive, because it is the best and the only explicit example in EU law concerning ecological duties. It will show that the Directive is a potentially powerful tool of implementation of ecological duties and of EU environmental law, and it provides a deterrent for polluters (Reiners, 2009).

2.2.3. Implementation by Environmental Liability Directive

The ordinary definition of liability is legal responsibility (Allen, 2000, p. 803), and Environmental Liability is the application of a liability mechanism for damage to the environment.[310]

Generally it is assumed that environmental liability results in the prevention of environmental damage by providing a financial incentive.[311] This is due to the fact that the obligation to pay for environmental damage in its aftermath reflects on the conduct of actors indirectly to not cause damage in the first place. It is, thus, a mechanism for the protection of the environment which works through

---

309   Directive 2008/99/EC of the European Parliament and the Council of 19 November 2008 on the protection of the environment through criminal law.

310   See the following authors on this field: Bergkamp, 2002, p. 216; De Sadeleer, 2002, p. 53; Kiss, & Shelton, 1993, p. 37.

311   COM(2000) 66 final, p. 11-12; Editorial Comment, 2007, p. 2; Hinteregger, 2008b,p.3.

financial pressure.[312] It is further seen as a mechanism to internalize the costs of environmental damage.[313] This means that the costs of environmental damage must be paid by the parties responsible for the damage and not financed by society in general.[314]

The first environmental liability scheme of the European Community was only narrowly concerned with sectorial environmental liability for damage caused by waste, and dates back to the 1970s.[315] It was necessary to wait until 2004 for a more comprehensive environmental liability scheme. Such a regime was established by Directive 2004/35/EC on Environmental Liability with Regard to the Prevention and Remedying of Environmental Damage.[316]

The system set up by the Directive is a liability system which establishes the liability of the operator of an occupational activity under administrative law. The legislation establishes a public law system in the form of administrative mechanisms.

The directive, hence, creates a liability system *sui generis* (Pirotte, 2004, p. 187), in other words an *administrative liability* system since it operates through administrative mechanisms (Lopatta, 2009, p. 3).

Such mechanisms are not new but applied in the Member States of the Community.[317] What is, however, new about the Directive is that is sets up these administrative mechanisms under the title *liability*, or more precisely under the title *environmental liability*.

The character of the Liability Directive as a *liability* directive is further underlined by the features reflecting the core of the Polluter Pays Principle. As

---

312   Calling it a marked-based mechanism in this sense Coroner, 2006, p. 226; Lee, 2005, p. 208.

313   COM(2000) 66 final, pp. 11-12; Coroner, 2006, p. 226; Lee, 2005, p. 206.

314   COM(2000) 66 final, pp. 11-12; Grossman, 2006, p. 1.

315   For a description see Betlem, 2005, p. 117; Clarke, 2003, p. 254; Doolittle, 1992, p. 20; Krämer, 2007. p. 187; Roller, 2006, p. 127; Wenk, 2005, p. 119; see in particular Commission Proposal on Environmental Liability in the Waste Sector on 22 May 1991 COM, 1991, 102 final – SYN 335.

316   OJ 2004, L 143/56 as amended by Directive 2006/21/EC of the European Parliament and of the Council of 15 March 2006 on the Management of Waste From Extractive Industries and Amending Directive 2004/35/EC, OJ 2006, L 102/15 and by Directive 2009/31/EC of the European Parliament and of the Council of 23 April 2009 On the Geological Storage of Carbon Dioxide and Amending Council Directive 85/337/EEC, European Parliament and Council Directives 2000/60/EC, 2001/80/EC, 2004/35/EC, 2006/12/EC, 2008/1/EC and Regulation (EC) No 1013/2006 OJ 2009, L 140/114.

317   For Portugal see Aragao, 2007, p. 8-9; for Hungary see Bándi, 2007, p. 1; for Finland see Ekroo, 2007, p. 1; for United Kingdom see Lee, & Macrory, 2007; for Italy see Montini, 2007, p. 1; for Spain see Moreno, & García Ureta, 2007, p. 1; for Denmark see Pagh, 2007, p. 1; for Estonia see Veinla, 2007, p. 2.

stated, the Polluter Pays Principle can be classified as a liability principle since it concerns the allocation of costs of environmental damage.

In line with the principle, the environment is not protected as such under the Directive but only in so far as the damage has been caused by an identifiable polluter. If the polluter is not identified and the damage in this case is a so-called *orphan damage*, the environment remains without restoration. Further in line with this principle, the obligation of the competent authority to prevent or to restore environmental damage was not inserted in the final text of the Liability Directive (Krämer, 2006a, p. 37-38).

The liability under administrative mechanisms has the feature of a *trusteeship system* (Brans, 2005, p. 7). It does not compensate the state as the owner of the environment, but the state enforces the interests of the environment as such as an interest of the general public. This liability system uses the traditional administrative mechanisms of an authority against the operator as a private party. The Directive describes the competences of a public authority, which is competent to request to the operator that has caused environmental damage or an imminent threat thereof to take the necessary preventive or restoration measures.

The competent authority, indeed, plays a central role in the Directive since it assures the implementation of the Directive and in other words the respect of fulfilment of ecological duties. According to Article 11 of such legislation, Member States shall designate the competent authority which determines if the requirements for liability of an operator of an occupational activity are met.[318] On the other hand, when the conditions for liability of the operator are fulfilled, the competent authority may require preventive or remedial actions from the operator.[319] It may further take the necessary preventive or remedial actions itself[320] and then recover the costs from the operator.[321] In particular, these mechanisms are injunctions, fines, suspensions and other such mechanisms (Kiss, & Shelton, 1993, p. 65).

It is, thus, a regulatory command and control system (Betlem, 2005, p. 121; Lee, 2005, p. 204).[322] In the environmental context this means that a state authority requires respect of the duty to prevent environmental damage caused by a private person.

---

318   Article 11(2) of the Liability Directive; on the competent authority see also Hinteregger, 2008b, p. 16.

319   Article 5(a)-(c) and Article 6(2) (a)-(d) of the Liability Directive.

320   Article 5(d) and Article 6(e) of the Liability Directive.

321   Article 8(2) of the Liability Directive; calls it the indirect financial liability of the operator Pirotte, 2004, p. 5.

322   See further description by C'M'S' McKenna, 1995, p. 11-12.

Hence, the features of focusing on the environment as an interest that needs to be protected regardless of any private interests,[323] and the role of the state authority as a *trustee* for protecting the environment as such, might give more environmental implications to the Liability Directive. Due to these characteristics the Liability Directive can be seen on one hand as a tool contributing to the principle of Sustainable Development which comprises the duty to preserve natural resources for the benefit of present and future generations,[324] and on the other hand contributing to the implementation of the duty to protect Earth itself.

2.2.3.1. The Polluter Pays Principle and the Preventive Principle in the Directive

The underlying principles of the Directive are the Polluter Pays Principle (PPP) and the Preventive Principle.[325] As seen above, both principles are, along with others, the ground on which ecological duties are based in Community Environmental Law (Larsson, 1999, p. 242).

The PPP can now be found in the Liability Directive in two ways. On the one hand, it is reiterated in the Preamble of the Directive[326] and in its Article 1. There, it is stated that the Liability Directive aims at establishing a framework of environmental liability based on the Polluter Pays Principle. Thus, such principle is the underlying principle of the Directive.

On the other hand, the principle is reflected in the obligation of the polluter to bear the costs of preventive and remediation action under Article 8 of the Liability Directive. It shall be said, that the costs the polluter has to pay according to the Directive do not include only the costs of prevention of an environmental damage but also the costs of remedial action. Therewith, Article 8 of the Directive reflects the just mentioned development of the principle from covering preventive costs to also covering remedial costs.

Contrary to the Polluter Pays Principle, the Liability Directive does not expressly mention the Preventive Principle, but implicitly formulates it as the

---

323   Except for damage to land, see above description of the material scope of the Directive concerning Article 2(1)(c) of the Liability Directive.

324   Report of the World Commission on Environment and Development: Our Common Future (Brundtland Report) of 1987, UN Doc. A/42/427, p. 40; Principle 2 of the New Delhi Declaration of Principle of International Law Relating to Sustainable Development of 2002 by the International Law Association, available at www.cisdl.org/pdf/new_delhi_declaration.pdf; Loibl, 2004, p. 97; Cordonier Segger, 2004, p. 61; Jóhannsdóttir, 2005, p. 27; Sands, 1995, p. 253; Wälde, 2004, p. 119.

325   Representative for others Hinteregger, 2008b, p. 8. For the polluter pays principle De Sadeleer, 2002, p. 30.

326   Preambular 2 and 18 of the Liability Directive.

objective of the Directive. Article 1 of the Liability Directive states that the Directive is "*based on the polluter pays principles*" and it reads further that it aims "*to prevent and remedy environmental damage*". This objective is enshrined already in the title of the Liability Directive "*with regard to the prevention and remedying of environmental damage*" and is recalled several times in the Preamble of the Directive.[327]

The Preventive Principle as an objective of the Liability Directive is also included in the Directive in two forms. First, Article 5 formulates the obligation to take the necessary preventive measures when environmental damage has not yet occurred but there is an imminent threat of such damage occurring. Moreover, Article 6(1)(a) applies when damage has already occurred, and establishes the obligation to immediately control, contain, remove or otherwise manage the damage in order to prevent further environmental damage.

Second, the Preventive Principle is reflected in the idea of the liability scheme as a mechanism preventing environmental damage.

2.2.3.2. The Personal, Material and Temporal Scope of the Liability Directive

The scope of the liability Directive can be described in terms of its personal application, its material application and its temporal application (Jans, & Vedder, 2008, p. 340).

The personal scope describes which person falls under the obligations of the Liability Directive. This scope of the Directive is limited to the operators of occupational activities.[328] Article 2(6) of the Liability Directive defines two types of operators. An operator is once defined as "*any natural or legal, private or public person who operates or controls the occupational activity*". An operator in the sense of the Directive is further a person "*to whom decisive economic power over the technical functioning of such an activity has been delegated*" if the national law foresees this person to be liable. The examples listed of such persons are the holder of a permit or authorisation of such an activity, or the person registering and notifying such an activity. Thus, the Directive does not differentiate between private and public persons if they are in control of an

---

327   Preambulars 1, 2, 3, 11, 15, 18, 20 21, 23, 28 and 29 of the Liability Directive.
328   Representative for others: Hinteregger, 2008b, p. 20; Jans, & Vedder, 2008, p. 340; Mullerat, 2005, p. 264; De Sadeleer, 2007, p. 68.

occupational activity.[329] The concept of the operator can certainly be seen to be a wide one (Mullerat, 2005, p. 264).

As stated above, only the operator of an occupational activity is liable according to the Directive. The term occupational activity is defined by Article 2(7) of the Liability Directive as "*any activity carried out in the course of an economic activity, a business or an undertaking, irrespective of its private or public, profit or non-profit character*".

This definition already appears to narrow down the scope of the Directive. Indeed, there are entities whose activities may result in an environmental damage which will not be involved in an economic activity (Jans, & Vedder, 2008, p. 340-341).[330]

The material scope is described by Article 3(1)(a) of the Liability Directive; the Directive covers *environmental damage* which is defined by Article 2(1) of the Liability Directive. The Directive does not cover the environment as a whole, so there is a limited ecocentric approach; in fact, only three elements of the environment are protected: protected species and habitats, counted as one element, water and land.[331] These three environmental elements are referred to under the Directive as natural resources.[332]

After the exclusion of the term biodiversity from the Liability Directive,[333] its merely partial application is reflected by the tutelage of certain species and habitats.[334] The species protected include only the species of birds under the Wild Birds Directive of 1979.[335] The habitats are limited to only the habitats of species under the Habitats Directive of 1992.[336] The material scope appears narrow in particular because in July 2009, the protected areas under both

---

329   Evaluating this as an achievement of the Directive Winter, Jans, Macrory, & Krämer, 2008, p. 6.

330   See *e.g.* case C-343/95 Diego Calì & Figli v. Servizi ecologici porto di Genova SpA (SEPG), Judgement of 18 March 1997, ECR [I-01574].

331   Protected species and natural habitats are defined in Article 2(3) of the Liability Directive.

332   Article 2(12) of the Liability Directive.

333   Term had been used by the Commission at earlier stages, Commission White Paper COM(2000) 66 final, p. 18; Commission Proposal COM(2002) 17 final, *inter alia* Article 2(1), (2), (8), (18).

334   They are elements of biodiversity, compare Questions and Answers Environmental Liability, Commission Memorandum MEMO/07/157 of 27 April 2007, p. 5; Thornton, & Beckwith, 2004, p. 91.

335   Council Directive 79/409/EEC of 2 April 1979 on the Conservation of Wild Birds, *OJ 1979, L 103/1*.

336   Council Directive 92/43/EEC of 21 May 1992 on the Conservation of Natural Habitats and of Wild Fauna and Flora, *OJ 1992, L 206/7*.

Directives covered 24,5 percent of the Community land area.[337] Nevertheless, it is possible to extend this by interpretation: not only the designated protection sites under the Habitats Directive come within the scope of the Liability Directive, but all habitat types listed there. Also, the habitats not listed in the Habitats Directive come within the scope of the environment under the Directive if a Member State includes such areas as protected areas under their national law (De Smedt, 2009, p. 7; Thornton, & Beckwith, 2004, p. 91).

Concerning water, Article 2(5) refers to the waters of the Water Framework Directive of 2000 and its regime. On the contrary, the term land is not further defined by the Liability Directive.

Compared with the definition of the environment made in Section I of the first Chapter, the definition of the environment of the Liability Directive must be called narrow. Thus, with this definition, the Liability Directive defines the environment which is protected as narrower compared to other secondary Community legislation[338] and the Convention on Biodiversity.[339]

Article 2(2) of the Liability Directive thus defines damage generally as a *"measurable adverse change in the natural resource or measurable impairment of a natural resource service which may occur directly or indirectly"*.

The term *damage* is further qualified by Article 2(1) for each of the protected natural resources. Damage to protected species and habitats is any damage that has *significant adverse effects* on reaching or maintaining their *favourable conservation status*.[340]

More in detail, water damage is defined as any damage that "*significantly adversely affects the ecological, chemical and/or quantitative status and/or ecological potential*" as defined in the Water Framework Directive. Damage to land is expressly defined as any land contamination that creates a significant risk of human health being adversely affected as a result of the direct or indirect introduction, in, on or under land, of substances, preparations, organisms

---

337   Natura 2000, European Commission DG Env. Nature Newsletter, no. 26, July 2009, available at www.ec.europa.eu/environment/nature/info/pubs/docs/nat2000newsl/nat26_en.pdf, pp. 8-9.

338   Article 3 of Council Directive 85/337/EEC of 27 June 1985 on the Assessment of the Effects of Certain Public and Private Projects on the Environment, OJ 1985, L 175/40 mentions *inter alia* the fauna and flora, soil, water, air, climate and the landscape, their inter-action and the cultural heritage.

339   Article 2 of the Convention of Biodiversity of 5 June 1992, 1760 UNTS, pp. I-30619, lists as biodiversity "the variability among living organisms from all sources including, inter alia, terrestrial, marine and other aquatic ecosystems and the ecological complexes of which they are part; this includes diversity within species, between species and of ecosystems"; on this also Hinteregger, 2008b, p. 14.

340   "Favourable conservation status" is defined in Article 2(4) of the Liability Directive.

or micro-organisms. Damage to land, thus, has an anthropocentric character because damage is considered as such when it poses a significant risk to human health. This reduces the application of the Directive to the protection of human health (Krämer, 2008, p. 7)[341] whereas the other definitions of damages cover damage to the environmental element as such.

According to Article 3 the Directive will only cover damage that is caused by an occupational activity listed in its Annex III. Such Annex covers 12 activities which are covered by other Community directives. These activities comprise the operation of polluting operations,[342] operations subject to permits for discharge of dangerous substances into water and groundwater,[343] waste management operations,[344] manufacturing, storage or use of dangerous substances and preparations,[345] plant protection products and biocidal products,[346] transport of

---

341 In particular on damage to land see Layard, 2006, p. 129.

342 Council Directive 96/61/EC of 24 September 1996 Concerning Integrated Pollution Prevention and Control, OJ 1996, L 257/26; Council Directive 84/360/EEC of 28 June 1984 on the Combating of Air Pollution from Industrial Plants, OJ 1984, L 188/20.

343 Council Directive 76/464/EEC of 4 May 1976 on Pollution Caused by Certain Dangerous Substances, Discharged into the Aquatic Environment of the Community, OJ 1976, L 129/23; Council Directive 80/68/EEC of 17 December 1979 on the Protection of Groundwater Against Pollution Caused by Certain Dangerous Substances, OJ 1980, L 20/43; Directive 2000/60/EC of the European Parliament and of the Council of 23 October 2000 Establishing a Framework for Community Action in the Field of Water Policy, OJ 2000, L 327/1.

344 Council Directive 75/442/EEC of 15 July 1975 on Waste, OJ 1975, L 194/39; Council Directive 91/689/EEC of 12 December 1991 on Hazardous Waste, OJ 1991, L 377/20; Council Regulation (EEC) No 259/93 of 1 February 1993 on the Supervision and Control of Shipments of Waste within, into and out of the European Community, OJ 1993, L 30/1; Council Directive 1999/31/EC of 26 April 1999 on the Landfill of Waste, OJ 1999, L 182/1; Directive 2000/76/EC of the European Parliament and of the Council of 4 December 2000 on the Incineration of Waste, OJ 2000, L 332/91; Directive 2006/21/EC of the European Parliament and of the Council of 15 March 2006 on the Management of Waste From Extractive Industries and Amending Directive 2004/35/EC, OJ 2006, L 102/15.

345 Council Directive 67/548/EEC of 27 June 1967 on the Approximation of the Laws, Regulations and Administrative Provisions of the Member States Relating to the Classification, Packaging and Labelling of Dangerous Substances, OJ 1967, L 196/1; Directive 1999/45/EC of the European Parliament and of the Council of 31 May 1999 Concerning the Approximation of the Laws, Regulations and Administrative Provisions of the Member States Relating to the Classification, Packaging and Labelling of Dangerous Preparations, OJ 1990, L 200/1; Directive 2009/31/EC of the European Parliament and of the Council of 23 April 2009 On the Geological Storage of Carbon Dioxide and Amending Council Directive 85/337/EEC, European Parliament and Council Directives 2000/60/EC, 2001/80/EC, 2004/35/EC, 2006/12/EC, 2008/1/EC and Regulation (EC) No 1013/2006, OJ 2009, L 140/114.

346 Council Directive 91/414/EEC of 15 July 1991 Concerning the Placing of Plant Protection Products on the Market, OJ 1991, L 230/1; Directive 98/8/EC of the European Parliament and of the Council of 16 February 1998 Concerning the Placing of Biocidal Products on the Market, OJ 1998, L 123/1.

dangerous goods by road, rail and vessels[347] and release of genetically modified organisms.[348]

This implies that the Directive does not cover damage which is caused by something other than an occupational activity and does not cover so called "orphan damage" (Pirotte, 2004, p. 7; Winter, Jans, Macrory, & Krämer, 2008, p. 6). In other words, this is damage for which it cannot be determined who or what caused it. Article 16(1) of the Liability Directive expressly points to the possibility of Member States adding more activities to the mentioned list.

Concerning the temporal application, Article 17 of the Liability Directive provides that the Directive only applies prospectively and not retroactively. This means that the Directive only covers damage which occurred after the entry into force of the Directive on April 30, 2007.[349]

Finally it is worth noting that this liability only arises when the operator was at fault or negligent. The Directive does not provide for a definition of fault and negligence and leaves room for the Members States' discretion.

2.2.3.3. Ecological Duties Under the Liability Directive

Ecological duty is expressed in the Directive by three obligations: obligation to prevent, to restore and to bear the costs of these measures (Winter, Jans, Macrory, & Krämer, 2008, p. 4; Betlem, 2006, p. 149), which derive in particular from the Preventive and the Polluter Pays Principle in the Directive.

---

347   Council Directive 94/55/EC of 21 November 1994 on the Approximation of the Laws of the Member States with Regard to the Transport of Dangerous Goods by Road, OJ 1994, L 319/7; Council Directive 96/49/EC of 23 July 1996 on the Approximation of the Laws of the Member States with Regard to the Transport of Dangerous Goods by Rail, OJ 1996, L 235/25; Council Directive 93/75/EEC of 13 September 1993 Concerning Minimum Requirements for Vessels Bound for or Leaving Community Ports and Carrying Dangerous or Polluting Goods, OJ 1993, L 247/19.

348   Council Directive 90/219/EEC of 23 April 1990 on the Contained Use of Genetically Modified Micro-organisms, OJ 1990, L 117/1; Directive 2001/18/EC of the European Parliament and of the Council of 12 March 2001 on the Deliberate Release into the Environment of Genetically Modified Organisms and Repealing Council Directive 90/220/EEC, OJ 2001, L 106/1.

349   Compare Article 19(1) of the Liability Directive. However, Article 17 of the Directive provides for two exceptions according to which the Directive does not apply to damages that occurred after the entry into force. One exception is made if damage occurs after the date of entry into force of the Directive but is derived from a specific activity that took place entirely before this date. It was intentionally completely left to the Member States national laws to deal with this so-called historic pollution. The other exception is made for a damage which is the result of an emission, event or incident which occurred more than 30 years ago.

Concerning the obligation to prevent environmental damage and to repair environmental damage, which of the obligations applies depends on the circumstances causing the liability of the operator.

If the operator has caused an imminent threat of environmental damage, he or she is to take the necessary preventive measures without delay under Article 5 of the Liability Directive. The Directive does not further define what the necessary preventive measures are. However, the costs the polluter has to pay for the environmental damage are determined by the costs of prevention and remediation. In this way, the Directive sidesteps the problem of determining the value of any particular environmental damage (Pirotte, 2004, p. 6). The obligation in Article 5 of the Liability Directive in particular reflects the Preventive Principle.

If the operator has already caused environmental damage, according to Article 6 he is under an obligation to inform the competent authority about the damage. Moreover, under Article 6(1)(a) the operator must take all practicable steps to control, contain, remove or otherwise manage the damage in order to prevent further damage. Furthermore, according to Article 6(1)(b) the operator must take the remedial measures provided by Article 7. This provision obliges the operator to decide for the remedial measures in accordance with Annex II of the Liability Directive and submit them to the competent authority for approval. Annex II sets out the aims of the restoration measures and criteria for determining the appropriate remedial measure.[350]

According to Article 8, the operator has to bear the costs of both preventive and restoration actions. What the costs are comprised of derives from the definition of costs in Article 2(16) of the Liability Directive. The definition of costs is very wide. Costs are all costs which are required by the need to prevent and restore the environment. They include *inter alia* the costs assessing the environmental damage or the imminent threat thereof, administrative, legal and enforcement costs, the costs of data collection and monitoring and supervision costs. Thus, the operator must pay for all possible costs which arise from the environmental damage or the threat thereto.

This provision implements the PPP. However, it might be criticised for not doing so adequately. One can argue that the Polluter Pays Principle is weakened by the fact that the public authority is, as seen above, not under obligation to take preventive or remedial measures itself in cases where the polluter is not able to restore the environment (Krämer, 2003b, p. 28).[351] If the competent

---

350   See in this topic: Hinteregger, 2008b, p. 17; Krämer, 2006a, p. 45-46; Mullerat, 2005, p. 265.
351   On the drawback of the Liability Directive Winter, Jans, Macrory, & Krämer, 2008, p. 7.

authority does not take any action then the operator as the polluter will never have to pay any costs.

Nevertheless, there is a partial remedy to this problem: the provisions relating to Access to Justice.

2.2.3.4. Access to Justice in the Liability Directive

While the White Paper of 2000[352] foresaw a possibility for public interest groups to bring a claim directly against the operator, this possibility does not exist anymore since the Commission proposal of 2002.[353] Nevertheless, there are two possibilities of natural or legal persons to take action concerning damage to the environment.

Article 12 gives natural or legal persons the possibility to submit any observation concerning an instance of environmental damage to the competent authority and request the competent authority to take action concerning environmental damage or an imminent threat thereof. This right of request for action is subject to the conditions that the person is affected or likely to be affected by the environmental damage, or has either a sufficient interest in an environmental decision relating to that damage or, alternatively, alleges the impairment of a right if this is required by national law. According to the norm, it is expressly up to the Member States to determine what falls under sufficient interest and impairment of a right.

In addition, in Article 13(1) natural and legal persons are entitled to initiate judicial or administrative review procedures concerning actions or omissions of the competent authority under the Directive. They are, thus, in a way controlling the competent authority. It is not so clear if any natural or legal person can bring an initiative under this norm. It could be concluded from the referral of the norm to Article 12(1) that only persons who made a request under Article 12 of this legislation can initiate the procedures under this norm (Brans, 2005, p. 9).

Against this interpretation stands the fact that the operator can also make use of this norm for his appeal against decisions of the competent authority (Fogleman, 2006, p. 127). The Commission explicitly confirmed that the norm also comprises the right of appeal of the operator.[354] Hence, despite the referral to Article 12 of the Liability Directive, the right under Article 13 of the Liability

---

352   COM(2000) 66 final, p. 22; Mullerat, 2005, p. 267.

353   Article 14 COM(2002) 17 final, p. 44; Brans, 2005, p. 8; De Smedt, 2009, p. 12; Lee, 2005, p. 208; Roller, 2006, p. 138.

354   Communication from the Commission to the European Parliament pursuant to the second subparagraph of Article 251(2) of the EC Treaty concerning the Common Position of the Council on the adoption of a Directive of the European Parliament and of the Council

Directive is not confined to natural or legal persons that made a request for action. In its second paragraph the norm reiterates that it is without prejudice to the national rules on access to justice, meaning the conditions for standing of persons before a court or administration and the potential exhaustion of administrative review possibilities before going to court.

Thus, individual and legal persons cannot bring an action against the operator directly but have the right to submit observations and request action from the competent authority, and initiate administrative and judicial review procedures against actions or omissions of the authority.

Conclusion of Chapter 2

In conclusion of this Chapter, it can be said that at the EU level, the Aarhus Regulation has only partially implemented the Aarhus Convention.

In fact, despite the fact that EU legislation relating to access to information is in the main in conformity with the Convention, the compliance with the second and third pillar of the Convention proves more challenging.

With regard to participation, indeed, the results are not satisfying, because the mechanisms are weak in themselves and strikingly inadequate for any attempt at democratisation in particular in the environmental field. Concerning access to justice, the Chapter has shown that the EU has a major problem of non-compliance with its obligations under Article 9(3) of the Aarhus Convention, also due to the strict interpretation of the ECJ. Thus this regulation is considered to be only a partial step forward in the access to justice in environmental matters on the level of the EC.

The second part of Chapter II has explored the implementation of environmental rights and duties at the national level. It has to be remarked that, also at the national level, the development of environmental procedural rights and the degree of implementing the three pillars of the Aarhus Convention differs from rather progressive advancements in the case of access to information to rather restrictive steps in the case of public participation and access to justice.

In fact, although all of the analysed Directives implementing the Convention follow Aarhus' path closely, they nevertheless leave a large degree of discretion to local and regional administrations in putting the provisions into practice.

---

on environmental liability with regard to the prevention and remedying of environmental damage of 19 September 2003, 2002/0021 (COD), p. 13.

Concerning the implementation of ecological duties, some steps have been made through Waste Regulations, Environmental Crimes and most important the Liability Directive.

Even if some aspects of the explored Directives can be criticised, it has to be kept in mind that it is quite a well-structured attempt, even if only partially so, to realise Environmental Democracy at the local level.

It is possible, therefore, to conclude that the theoretical model of Environmental Democracy does not yet exist at the European level, but nevertheless, despite mentioned limits, there is a shift towards this new form of Democracy and towards a green Europe.[355]

---

355   For the theoretical model see in detail Parola, 2013.

Conclusion

EU environmental law offers a good example of an attempt to develop an Environmental Democracy at the local level which is better suited to answer to present environmental trans-boundary problems.

Although the construction of an Environmental Democracy in Europe is taking place through a cautious, step-by-step process, this can help the progress of its construction at the international level. In this respect, the EU has accomplished more than other international organisations; nevertheless, the analysis of the provisions of EU environmental law has shown a mixed record concerning the effectiveness of this shift.

From a formal point of view, the EU, despite having a relatively substantial democratic deficit, has tried to find a solution by introducing some elements of participatory and deliberative democracy which little by little have been consolidating at a European level.

The democracy recognised at the EU level, in particular confirmed and extended by the Lisbon Treaty, is on one hand the representative democracy which encompasses elections, political parties, and government by elected officials; on the other hand, it is the participatory and deliberative democracy which involves, for example, citizen initiatives, access to information or civil society in its day-to-day government decision-making.

It is possible to affirm that considerable progress has been made in responding to the expectations of openness and consultations at the EU level; nevertheless, any talk about general "democratisation" sounds somewhat ambitious. The described movement of implementation of participatory democracy cannot be viewed as an achieved goal; participation is not just a movement, but it requires many more tools which could lead first to an increase in the relationship between European institutions and citizens, and second to more effective mechanisms to reach participation.

In fact, from a legislative perspective, the modest expansion of procedural rights as a result of the above-mentioned Treaty provisions plays a limited role in challenging the EU's democratic deficit.

On the contrary, from an environmental point of view, it has been noted that a development in the granting of environmental participatory rights has occurred and that such a situation has increased the level of participation in the environmental field.

The relationship between "Europe" and "Environment" has also been explored; in particular the notion "Environment" which can be found within the European context. It has been observed, in this regard, that the notion can be divided into broad and narrow definitions. Broad definitions comprise natural resources and human beings, man-made things or both, while the narrow one only comprises natural resources. However, broad definitions of the environment seem to be more common.

Furthermore, the European notion of "Environment" has mainly an anthropocentric character, focusing on protection of human health rather than on protection of the environment for its own sake. This can be seen for instance in the Habitats Directive, in which the destruction of a habitat for development is provided for, so long as certain procedural requirements are fulfilled.

Nevertheless, this strong anthropocentric orientation should be reduced with the increase of EU actions in certain fields which entail a more ecocentric approach, for instance Climate Change; and also, some traces of the ecocentric approaches have entered into EU environmental law provisions, in particular through ECJ jurisprudence.

Additionally, it can be affirmed that the theoretical model of Environmental Democracy and also some features of the new citizenship and its environmental rights and ecological duties are starting to be recognised within the European Union. There are, as well, some signs of the EU's efforts to foster the role for citizens and NGOs in environmental fields through the explored directives which implement the Aarhus Convention.

In particular, concerning environmental rights, it has also been seen that EU environmental law does not explicitly recognise a substantive right to an adequate environment, and where it has made attempts to accommodate such right, this has taken the shape of a policy statement rather than a specific right.

Instead, the EU has adopted another way to grant it: a substantive right to the environment which can be derived from the existing environmental procedural rights in EU law. Hence, those rights have the potential to achieve the same positive environmental behaviour as substantive rights in terms of citizen enforcement. They could help to "shed light on the vague right" enshrined in the Charter of Fundamental Rights and to facilitate focusing on a substantive right (Pedersen 2010, p. 46).

With regard to ecological citizenship, it can be affirmed that some aspects of this theoretical legal status already exist in the recognition that European Citizenship extends beyond territorial boundaries of national States.

Concerning ecological duties, it is evident that they are not yet explicitly recognised, but there are some principles, such as the Polluter Pays Principle, which embody the duty to protect and repair the environment.

The book gives also an overview over the implementation of the substantive provisions in its so-called three pillar rights, firstly at the EU level and then at the Member States level, and finally, the implementation of ecological duties at the Member States level.

At the EU level, the adoption of the Aarhus Regulation has only partially implemented the Aarhus Convention., despite the optimism of some commentators who considered it as a potentially "ground-breaking development" in the field of Environmental Democracy in the EU.

In fact, despite the fact that EU legislation relating to the access to information has a long history in Europe and it is largely in conformity with the Convention, compliance with the second and third pillars of the Convention proves more challenging.

With regard to participation, though one is generally enthusiastic at the EU level concerning increased participation rights, the results are not satisfying. In fact, the mentioned available mechanisms are weak in themselves and strikingly inadequate for any attempt at democratisation, in particular in the environmental field. The participation pillar is far from being a sufficiently robust instrument to beat the weight of democratising the Union.

Concerning access to justice, the EU has a major problem of non-compliance with its obligations under Article 9(3) of the Aarhus Convention, also due to a strict interpretation of the ECJ. Thus, this regulation is considered to be only a partial step forward towards access to justice in environmental matters on the level of the EC.

Also, the mentioned amendment of the European Treaty will not resolve the lack of effective access to justice. In particular, the accession to the European Convention on Human Rights will not improve access to justice, especially concerning time issues, due to the necessity for potential applicants to exhaust domestic remedies before being in a position to take a case to Strasbourg.

Furthermore, while the EU Charter of Fundamental Rights should help to reinforce the EU's obligations in respect to environmental protection once a case is before the Courts, it does not appear likely that it will create any new mechanisms for gaining admissibility. In short, neither the Charter nor ratification of the European Convention on Human Rights replaces the necessity of the EU to comply fully with its Aarhus obligations.

In conclusion, it could be argued that although EU environmental law has been undertaking some steps to implement environmental rights at an EU Level, reflecting a growing attempt to democratise European law, especially by enhancing the status of Environmental Citizens and their participatory rights, the construction of an Environmental Democracy and the affirmation of a Europe in Green is still far away.

Concerning the implementation of environmental rights and duties at the national or Member States level, it has to be remarked that also at this level the development of environmental procedural rights and the degree of implementing the three pillars of the Aarhus Convention defers: from rather progressive advancements in the case of access to information to rather restrictive steps in the case of public participation and access to justice.

In fact, although all of the analysed Directives implementing the Convention follow Aarhus' path closely, they nevertheless leave a large degree of discretion to local and regional administrations in putting the provisions into practice.

This leads to the conclusion that the practical application of the Directive is the decisive and only criterion for assessing its efficiency. If national authorities show their will to approach the model of Environmental Democracy in environmental matters, the directive can constitute a useful instrument.

Concerning the implementation of ecological duties, some achievements have been made through Waste Regulations, Environmental Crimes and the Liability Directive. Although various problems exist relating to the fulfilment of the above mentioned Directive, it constitutes an innovative tool to concretise the ecological duties since it establishes a liability for purely environmental damage by relying upon classical administrative procedures.

Even if some aspects of the explored Directives can be criticised, it has to be kept in mind that they are quite a well-structured attempt to realise, though in a partial way, Environmental Democracy at the local level.

Framework directives, indeed, only aim at a minimum harmonisation of the Member States' national laws, and Member States are free to expand the narrow scope of application in any way they want and improve the implementation of the Environmental Democracy.

Following the above analysis, it is possible to conclude that the theoretical model of Environmental Democracy does not exist yet in the European Union, but despite mentioned limits of implementation within the European Union and its legislation, the potential exists to influence legal developments inside of the European Union and also beyond Europe, and to contribute to a shift towards this new form of Democracy and towards a Europe in Green.

Index

A

Aarhus Convention 12, 13, 14, 39,
55, 61, 62, 65, 69, 81, 82, 83, 84, 85,
88, 89, 90, 91, 94, 96, 98, 99, 103,
104, 105, 106, 107, 108, 109, 113,
114, 116, 117, 118, 119, 120, 121,
122, 123, 124, 126, 128, 129, 130,
131, 132, 133, 134, 135, 137, 138,
140, 142, 158, 161, 162
    The Convention 106
Aarhus Regulation 83, 84, 88, 89, 90,
91, 92, 93, 94, 96, 99, 104, 105, 107,
108, 109, 111, 114, 115, 116, 117,
118, 119, 120, 121, 123, 124, 142,
158, 161
    Aarhus Regulation Proposal 120
    Article 10 111, 115
    Article 11 116
    Environmental Law 114
    Regulation 1367/2006 83, 98,
    105, 106
Access to information
    Active access to information 86,
    94
    Passive access to information 86,
    89
    Transparency Regulation 29, 89,
    91, 92, 93
Acquis communautaire 86
Actio popularis 116, 140, 142
Amsterdam Treaty 28, 33, 47, 88
Article 37 of Charter of Fundamental
Rights 61

Atomstopp 48

B
Beck 16

C
Charter of Fundamental Rights 29,
61, 64, 124, 126, 161, 162
Citizens' initiative 31, 33, 34, 48, 53,
54
ClientEarth 123
Commission White Paper on Euro-
pean Governance 26
    White Paper 26, 27, 28, 29, 30,
    32, 96, 157
Constitution for Europe 30, 35, 48
Convention on Biological Diversity
37
Court First Instance 90, 99, 101, 102,
103, 104, 111, 117, 120, 121

D
Dahl 17
Demmke 25
Direct concern 34, 35, 115, 124, 125
Direct effect 18
Directive 85/337 131, 138
Directive 90/313 127, 137
Directive 96/61 131, 138
Directive 2003/4 39, 128, 129, 137
Directive 2003/35 131, 138
Directive 2003/35/ 132, 133, 138

Directive 2004/35 148
Directive 2008/99 147
Directive on Environmental Impact
Assessment 74, 127

E

Ebbesson 116
Ecocentric approach 78
Eco-labelling 75
Ecological citizenship 12, 14, 59, 72,
75, 161
Ecological duties 12, 14, 55, 57, 72,
74, 75, 76, 77, 127, 144, 145, 147,
149, 150, 155, 159, 161, 163
Ecological European Citizens 71
EIA Directive 131, 133, 134, 138
Environment 99, 108, 109
    Anthropocentric approach 80
    Anthropocentric character 42,
    154, 161
    Ecocentric approach 43, 80, 152,
    161
    Ecocentric character 36, 42
    Narrow definition 36, 40, 41
    Wide definition 38, 40, 114, 160
Environmental Citizenship 12
Environmental crimes 75, 144, 145
Environmental Democracy 12, 13,
14, 15, 36, 53, 55, 57, 59, 72, 81, 82,
83, 86, 126, 127, 159, 160, 161, 162,
163
    Environment 97
    Form 108
Environmental liability 75, 147, 148,
150
Environmental rights 12, 14, 55, 57,
59, 65, 69, 71, 72, 74, 81, 85, 125,
126, 127, 142, 158, 161, 162
    European environmental rights
    59
Eu Level
    Implementation First pillar 86
    Implementation Fourth pillar 108
    Implementation Second pillar 96
    Implementation Third pillar 98
European Central Bank 33

European civil society 25, 27, 31
European Community 14, 36, 41, 61,
77, 78, 83, 84, 103, 114, 120, 121,
122, 126, 137, 148
European Consultative Forum on the
Environment and Sustainable Devel-
opment 30
European Convention of Human
Rights 52
European Convention on Human
Rights 51, 59, 60, 66, 125
European Court of Human Right 52
European Court of Human Rights 66,
67, 68, 69, 71, 125
European Court of Justice 18, 33, 44
    ECJ 19, 34, 35, 43, 45, 65, 80, 85,
    91, 98, 99, 101, 102, 103, 104,
    106, 107, 109, 111, 112, 113,
    114, 115, 117, 119, 120, 122,
    123, 124, 125, 130, 136, 158,
    161, 162
European Economic Community 15,
43
European Environmental Democracy
53, 83, 84
    Form of democracy 12, 53
    Space dimention 55
European Environmental Substantive
Right 66
European Investment Bank 33
European Union 13, 15, 22, 29, 32,
34, 44, 51, 59, 61, 66, 77, 81, 161,
163
    Deliberatory democracy 23, 30
    Democratic deficit 16, 17, 18, 20,
    21, 22, 23, 24, 28, 31, 80, 86, 96,
    160
    E-democracy 24
    EU 13, 14, 15, 16, 17, 18, 19, 20,
    21, 22, 23, 24, 27, 28, 30, 31, 32,
    34, 35, 36, 37, 38, 41, 42, 43, 45,
    46, 47, 48, 49, 50, 51, 52, 53, 54,
    55, 57, 58, 59, 60, 61, 62, 64, 65,
    66, 72, 73, 74, 75, 77, 78, 80, 81,
    82, 83, 84, 85, 86, 87, 88, 89, 90,
    95, 96, 98, 99, 100, 101, 102,
    106, 114, 117, 119, 122, 123,

124, 125, 126, 127, 129, 131,
133, 134, 135, 139, 143, 144,
146, 147, 158, 160, 161, 162
EU level 14, 17, 18, 20, 23, 24,
28, 34, 35, 53, 54, 59, 62, 66, 80,
83, 87, 120, 126, 127, 146, 158,
160, 161, 162
European Parliament 21, 27, 28,
29, 34, 84, 88, 89, 139, 142
EU Treaty 22
Member States 14, 15, 16, 22, 31,
32, 34, 35, 42, 44, 46, 47, 51, 56,
59, 60, 62, 73, 74, 77, 82, 90, 93,
97, 98, 102, 103, 125, 128, 131,
135, 136, 138, 139, 140, 141,
142, 146, 148, 149, 155, 157,
163
Participatory democracy 23, 24,
27, 28, 31, 33, 54, 55, 96, 160
Representative democracy 21,
22, 27, 30, 31, 33, 54, 80, 160

F
First Action Programme on the Envi-
ronment 44
First Environmental Action Pro-
gramme 55
Friends of the Earth 48

G
Greenpeace 48, 101, 102, 117

H
Habitats Directive 40, 42, 152, 153,
161

I
IPPC Directive 131, 133, 134, 138

J
Jans 98

L
Liability Directive 77, 147, 148, 149,

150, 151, 152, 153, 155, 156, 157,
159, 163
Lisbon Treaty 21, 22, 23, 28, 31, 32,
33, 34, 35, 42, 49, 50, 51, 53, 60, 61,
66, 80, 124, 126, 160
Lugano Convention 39

M
Maastricht Treaty 26, 46
Miller 66

N
National level 18, 42, 49, 57, 114,
126, 158, 162
    Ecological Duties 143
    Implementation First pillar 127
    Implementation Fourth pillar 139
    Implementation Second pillar
    131
    Implementation Third pillar 137
NGO 71, 102, 109, 111, 114, 115,
116, 117, 121, 123, 124
NGOs 35, 48, 49, 58, 81, 84, 98, 99,
102, 104, 109, 111, 114, 115, 116,
117, 118, 119, 120, 121, 122, 123,
124, 125, 131, 138, 140, 161
Nice Treaty 29, 35

O
Ombudsman 86, 105, 106

P
Participation 108
    Citizen s forums 24
    Citizens initiatives 24
    Procedural rights 21, 59, 60, 62,
    65, 71, 124, 158, 160, 161, 162
    Public participation 17, 18, 23,
    48, 60, 65, 72, 82, 84, 96, 97, 98,
    131, 132, 133, 134, 136, 139
Pereira 145
Plan D 30
Polluter Pay Principle 79, 150, 156
Polluter Pays Principle 45, 75, 79,
148, 149, 150, 155, 156, 161

Precautionary principle 66, 75, 76, 77, 145
Preventive Action Principle 45
Preventive principle 75, 76, 150, 151, 156
Principle of Subsidiarity 55
Principle of Subsidiarity. 55
Procedural rights
    Access to information 18, 28, 29, 33, 53, 60, 65, 72, 80, 86, 87, 88, 89, 91, 106, 127, 128, 137, 158, 160, 162
    Access to Information 12, 14, 28, 86, 90, 91, 128, 130
    Access to justice 28, 34, 35, 53, 61, 65, 82, 98, 99, 102, 104, 106, 107, 109, 116, 118, 119, 120, 122, 123, 126, 128, 132, 134, 138, 141, 158, 162
    Access to Justice 13, 14, 34, 98, 137, 139, 141, 157
    Public participation 28
    Public Participation 29
    Public Participation in Decision-Making 12, 14
Proposal for a Directive of the European Parliament of Council on Access to Justice in environmental matters 139

R
Rhodes Summit 77
Rio Declaration271 69

S
SEA Directive 132, 135
Single European Act 45, 46, 47, 55, 76, 79
Sixth Environment Action Program 57
Sixth Environmental Action Programme 47, 80
Substantive environmental right 60, 62
Substantive Environmental Right 60
Supremacy 18
Sustainable Development 30, 49, 50, 61, 77, 78, 144, 150
Sustainable Development Principle 75

T
Transparency Regulation 88, 89, 90, 92, 93, 94, 95

W
Waste Legislation 143
Water Framework Directive 56, 73, 133, 135, 136, 153
Wild Birds Directive 40, 43, 139, 152

Bibliography

1. Books and Articles

Abels, G. (2008). Citizens' deliberations and the Eu democratic deficit. Is there a model for participatory democracy?. Paper presented at the Fourth Pan-European Conference on Eu Politics Panel "Governance and Participation", Standing Group on the European Union, 25–27 September, Latvia, TAIF n. 1/2009.

Abromeit, H., & Wolf S. (2005). Will the Constitutional Treaty Contribute to the Legitimacy of the European Union?. Available at www.eiop.or.at, 9, 11.

Accame, S. (1998). La prima assemblea politica del mondo occidentale". In A. D'Atena, & E. Lanzillotta (Eds.), Alle radici della democrazia. Dalla polis al dibattito costituzionale contemporaneo (p. 11), Roma, Carocci.

Aderson, K. (2005). Book Review: Squaring the Circle? Reconciling Sovereignty and Global Governance through Global Government Networks: A New World Order. Harvard Law Review, 1255.

Agarwal, A., & Narain, S. (1992). A proposal for global environmental democracy. Earth Island Journal, 7, 1.

Agius, E., & Busuttil, S. (1994). What future for future generations?. Foundation for International Studies, Malta. Engelhardt, HT, Jr.

Allegri, M. R. (2008). Democracy at Union Level: an open question. Political Perspectives, 2, 1.

Allen, R. (2000). The New Penguin English Dictionary. London, Penguin.

Alston, P. (1982). A third Generation of Solidarity Rights. Netherlands International Law Review, 307.

Alves, C. M. (2003). La protection intégrée de l'environnement en droit communautaire. Revue Juridique de l'Environnement, 129.

Anagnostaras, G. (2001). The Principle of State Liability for Judicial Breaches: the Impact of European Community Law. European Public Law. 281.

Anaya, S. J. (2004). Indigenous Peoples in international law. New York, Oxford University Press.

Anderson, M. R. (1996). An overview. In: A, Boyle, & M. R. Anderson (Eds.), Human Rights Approaches to Environmental Protection (p. 21). Oxford, Oxford University Press.

Anderson, M. R. (1996). Human Rights Approaches to Environmental Protection: An Overview. In: A. Boyle, & M. Anderson (Eds.), Human Rights Approaches to Environmental Protection (p.1)., Oxford, Oxford University Press.

Andeweg, R. B. (2007). A Comment on Auel, Benz and Maurer. in: B. Kohler-Kock, & B. Rittberger (Eds.), Debating the Democratic Legitimacy of the European Union (p. 102). Plymouth, Rowman & Littlefield.

Annan, K. (2000). Foreword. In: S. Stec, S. Casey-Lefkowitz (Eds.), The Aarhus Convention: An Implementation Guide (p. 17). New York, Geneva, United Nations Publication.

Anton, D. K. (1993). The Internationalization of Domestic Law: The Shrinking Domaine Réservé. American Society of International Law Proceedings, 553.

Anton, D. K. (2008). Observations about expanding public participation in the international environmental law-making process. Public Law and Legal Theory Working Paper, Series Working paper n. 112, 8, June 2008. Available at www.ssrn.com/abstract=1145066.

Aragao, A. (2007). Environmental Liability Directive in Portugal. Paper for the Avosetta Group Meeting 1-2 June. Available at www.avosetta.org/, p. 8

Arblaster, A. (1994). Democracy. Buckingham, Open University Press.

Arditi, S. (2010). Enforcing Individual Producer Responsibility. American Society of International Law Proceedings 2010 Newsletter # 56 European Environmental Bureau, Metamorphosis, also on line available at www.eeb.org/?LinkServID=ADC892EB-C574-5800-28F68DA461162AA2&showMeta=0

Arend, A. C. (1999). Legal Rules and International Society. Oxford, Oxford University Press.

Aristotele, (1946). The Politics of Aristotle. Oxford, Oxford University Press.

Armstrong, K.A. (2002). Rediscovering Civil Society: the European Union and the White Paper on Governance. European Law Journal, 113.

Armstrong, K.A. (2008). Civil Society and the White Paper–Bridging or Jumping the Gaps. Available at www.jeanmonnetprogram.org.

Arrhenius, G. (2007). The boundary problem in democratic theory, Stockholm. Available at www.people.su.se/*guarr/texter/boundary. pdf.

Attfield, R. (1983). The Ethics of Environmental Concern. Athens, University of Georgia Press.

Attfield, R. (2003). Environmental Ethics, Polity. Cambridge, Wiley.

Aubin, D., & Varone, F. (2002). European Water Policy. A path towards an integrated resource management. Louvain-la-neuve. Euwareness, 28.

Auel, K., & Benz, A. (2007). Expanding National Parliamentary Control: Does it Enhance European Democracy?. In: B. Kohler-Kock & B. Rittberger (Eds.), Debating the Democratic Legitimacy of the European Union (p. 57). Plymouth, Rowman & Littlefield.

Baber, W. F., & Bartlett, R. V. (2005). Deliberative Environmental Politics. London, MIT Press.

Baber, W. F., & Bartlett, R. V. (2009). Global Democracy and Sustainable Jurisprudence. London, MIT Press

Bacqué, M.H., Rey, H., & Sintomer, Y. (2005). Gestion de proximité et démocratie participative. Une perspective comparative. Paris, La découverte.

Balck, E. C. (2010). Climate Change Adaptation: Local Solution for a Global Problem. Georgetown International Environmental Law Review, 359.

Baldwin, L. D. (1956). Best Hope of Earth, A Grammar of Democracy. Pittsburgh, University of Pittsburgh Press.

Ballesteros, M. (2009). EU Enforcement Policy of Community Environmental law as presented in the Commission Communication on implementing European Community Environmental law. Environmental Law Network International Review, 54.

Ballesteros, M., & Luk S. (2010). The impact of the Lisbon Treaty–an environmental perspective. Available at www.clientearth.org/.

Balme, R., & Chanet, D. (2008). European Governance and Democracy. Plymouth, Rowman & Littlefield.

Bandi, G. (1993). The Right to Environment in Theory and Practice: The Hungarian Experience. Connecticut Journal of International Law. 439.

Bándi, G. (2007). Environmental Liability Directive – Hungary. Paper for the Avosetta Group Meeting 1-2 June 2007. Available at www.avosetta.org/, 1.

Bankowski, Z., & Christodoulidis, E. (1998). The European Union as an Essentially Contested Project. European Law Journal, 4, 4, 341.

Barber, B. (1984). Strong Democracy: Participatory Politics for a New Age. London, California University Press.

Barbi, P. (2005). L'elaborazione della Costituzione Europea. Napoli, Editoriale Scientifica.

Barker, E. (1942). Reflections on Government. Oxford, Oxford University Press.

Barker, M. J. (1970). The Environmental Citizenship Where to Begin. Art Education, 23, 33.

Barnard, C. (2007). The Fundamentals of EU Law Revisited: Assessing the Impact of the Constitutional Debate. Oxford, Oxford University Press.

Barresi, P. A. (1997). Beyond fairness to future generations: An intergenerational alternative to intergenerational equity in the intergenerational environmental arena. Tulaine Environmental Law Journal, 11, 3.

Barry, B. (1978). Circumstances of justice and future generations. In: R. Sikora, & B. Barry (Eds.), Obligations to future generations (p. 204). Philadelphia, White Horse Press.

Barry, H. (2002). Democracy and global warming. London, Biddles Ltd, Guildford and King's Lynn.

Barry, J. (1999). Rethinking Green Politics. London, SAGE.

Barry, J. (2002). Vulnerability and virtue: democracy, dependency, and ecological stewardship. In: B. A. Minteer, & B. Pepperman Taylor (Eds.), Democracy and the Claims of Nature: Critical Perspectives for a New Century (p. 133). Oxford, Rowman & Littlefield Publishers Inc.

Barry, J. (2006). Resistance is fertile: from Environmental to Sustainability Citizenship. In: A. Dobson A., D. Bell (Eds.), Environmental Citizens (p. 21). Cambridge, MIT Press.

Barry, J., Baxter, B. & Dunphy, R. (2004). Europe, Globalisation and Sustainable Development. London, Routledge.

Barstow, Magraw, D., Hawke, L. D. (2007). Sustainable Development. In: D. Bodansky, J. Brunné (Eds.). International Environmental Law (p. 614). Oxford, Oxford University Press.

Bartenstein, K. (2005). Les origines du concept de développement durable. Revue Juridique de l'Environnement, 3, 294.

Barton, B. (2002). Underlying Concepts and Theoretical Issues in Public Participation in resource Development. In: D. Zillman (Ed.), Human Rights in Natural Resource Development: Public participation in the Sustainable Development of Ming and Energy Resources (p. 84). Oxford, Oxford University Press.

Bates, D. C. (2002). Environmental refugees? Classifying human migrations caused by environmental change. Population and Environment, 465.

Beck, U. (1998). Politik der Globalisierung. Frankfurt, Suhrkamp.

Becker, M. L. (1993). The International Joint Commission and Public Participation: Past Experiences, Present Challenges, Future Tasks. Natural Resources Journal, 235.

Beckerman, W. (1999). Sustainable Development and Our Obligations to Future Generations. In: A. Dobson (Ed.), Fairness And Futurity (p. 85). Oxford, Oxford University Press.

Beckman, L. (1994). Democracy and future generations. Why tomorrow's people should not vote today. In: M. Coppens, A. Gosseries, & J-C. Merle (Eds.), Intergenerational justice, Oxford, Oxford University Press.

Beckman, L. (2006). Citizenship and voting rights: should resident aliens vote?. Citizenship Studies, 10 (2), 153.

Beckman, L. (2007). Democracy, future generations and global climate change. In: Prepared for the workshop "Democracy on the day after tomorrow" at the ECPR Joint Sessions, Helsinki.

Beigbeder, Y. (1992). Le rôle international des organisations non gouvernementales. Paris, Bruylant.

Bell, D. R. (2004 a). Environmental Refugees: What Rights? Which Duties. Res Publica, 135.

Bell, D. R. (2004 b). Sustainability through democratisation? the Aarhus convention and the future of environmental decision-making in Europe. In: J. Barry, B. Baxter, & R. Dunphy (Eds.), Europe, Globalisation and the Challenge of Sustainability (p. 94). London, Routledge.

Bell, D. R. (2005). Liberal Environmental Citizenship. Environmental Politics, 14(2), 179.

Belrhali-Bernard, H. (2009). Le droit de l'environnement: entre incitation et contrainte. Revue Droit Public, 1683.

Benson, D., & Jordan, A. (2008). A Grand Bargain or an Incomplete Contract? European Union Environmental Policy after the Lisbon Treaty. European Energy and environmental Law Review, 280.

Benvenisti, E. (2005). The Interplay between Actors as a Determinant of the Evolution of Administrative Law in International Institutions. Law and Contemporary Problems, 319.

Berge, E. (1994). Democracy and Human Rights: Conditions for Sustainable Resource Utilisation. In: B.R. Johnson (Ed.), Who Pays the Price? The Socio cultural Context of Environmental Crisis (p. 187), Covelo. Island Press.

Bergesen, H.O., & Parmann, G. (1992). In Green Globe Yearbook of International Cooperation on Environment and Development. Oxford, Oxford University Press.

Bergkamp, L. (2001). Liability and Environment – Private and Public Law Aspects of Civil Liability for Environmental Harm in an International Context. The Hague, Kluwer Law International.

Bergkamp, L. (2002). Corporate Governance and Social Responsibility: a New Sustainability Paradigm?. European Environmental Law Review, p. 136

Bering Liisberg, J. (2010). The EU Constitutional Treaty and its Distinction Between Legislative and Non-Legislative Acts–Oranges into Apples?. Jean Monnet Working Paper, no. 01/06.

Bernstein, S. (2005). Legitimacy in Global Environmental Governance. Journal of International Law and International Relations, 139.

Bessette, J. (1980). Deliberative Democracy: The Majority Principle in Republican Government. In: How Democratic is the Constitution? (p. 102). Washington, American Enterprise Institute.

Besson, S., & Utzinger A. (2007). Introduction: Future Challenges of European Citizenship: Facing a Wide-Open Pandora's Box. European Law Journal, 573.

Betlem, G. (2005). Environmental Liability and Private Enforcement – Lessons from International Law, the European Court of Justice, and European Mining Laws. Yearbook European Environmental Law, 4, 117.

Betlem, G. (2006). Transnational Operator Liability. In: G. Betlem, & E.H.P. Brans (Eds.), Environmental Liability in the EU – The 2004 Directive compared with US and Member States Law (p. 149). London, Cameron May.

Betlem, G., Brans E.H.P. (2002). The Future Role of Civil liability for Environmental Damage in the EU. Yearbook of European Environmental Law, 2, 183.

Beyer, P., Coffey, C., Klasing, A., & Homeyer, I. (2004). The Draft Constitution for Europe and the Environment – the impact of institutional changes, the reform of the instruments and the principle of subsidiary. European Environmental Law Review, 218.

Bignami. F. (2004). Three generations of participation rights before the European Commission. Law and Contemporary Problems, 61.

Birch A. H (1993). The Concepts and Theories of Modern Democracy. London, Routledge.

Birkin-Shaw, P. (2004). A Constitution for the European Union? A Letter from Home. European Public Law, 57.

Birkin-Shaw, P. (2006). Freedom of Information and Openness: Fundamental Human Rights. Administration Law Review, 177.

Birnie, P., Boyle A. (2002). International Law and the Environment. Oxford, Oxford University Press.

Birnie, P., Boyle A., Redgwell, C. (2009). International law and the environment. Oxford, Oxford University Press.

Bjerler, N. (2009). Do Europeans Have a Right to Environment?. Available at www. esil-sedi.eu/fichiers/en/Bjerler_455.pdf.

Blanc-Jouvan, X. (1971). Problems of harmonisation of traditional and modern concepts in the land law of french-speaking Africa and Madagascar, integration of customary and modern legal systems in Africa. New York, African Pub. Corp.

Bleeker, A. (2009). PPP. European Energy & Environmental Law Review, 18, 289 -306.

Bobbio, N. (1978). Democrazia rappresentativa e democrazia diretta. In: G. Quazza (Ed.), Democrazia e partecipazione (p. 22). Torino, Giappichelli.

Bobbio, N. (1984). Il futuro della democrazia. Una difesa delle regole del gioco. Torino, Giappichelli.

Bobbio, N. (1997). L'età dei diritti. Torino, Einaudi.

Bodansky, D. (2007). Legitimacy. In: Bodansky D., & J. Brunnée (Eds.), International Environmental Law (p. 704). Oxford, Oxford University Press.

Bodansky, D. (2009). Is There an International Environmental Constitution?. Indiana Journal of Global Legal Studies, 16, 565.

Bohman, J. (1996). Public Deliberation: Pluralism, Complexity and Democracy. Cambridge, MIT Press.

Boiteux, M. (2003). L'homme et sa planèt. Paris, Académie des sciences morales et politiques.

Bolton, J. R. (2000). Should We Take Global Governance Seriously?. Chicago Journal of International Law, 205.

Bonine, J. E. (2003). The public's right to enforce environmental law. In: S. Stec (Ed.), Handbook on Access to Justice under the Aarhus Convention (p. 31), Szentendre, Unites Nation Publication.

Bookchin, M. (1971). Ecology and Revolutionary Thought. In: his Post-Scarcity Anarchism. San Francisco.

Bookchin, M. (1988). Toward and Ecological Society. California, Black Rose Books

Bookchin, M. (1990). Ecology and Revolutionary Thought. In: M. Bookchin (Ed.), Post-Scarcity Anarchism. San Francisco, AK Press.

Boon, E. K., & Le Tran, T. (2007). Are Environmental Refugees Refused?. Studies of Tribes and Tribals, 89.

Borloo, J.L. (entretien avec) (2008). Le développement durable n'est plus une question parmi d'autres mais bien une préoccupation placée au cœur de toutes les autres. Les Petites Affiches, 22 avr. 81, 9.

Boscheck, R. (2006). The EU Water Framework Directive: Meeting the Global Call for Regulatory Guidance?. Intereconomics, 268.

Bosselmann, K. (2008). The Principle of Sustainability. Aldershot, Ashgate Publishing Company.

Bosselmann, K. (2009). The Way Forward: Governance for Ecological Integrity. In: L. Westra, K. Bosselmann, & R. Westra, (Eds.), Reconciling Human Existence with Ecological Integrity (p. 319). London, Earthscan.

Bouleaul, G. (2008). Water Framework Directive paper The WFD dreams: between ecology and economics. Water and Environment Journal. 235

Boyle, A. E. (1996). The role of International Human Rights Law in the Protection of the Environment. In: A. Boyle, & M. Anderson (Eds.), Human rights Approaches to environmental protection (p. 43). Oxford, Oxford University Press.

Bradford, M. (1996). Protecting the environment for future generations: A proposal for a republican superagency. New York University Environmental Law Journal, 5.

Braibant, G. (2003). L'environnement dans la Charte des droits fondamentaux de l'Union européenne. Les Cahiers du Conseil Constitutionnel, 15, 262.

Brandl, E., & Bungert, H. (1992). Constitutional Entrenchment of Environmental Protection: A Comparative Analysis of Experiences Abroad. Harvard Environmental Law Review, 16, 4.

Brans, E.H.P. (2005). Liability for Damage to Public Natural Resources Under the 2004 EC Environmental Liability Directive: Standing and Assessment of Damages. Environmental Law Review, 7(2), 90.

Breitmeier, H., & Rittberger, V. (2000). Environmental NGOs in an Emerging Global Civil Society. In: P. S. Chasek (Ed.), The Global Environment In The Twenty-First Century: Prospects For International Cooperation (p. 130). New York, Institut für Politikwissenschaft.

Breton-Le Goff, G. (2001). L'influence des organisations non gouvernementales (ONG) sur la négociation de quelques instruments internationaux. Brussels, Bruylant.

Brooke, D. (2006). Hall Memorial Lecture, Environmental Justice: The Cost Barrier. Journal of Environmental Law, 341.

Bruch, C.E., & Czebiniak, R. (2002). Globalising Environmental Governance: Making the Leap from Regional Initiatives on Transparency, Participation, and Accountability in Environmental Matters, XXXII. Environmental Law Reporter, 1428.

Bugge, H. C., & Voigt, C. (2008). Sustainable Development in International and National Law. Groningen, Europa Law Publishing.

Bullard, R. D. (1996). Unequal protection: Environmental justice and communities of color. San Francisco, Sierra Club Books.

Burhenne, W. E., & Tarasofsky, R. G. (1998). Codification and Progressive Development of International Law – An Example from the Field of the Environment. Environmental Policy and Law, 77.

Burker, M., & Rees, A. (1996). Citizenship Today: The Contemporary Relevance of T.H. Marshall. London, University of London Press.

Burnett-Hall, R., & Jones, B. (2009). Environmental Law. London, Thomson Reuters.

Butler, J., & De Schutter, O. (2008). Binding the Eu to International Human Rights Law. Yearbook of European Law, 277.

Caldwell, L. K. (1980). International Environmental Policy and Law. Durham, Duke University Press.

Callicott, J.B. (1980). Animal Liberation: A Triangular Affair. Environmental Ethics, 2, 311.

Cameron, J. (1996). Compliance, Citizens and NGOs. In: J. Cameron, J. Werksman, & P. Roderick (Eds.), Improving Compliance With International Environmental Law (p. 29). London, Earthscan Pub.

Cameron, J., & Mackenzie, R. (1996). Access to Environmental Justice and Procedural Rights in International Institutions. In: A. Boyle, & M. Anderson (Eds.), Human Rights Approaches to Environmental Protection (p. 129). Oxford, Oxford University Press.

Camm, T., & Bowles, D. (2000). Animal welfare and the Treaty of Rome – a legal analysis on the Protocol on Animal Welfare and welfare standards in the European Union. Journal of Environmental Law, 195.

Campiglio, L., Pineschi, L., Siniscalco, D. & Trevest, T. (1994). The Environment After Rio. Dordrecht, London, Graham & Trotman/martinus Nijhoff.

Cancado Trindade, A. A. (1992). The contribution of international human rights law to environmental protection, with special reference to global environmental change. In: E. B. Weiss (ed.), Environmental Change and International Law (p. 244). Hong Kong, United Nations University Press.

Caney, S., & Simons, C. (2005). Cosmopolitan justice, responsibility, and global climate change. Leiden Journal of International Law, 18, 747.

Cano, G. J. (1975). A Legal and Institutional Framework for Natural Resources Management. FAO Legislative Studies, Rome, 9, 1.

Cantat, O. (2008). Développement durable: une pensée de référence difficile à mettre en œuvre. Droit de l'Environnement, 1 juillet, n° spéc.

Caranta, R. (1993). Governmental liability after Francovich. Cambridge Law Journal, 272.

Caranta, R. (2008). Interest representation in administrative proceeding. Napoli, Jovene.

Carolan, M. (2006). Ecological representation in deliberation: the contribution of tactile spaces. Environmental Politics, 15 (3), 345.

Carson, R. (1962). Silent Spring. Boston, Houghton Mifflin Harcourt ,

Cassin, R. (1974). Les droits de l'Homme., IV Recueil des Cours, 323, 327. Leyden.

Ceiner, G. (1984). Porte, Portici e Logge. Urbino, Spilimberc.

Chalmers, D. (1999). Inhabitants in the Field of EC Environmental Law. In: P. Craid, & G. Burca (Eds.), The Evolution of EU Law, Oxford, Oxford University Press.

Chambers, N., Simons, C., & Wackeragel, M. (2000). Sharing Nature's Interest: Ecological Footprints as an Indicator of Sustainability. London, Earthscan.

Chambers, S. (2003). Deliberative democratic theory. Annual Review of Political Science, 6, 307.

Chamboredon, A. (2007). Du Droit de l'Environnement au droit à l'Environnement, A la recherche d'un juste milieu. Paris, L'Harmattan.

Charney, J. I., Anton, D. K. & O'Connell, M. E. (Eds.), Politics, Values And Functions: International Law In The 21st Century: Essays In Honor Of Professor Louis. Henkin. Martinus Nijhoff Publishers.

Charnovitz, S. (1997). Two Centuries of Participation: NGOs and International Governance. Michigan Journal of International Law, 183.

Charnovitz, S. (2003). The Emergence of Democratic Participation in Global Governance (Paris 1919). Indiana Journal of Global Legal Studies, 45.

Charnovitz, S. (2006a). Centennial Essay: In Honour of the Tenth Anniversary of the AJIL and the ASIL. American Journal of International Law, 348.

Charnovitz, S. (2006b). Nongovernmental organisations and International Law. American Journal of International Law, 348.

Chekki, D. A. (1979). Participatory Democracy in Action: International Profiles of Community Development. Bombay, Vikas Publishing House.

Chioma Steady, F. (2009). Environmental justice in the new millennium: global perspectives on race, ethnicity and human rights. New York, Palgrave Macmillan.

Chiti, E. (1998). Il nodo irrisolto dell'accesso ai documenti di Commissione e Consiglio dell'Unione europea. Giornale di diritto amministrativo, 11, 1027.

Chiti, E. (2002). Legittimazione ad agire ex art. 230 del Trattato ed effettività della tutela giurisdizionale. Giornale di diritto amministrativo, 11, 1169.

Chiti, E. (2003). On "European Agencies". In: E.O. Eriksen, C. Joerges, & J. Neyer (Eds.), European Governance, Deliberation and the Quest for Democratisation (n. 2, p. 271), Arena Report.

Chiti, E. (2005). The Relationship between National Administrative Law and European Administrative Law in Administrative Procedures. In: J. Ziller (Ed.), What's New in European Administrative Law?, European University Institute, Department of Law, Working Paper, 10, 7.

Chiti, E. (2007). Citizenship in Europe: Are New Layers of Complexity Emerging?. European Public Law Review, 99.

Chiti, E. (2008). I problemi. In: E. Chiti (Ed.), Il regime linguistico dei sistemi comuni europei. Multilinguismo e monolinguismo nell'Unione europea (p. 1). Milano, Giuffré.

Chiti, E. (2008). Il regime linguistico del sistema comune europeo per l'informazione ambientale. La disciplina giuridica. In: E. Chiti (Ed.), Il regime linguistico dei sistemi comuni europei. Multilinguismo e monolinguismo nell'Unione europea (p. 11). Milano, Giuffré.

Chiti, E. (2010). Trattato di Lisbona. La Cooperazione Amministrativa. Giornale di diritto amministrativo, 241.

Christoff, P. (1996). Ecological citizens and ecologically guided democracy. In: B. Doherty, & M. De Geus (Eds.), Democracy and Green Political Thought. Sustainability, Rights and Citizenship (p. 151). London, Routledge.

Clarke, C. (2003). The Proposed EC Liability Directive: Half-Way Through Co-Decision. Review of European Community and International Environmental Law, 12(3), 254.

Clarke, P.B. (1999). Deep Citizenship. London, Pluto Press.

Clientearth (2009). The impact of the Lisbon Treaty–an environmental perspective. Available at www.clientearth.org/.

Closa, C. (2005).Constitution and Democracy in the Treaty Establishing a Constitution for Europe. European Public Law, 145.

Coenen, F. (2008), Public Participation and Better environmental Decisions. Enschede, Springer

Coffey, C., & Newcombe, J. (2001). The Polluter Pays Principle and Fisheries: the Role of Taxes and Charges. London, Routledge.

Cohen, J. (1989). Deliberative Democracy and Democratic Legitimacy. In: A. Hamlin, & P. Pettit, (Eds.), The Good Polity (p. 17). Oxford, John Wiley & Sons, Limited.

Cohen, J., & Rogers, J. (2003). Power and Reason. In: A. Fung, & E. Olin Wright (Eds.), Deepening Democracy: Institutional Innovations in Empowered Participatory Governance (p. 237). New York, Princeton University Press.

Cohen, M. & Murphi, J. (2001). Exploring sustainable consumption: environmental policy and the social sciences. Oxford, Emerald Group Publishing Limited.

Collins, L. (2006). The Constitution: A Carter for Sustainable development in Europe?. In: M. Pallemaerts, & A. Azmanova (Eds.), The European Union and Sustainable Development: Internal and External Dimension (p. 93). Brussels, ASP-VUB Press.

Collins, L. (2007a). Are We There Yet? The Right to Environment International and European Law. McGill International Journal of Sustainable Development Law and Policy, 120.

Collins, L. (2007b). Environmental Rights for the Future? Intergenerational Equity in the EU. Review of European Community and International Environmental Law, 16, 321.

Comba, D. (2009). Prochaine entrée en vigueur du protocole de Kiev sur les registres des rejets et transferts de polluants. Sentinelle 27 September. Available at www.sfdi.org/actualites/a2009/Sentinelle%20197.htm#kiev

Commoner, B. (1992). Making peace with the planet. New York, The New Press.

Comte, F. (2003). Criminal Environmental Law and Community Competence. European Environmental Law Review, 147.

Comte, F. (2006). Environmental Crime and the Police in Europe: A Panorama and Possible Paths for Future Action. European Environmental Law Review, 190.

Cooper, D. E., & Palmer, J. (1998). Spirit of the Environment. London, Routledge.

Corazza, C. (2009). EcoEuropa, Le nuove politiche per l'energia e il clima. Milano, Egea.

Cordonier Segger, M.-C & Weeramantry, C.G. (2005). Sustainable Justice: Reconciling Economic, Social and Environmental Law. London, Martinus Nijhoff.

Cordonier Segger, M.C. (2004). Significant Developments in Sustainable Developments Law and Governance: A Proposal. Natural Resources Forum, 28, 61.

Coroner, F. (2006). Environmental Liability Directive: how well are Member States handling transposition?. Environmental Liability, 6, 226.

Craig, P. (1991). Francovich, remedies and the scope for damages liability. Law Quarterly Review, 595.

Craig, P. (1997). Democracy and Rule-making Within the EC: an empirical and normative assessment. European Law Journal, 105.

Craig, P. (1999). The Nature of the Community: Integration, Democracy and Legitimacy. In: P. Craig, & G. De Burca (Eds.), The Evolution of EU Law (p. 41). Oxford, Oxford University Press.

Craig, P., & De Burca, G. (1999). The Evolution of EU Law. Oxford, Oxford University Press.

Craig, P., & De Burca, G. (2008). EU Law. Text, cases and materials. Oxford, Oxford University Press.

Cramer, B. W. (2009). The Human Right to information, the environment and information about the environment: from the Universal Declaration to the Aarhus Convention. Communication Law and Policy, 14, 73.

Cremona, M. (2003). The Draft Constitutional Treaty: external relations and external action. Common Market Law Review, 1347.

Cremona, M. (2004). The Union as a Global Actor: roles, models and identity. Common Market Law Review, 553.

Crosetti, A. & Fracchia, F. (2002). Procedimento amministrativo e partecipazione. Problemi, prospettive ed esperienze. Milano, Giuffré.

Cross, G. (1995). Subsidiarity and the Environment. Yearbook of European Law, 107.

Crossen, T., & Niessen, V. (2007). NGO Standing in the European Court of Justice – Does the Aarhus Regulation Open the Door?. Review of European Community & International Environmental Law, 3, 332.

Crum, B. (2005). Tailoring Representative Democracy to the European Union: does the European constitution reduce the democratic deficit?. European Law Journal, 452.

Cullet, P. (1995). Definition of an Environmental Right in a Human Rights Context. Netherlands Q. Human Rights, 25.

Czech, E.K. (2007). Liability for Environmental Damage according to Directive 2004/35/EC. Polish Journal of Environmental Studies, 16 (2), 321.

D'Amato, A. (1990). Do We owe a Duty to Future generations to Preserve the global Environment?. American Journal of International Law, 190.

Dahl, R. (1956). A Preface to democratic Theory. Chicago, University Of Chicago Press.

Dahl, R. (1991). Modern Political Analysis. London, Pearson.

Dahl, R. (1998). On democracy. Yale, Yale University Press.

Daly, H. E. (1973).Toward a Steady State Economy. San Francisco, W.H.Freeman & Co Ltd.

Dannenmaier, E. (1997). Democracy in Development: Toward a Legal Framework for the Americas. Tulane Environmental Law Journal, 111.

Dannenmaier, E. (2007). A European Commitment to Environmental Citizenship: Article 3.7 of the Aarhus Convention and Public Participation in International Forums. Yearbook of International Environmental Law, 33.

Daswood, A., & Johnston, A. (2004). The Institutions of the Enlarged EU under the Regime of the Constitutional Treaty. Common Market Law Review, 1481.

Davies, S. (2007). In Name or Nature? Implementing International Environmental Procedural Rights in the Post-Aarhus Environment: A Finnish Example. Environmental Law Review, 190.

Davis, J. (2007). Conceptual Change, Emerging Perspectives on Learning, Teaching and Technology. University of Georgia. 3 October, 2007. Available at www.projects.coe.uga.edu/epltt/index.php?title=Conceptual_Change.

De Abreu Ferreira, S. (2007a). Fundamental Environmental Rights in EU Law. 6th Global Conference (2007) Monday 2nd July – Thursday 5th July 2007, Mansfield College, Oxford. Available at www.inter-disciplinary.net/ptb/ejgc/ejgc6/Ferreira%20paper.pdf, p.5.

De Abreu Ferreira, S. (2007b). The Fundamental Right of Access to Environmental Information in the EC: A Critical Analysis of WWF-EPO v. Council. Journal of Environmental Law, 19, 399.

De Abreu Ferreira, S. (2008). Passive Access to Environmental Information in the EU – An Analysis of Recent Legal Developments. European Energy and Environmental Law Review, 186.

De Burca, G. (1996). The Quest for Legitimacy in the EU. Modern Law Review, 349.

De Burca, G. (2006). After the Referenda. European Law Journal, 6.

De Geus, M. (1996). The ecological restructuring of the state. In: B. Doherty, & M. De Geus (Eds.) Democracy and Green Political Thought (p. 190). London, Routledge.

De La Fayette, L. (2002). The Concept of Environmental Damage in International Liability Regimes. In: M. Bowman, & A. Boyle (Eds.), Environmental Damage in International and Comparative Law – Problems of Definition and Valuation (p. 149), New York, Oxford University Press.

De Lange, F. (2003). Beyond Greenpeace, Courtesy of the Aarhus Convention, in EC Environmental Law. Yearbook European Environmental law, 227.

De Leeuw, M.E. (2007). Openness in the legislative process in the European Union. European Law Review, 295.

De Sadeleer, N. (1999). Les principes du pollueur-payeur, de prévention et de précaution. Bruxelles, Emile Bruylant.

De Sadeleer, N. (2002). Environmental Principles – From Political Slogans to Legal Rules. Oxford, Oxford University. Press.

De Sadeleer, N. (2005). Access to justice in environmental matters and the role of NGOs. Groningen, Europa Law Pub.

De Sadeleer, N. (2007). The Birds, Habitats and Environmental Liability Directives to the Rescue of the Wildlife Under Threat. Yearbook European Environmental Law, 7, 36.

De Sadeleer, N. (2008). Sustainable Development and EU Waste law. In: H. C. Bugge, & C. Voigt (Eds.), Sustainable Development in International and National Law p. 399. Groningen, Europa Law Publishing.

De Schutter, O. (1996). Sur l'émergence de la société civile en droit international: la Cour européenne des droits de l'homme. European Journal of International Law, 372.

De Smedt, K. (2009). Is Harmonisation always Effective? The Implementation of the Environmental Liability Directive. American Journal of International Law, 2.

Dean, H. (2001). Green Citizenship. Social Policy and Administration, 35, 490.

Déjeant-Pons, M. (1999). La Convention de Berne relative à la conservation de la vie sauvage et du milieu naturel en Europe. In: Déjeant-Pons, M. (Ed.): Vers l'application renforcée du droit international de l'environnement/Towards strengthening application of international environmental law (p. 58). Paris, Edition Frison Roche.

Déjeant-Pons, M. (2002). Human Rights to Environmental Procedural Rights. In: M. Déjeant-Pons, & Pallemaerts M. (Eds.), Human Rights and the Environment (p. 23). Strasbourg, Council of Europe.

Del Rey, M.-J. (2010). « Développement durable »: l'incontournable hérésie. Droit, 1493.

Delreux T. (2009). The Eu in Environmental Negotiations in UNECE: An Analysis of its Role in the Aarhus Convention and the SEA Protocol Negotiations. Review of European Community and International Environmental Law, 328.

Demmke, C. (1998). The Secret Life of Comitology or the Role of Public Officials in EC Environmental Policy. European Institute of Public Administration. Available at www.eipa.nl/eipascope/98/scop-3/secret-comitology.htm

Descartes, R. (1931). Discourse on Method. In: The philosophical Works of Descartes. Cambridge, Cambridge University Press.

Desgagne R. (1995). Integrating Environmental Value into the European Convention on Human Rights. Am Journal international Law, 263.

Dette, B. (2004). Access to Justice in Environmental Matters. In: M. Onida (Ed.), Europe and the Environment – Essays in Honour of Ludwig Krämer (p. 3), Groningen, Europa Law Publishing.

Devall, B., & Sessions, G. (1984). The Development of Natural Resources and the Integrity of Nature. Environmental Ethics, 6, 296.

Dobson, A. (1995). Green political thought. London, Routledge.

Dobson, A. (1996). Representative democracy and the environment. In: W.M. Lafferty, & Meadowcroft, J. (Eds.), Democracy and the environment: problems and prospects (p. 125), Cheltenham, Edward Elgar Publishing Ltd.

Dobson, A. (1998). Justice and the Environment: Conceptions of Environmental Sustainability and Dimensions of Social Justice. Oxford, Clarendon Press.

Dobson, A. (1999). Fairness And Futurity. Oxford, OUP.

Dobson, A. (2003). Citizenship and the Environment. London, Oxford University Press.

Dobson, A. (2004). Social inclusion, environmental sustainability and citizenship education. In: J. Barry, B. Baxter, & R. Dunphy (Eds.), Europe, Globalisation and Sustainable Development (p. 115), London, Routledge.

Dobson, A. (2005). Citizenship. In: Dobson, A., & Eckersley, R. (Eds.), Political Theory and the Ecological Challenge (p. 481). Cambridge, Cambridge University Press.

Dobson, A. (2010). Ecological citizenship: a disruptive influence?. Available at www.vedegylet.hu/okopolitika/Dobson%20-%20Ecological%20Citizenship.pdf

Dobson, A., & Bell, D. (2006). Environmental Citizens. Oxford, OUP.

Dobson, A., & Bell, D. (2006). Introduction. In: A. Dobson., & D. Bell (Eds.), Environmental Citizenship (p. 1). Cambridge, Cambridge University Press.

Dobson, A., & Saiz, A.V. (2005). Introduction. Environmental Politics, 157.

Dodeller, S., & Pallemaerts, M. (2005). L'accès des particuliers à la Cour de Justice et au Tribunal de Première Instance des Communautés européennes en matière d'environnement: bilan du droit positif et perspectives d'évolution. In: C. Larssen, & M. Pallemaerts (Eds.), L'accès à la justice en matière d'environnement/Toegang tot de rechter in milieuzaken (p. 287). Brussels, Emile Bruylant.

Donald, K. A. (2008). Observations About Expanding Public Participation In The International Environmental Law-Making Process. The Social Science

Research Network Electronic Paper Collection. Available at www.ssrn.com/abstract=1145066.

Donnelly, B., & Bishop, P. (2007). Natural Law and Ecocentrism. Journal of Environmental Law, 89.

Doolittle, I. (1992). A Guide to EC Regulation: Environmental Liability. International Financial Law Review, Suppl. June, 20.

Douglas-Scott, S. (1996). Environmental Rights In the European Union – Participatory Democracy or Democratic Deficit?. In: Boyle, A., & Anderson, M. (Eds.), Human rights Approaches to environmental protection (p. 109). Oxford, Oxford University Press.

Dozer, R. (1976). Property and Environment: The Social Obligation Inherent in Ownership. Morges, International Union for Conservation of Nature.

Drengson, A.R. (1998). Shifting Paradigms: from the technocratic to the person-planetary. Environmental Ethics, 221.

Drevensek, M. (2005). Negotiation as the Driving Force of Environmental Citizenship. Environmental Politics, 14(2), 226.

Dross, M. (2005). Access to Justice in EU Member States. Journal for European Environmental Planning Law, 22.

Dryzek, J. (2000). Deliberative democracy and beyond: liberals, critics, contestations. Oxford, Oxford University Press.

Dunoff, J. L. (2007). Levels of Environmental Governance. In: D., Bodansky, & J. Brunnée (Eds.), International Environmental Law (p. 85). Oxford, Oxford University Press.

Dwivedi, O. P. (2006). Hindu Religion and Environmental Well-Being. In: R. S. Gottlieb (Ed.) Religion and Ecology (p. 160). Oxford, Routledge.

Ebbesson, J. (2006). Access to justice at the level of the EU: progress or stagnation?. In: A. Gourtin, (Ed.) The Aarhus Regulation: New Opportunities for Citizens in the EU and Beyond?. Report of the ECOSPHERE Forum held in Brussels, 27 October 2006, Brussels, ECOSPHERE.

Ebbesson, J. (2007). Public Participation. In: D. Bodansky,& J. Brunnée (Eds.), International Environmental Law (p. 683). Oxford, Oxford University Press.

Ebbesson, J. (2009). Environmental law and justice in Context. Cambridge, Cambridge University Press.

Eberhard, C. (2008). Traduire nos responsabilités planétaires, recomposer nos paysages juridiques. Bruxelles, Emile Bruylant.

Eckersley, R. (1992). Environmentalism and Political Theory. London, Routledge.

Eckersley, R. (1996). Greening Liberal Democracy: The Rights Discourse Revisited. In: B. Doherty, & M. De Geus (Eds.), Democracy and Green Political Thought (p. 214), London, Routledge.

Eckersley, R. (2000). Deliberative Democracy, Ecological Representation and Risk: Towards a Democracy of the Affected. In: M. Saward (Ed.), Democratic Innovation: Deliberation, Representation and Association (p. 230). London, Routledge.

Eckersley, R. (2001). Ecofeminism and Environmental Democracy: Exploring the Connections. Women & Environments International Magazine, 52.

Eckersley, R. (2004). The Green State: Rethinking Democracy and Sovereignty. Cambridge, MIT Press.

Eder, K., & Trenz, H. J. (2007). Prerequisites of Transnational Democracy and Mechanisms for Sustaining It: The Case of the European Union. In: B. Kohler-Kock, & B. Rittberger (Eds.), Debating the Democratic Legitimacy of the European Union (p. 167) Plymouth, Rowman & Littlefield.

Editorial (2007a). What should replace the Constitutional Treaty?. Common Market Law Review, 561.

Editorial (2007b). Democracy and the Union: Dressing up Cinderella. European Constitutional Law Review, 3, 353.

Editorial Comment (2007). Environmental Liability Directive enters into force. EUF, 209, 2.

Egger, R. (2007). Press Officer Atomstopp – Initiative "1 Million against Nuclear Power", June 28.

Ekross, A. (2007). Environmental Liability Directive – Finland. Paper for the Avosetta Group Meeting 1-2 June, available at www.avosetta.org/, p. 1.

El-Hinnawi, E. (1985). Environmental Refugees. Nairobi, Kenya: United Nations Environmen- tal Programme.

Eleftheriadis P. (2007). Environmental Rights in the EC Legal Order. University of Oxford Faculty of Law Legal Studies Research Paper Series Working Paper No 24/2007. Available at www.ssrn.com/abstract=1015923

Elgar, E., Doeleman J., & Sandler, T. (1998). The intergenerational case of missing markets and missing voters. Land Economics, 1.

Ellickson, R. (1991). Order Without Law: How Neighbors Settle Disputes. Harvard, Harvard University Press.

Emiliou, N. (1992). Subsidiarity: An Effective Barrier Against the "The Enterprises of Ambition"?. European Environmental Law Review, 383.

Emiliou, N. (1996). State liability under Community law: shedding more light on the Francovich principle?. European Environmental Law Review, 399.

Engin, F., & Turner, S. (2002). Handbook of Citizenship Studies. London, SAGE Publications Ltd.

Engle, E. (2007). Ecotaxes and the European Union. European Environmental Law Review, 298.

Epstein, R. (1998). Justice across generations. Texas Law Review, 67.

Ermacora, F. (2003). The right to a Clean Environment in the Constitution of the European Union. In: J.H. Jans (Ed.), The European Convention and the Future of European Environmental Law, Proceedings of the Avosetta Group of European Environmental Lawyers (p. 29). Groningen, Europa Law Publishing.

Estella De Noriega, A. (2002). The EU Principle of Subsidiary and its Critique. Oxford, Oxford University Press.

Estlund, D. (2003). The democracy/contractualism analogy. Philosophy and Public Affairs, 31.

Estyd, C. & Ivanova, M.H. (2002). Global Environmental Governance, Options and Opportunities. New Haven, Yale School of Forestry.

Europa. The E.U. at a glance, Treaties & Law. Available at www.europa.eu/abc/treaties/index_en.htm

Exell Pirro, D. (2008). Introduction Women and an International Court of the Environment. In: A. Postiglione (Ed.), The Protection and Sustainable Development of the Mediterranean Black Sea Ecosystem (p. 833). Bruxelles, Bruylant.

Farrell, H., & Heritier, A. (2002). Formal and Informal Institutions under Codecision: Continuous Constitution Building in Europe, European Integration online Papers (EIoP), 6.

Farrelly, C. (2004). Introduction to Contemporary Political Theory. London, Sage Publications Ltd.

Faure, M. (2004). European Environmental Criminal law. Do we really need it?. European Environmental Law Review, 18.

Faure, M. (2008). The Continuing Story of Environmental Criminal Law in Europe after 23 October 2007. European Energy and Environmental Law Review, 69.

Fedrigo, D., & Tukker, A. (2009). Blueprint for Europe, Sustainable consumption and Production: Finding the path of transition to a sustainable society. Brussels, European Environmental Bureau.

Feinberg, J. (1998). Harmless wrongdoing: The moral Limits of the Criminal Law. Oxford, Oxford University Press.

Fergusson, R., Manser, M., & Pickering, D. (2000). The New Penguin Thesaurus. Harmondsworth, Penguin Books Ltd.

Fievet, G. (2001). Réflexions sur le concept de développement durable: prétention économique, principes stratégiques et protection des droits fondamentaux. Revue belge de droit international, 128.

Finger, M. (2008). Which governance for sustainable development?. In: J. Park, K. Conca, & M. Finger (Eds.), The crisis of Global Environmental Governance (p. 35). London, Routledge.

Finley, M.I. (1973). Democracy Ancient and Modern. New York, Rutgers University Press.

Finley, M.I. (1983). Politics in the Ancient World. Cambridge, Cambridge University Press.

Fischer, C., & Lichtblau, T. (2008). European Citizens' Initiative – interim results. In: J. W. Pichler (Ed.), We Change Europe, The European Initiative- Art. 8b(4) Treaty of Lisbon (p. 333). Vienne, BWV Berliner Wissenschafts-Verlag.

Fish, S. (1999). Mutual respect as a device of exclusion. In: S. Macedo (Ed.), Deliberative politics: essays on democracy and disagreement (p. 88). New York, OUP USA.

Fitzmaurice, M. (2003). Public Participation in the North American Agreement on Environmental Cooperation. International Law & Comparative Law Quarterly, 333.

Fitzmaurice, M. (2009). Contemporary Issues in International Environmental Law. Cheltenham, Edward Elgar Publishing Ltd.

Fitzmaurice, M. (2009). Environmental justice through international complaint procedure? Comparing the Aarhus Convention and the North American Agreement on Environmental Cooperation. In: J. Ebbesson, (ed.), Environmental law and justice in Context (p. 211). Cambridge, Cambridge University Press.

Flynn, B. (2008). Planning Cells and Citizen Juries in Environmental Policy: Deliberation and Its limits. In: F. Coenen (Ed.), Public Participation and Better environmental Decisions (p. 57). Enschede. Springer.

Flynn, R., Bellaby, P., & Ricci, M. (2008). Environmental citizenship and public attitudes to hydrogen energy technologies. Environmental Politics, 17, 766.

Fogleman, V. (2006). Enforcing the Environmental Liability Directive: Duties, Powers and Self-Executing Provisions. Environmental Liability, 127.

Ford K. (1998). Can a Democracy Bind Itself in Perpetuity? Paine, the Bank Crisis, and the Concept of Economic Freedom. Proceedings of the American Philosophical Society, 142.

Fossum, J.E., & Menendez, A.J. (2005). The Constitution's Gift? A Deliberative Democratic Analysis of Constitution Making in the European Union. European Law Journal, 380.

Foster, J. (1997). Valuing nature? Economics, ethics and environment. London, Routledge.

Fowles, B. (2002). Meeting Human and Ecological Rights in Creating the Sustainable Built Environment. 1er Global Conference "Environmental Justice and Global citizenship", 14th – 16th February 2002 Copenhagen. Oxford, Oxford University Press.

Fox, W. (1989). The Deep Ecology-Ecofeminism Debate and Its Parallels. Environmental Ethics, 5.

Fraccia, F. (2009). The Legal Definition of Environment: From Rights to Duties. Research Paper, n. 2009. Available at www.ssrn.com/abstract=850488.

Fralin, R. (1978). Rousseau and Representation. A Study of the Development of his concept of Political Institutions. New York, Columbia University Press.

Francioni, F. (2008). Access to Justice in International environmental law. In: A. Postiglione (Ed.), The Protection and Sustainable Development of the Mediterranean Black Sea Ecosystem (p. 25). Bruxelles, Bruylant.

Francioni, F. (2009). Access to Justice as a Human Right. Oxford, Oxford University Press.

French, H. (1996). The Role of Non-State Actors. In: J. Werksman (Ed.), Greening International Institutions (p. 251). London, Earthscan.

Frost, A. (2003). Restoring Faith in Government – Transparency Reform in the United States and the European Union. European Public Law, 89.

Frumer, P. (1998). Protection de l'environnement et droits procéduraux de l'homme: des relations tumultueuses?. Revue Trimestrielle Droit Homme, 813.

Gallego, G. (2002). Waste Legislation in the European Union. European Environmental Law Review, 8.

Gamble, A. & Wright, T. (1999), The New Social Democracy. Oxford, Wiley.

Gardner, G., & Stern, P. (2002). Environmental Problems and Human Behaviour. Boston, Pearson Custom Publishing.

Gardner, J. (1978). Discrimination against future generations: The possibility of constitutional limitations. Environmental Law, 9.

Gates, S., Gleditsch, N. P., & Neumayer, E. (2003). Environmental Commitment, Democracy and Inequality, Background Paper, World Development Report 2003, World Bank. Washington. Work Bank Publication.

Gbikpi, B. , & Grote, J. R. (2002). From Democratic Government to Participatory Governance. In: H. Heinelt, & A. Opladen (Eds.), Participatory Governance in Multi-Level Context: Concept and Experience (p. 17). Leverkusen, Leske + Budrich.

Geisinger, A. (2002). A Belief Change Theory of Expressive Law. Iowa Law Review, 88, 35.

Geisinger, A. (2009). Expressive Environmental Regulation: How Law Influences Beliefs About How to Live Sustainably. 8th Global Conference "Environmental Justice and Global Citizenship", 10th – 12th July 2009. Oxford, Oxford University Press.

Gemmill, B., & Bamiele-Izu, A. (2002). The Role of NGOs and Civil Society in Global Environmental Governance. In: C. Estyd, & M.H. Ivanova (Eds.), Global Environmental Governance, Options and Opportunities (p. 77). New Haven, Yale School of Forestry & Environmental Studies.

Gendron, C., Vaillancourt, J.G., & Audet, R. (2010). Développement durable et responsabilité sociale, de la mobilisation à l'institutionnalisation. Quebec, Presses Internationales Polytecnique.

Getliffe, K. (2002). Proceduralisation and the Aarhus Convention Does increased participation in the decision-making process lead to more effective EU environmental law?. Environmental Law Review, 4, 101.

Giagnocavo, C., & Goldstein, H. (1990). Law Reform or World Reform: The Problem of Environmental Rights. McGill Law Journal, 345.

Gillespie, A. (1997). International environmental law, policy, and ethics. Oxford, Oxford University Press.

Gilpin, A. (2000). Dictionary of Environmental Law. Cheltenham, Edward Elgar Publishing Ltd.

Gleditsch, N. P. (1998). Armed Conflict and the Environment: A Critique of the Literature. Journal of Peace Research, 381.

Gleditsch, N. P., & Sverdlop, B.O. (2003). Democracy and the Environment. In: E. Paper, & M. Redclift (Eds.), Human Security and the Environment: International Comparisons (p. 70). London, Edward Elgar Publishing Ltd.

Goodin, R. E. (1992). Green Political Thought. Cambridge, Routledge.

Goodin, R. E. (1996) Institutionalizing the public interest: the defense of deadlock and beyond. The American Political Science Review, 90, 2 June, 331.

Goodin, R. E. (2003). Reflective Democracy. Oxford, Oxford University Press.

Goodin, R. E. (2007). Enfranchising the all-affected and its alternatives. Philosophy and Public Affairs. 35, 40.

Gormley, W. P. (1976). Human Rights and Environment: The Need For International Co-operation. Amsterdam.

Gormley, W. P. (1990). The legal Obligation of the International Community to Guarantee a Pure and Decent Environment; The Expansion of Human Rights Norms. Geo International Environmental Law Review, 85.

Gouguet, J.J. (2007). Développement durable et décroissance, deux paradigmes incommensurables. In: Pour un droit commun de l'environnement, Mélanges en l'Honneur de Michel Prieur (p. 124). Paris, Dalloz.

Gourtin, A. (2006). The Aarhus Regulation: New Opportunities for Citizens in the EU and Beyond? Report of the ECOSPHERE Forum held in Brussels, 27 October . Brussels, ECOSPHERE.

Graham, S. (2003). Deliberative Democracy and the Environment. London, Routledge.

Green, J.F. (2004). Engaging the Disenfranchised: Developing Countries and Civil Society in International Governance for Sustainable Development–An Agenda for Research, UNU-IAS Report, United Nations University, Tokyo, UNU/IAS.

Greven, M. TH. (2007). Some Considerations on Participation in Participatory Governance. In: B. Kohler-Kock, & B. Rittberger (Eds.). Debating the Democratic Legitimacy of the European Union (p. 233). Plymouth, Rowman & Littlefield.

Gros, M. (2009). Quel degré de normativité pour les principes environnementaux?. Revue Droit Public, 425.

Grossman, M.R. (2006). Agriculture and the Polluter Pays Principle: An Introduction. Oklahoma Law Review, 59, 1.

Grubb, M. (1993). The Earth Summit Agreements: A Guide and Assessment. London, Earthscan Publications Ltd.

Guha, R. (1989). Radical American Environmentalism and Wilderness Preservation. A third World Critique. Environmental Ethics, 11, 71.

Gupte, M., & Bartlett, R.V. (2007). Necessary Preconditions for Deliberative Environmental Democracy? Challenging the Modernity Bias of Current Theory. Global Environmental Politics, 94.

Gutmann, A., & Thompson, D. (1996). Democracy and disagreement. Cambridge, Belknap Press of Harvard University Press.

Habermas, J. (1973) Legitimation Crisis. Boston, Beacon Press.

Habermas, J. (1987a). The Philosophical Discourse of Modernity. Cambridge, The MIT Press.

Habermas, J. (1987b). Theory of Communicative Action. Boston, Beacon Press.

Habermas, J. (1991). Citizenship and National Identity: Some Reflections on the Future of Europe. Praxis International, 12, 1.

Habermas, J. (1996). Between Facts and Norms. Cambridge, The MIT Press.

Habermas, J. (1998). The inclusion of the Other: Studies in Political Theory. Cambridge, The MIT Press.

Habermas, J. (1996). Environmental citizenship as reasonable citizenship. Environmental Politics, 14, 195.

Hall, N. D. (2007). The evolving role of citizens in united states-canadian international environmental law compliance. Pace Environmental Law Review,131.

Hall, P. (1997). Sustainable Cities for Europe. In: V. P. Mega, & R. Petrella (Eds.), Utopias and Realities of Urban Sustainable Development, New Alliances between Economy, Environment, and Democracy for small and Medium-sized Cities (p. 24). Dublin, European Foundation for the Improvement of Living and Working Conditions.

Hall, P. (1997). Sustainable Cities for Europe. In: V. P. Mega, & R. Petrella (Eds.), Utopias and Realities of Urban Sustainable Development, New Alliances between Economy, Environment, and Democracy for small and Medium-sized Cities (p. 24). Dublin, European Foundation for the Improvement of Living and Working Conditions.

Hallo, R. E. (2007). How far has the EU applied the Aarhus Convention?. Brussels, European Environmental Bureau.

Hallo, R. E. (2008). Unwelcome Guests: Etiquette in Public Participation processes. In: Proceedings of the Conference on Environmental Governance and Democracy (10). Yale, Yale University Press.

Hancock, J. (2003). Environmental Human Rights: Power, Ethics and Law. London, Ashgate Publishing Limited.

Handl, G. (1992). Human Rights and Protection of the Environment: A mildly "revisionist" View. In: A. A. Cancado Trindade (Ed.) Human Rights, Sustainable Development and the Environment (p. 117). San Jose de Brasilia.

Hansen, M.H. (1991). The Athenian Democracy in the Age of Demosthenes. Oxford, University of Oklahoma Press.

Harden, I. (2009). The Revision of Regulation 1049/2001 on Public Access to Documents. European Public Law, 239.

Hardin, G. (1968). The Tragedy of the Commons. Science, 1243.

Hargrone, J. L. (1972). Law Institutions and global environment. New York, Kluwer Academic Publishers.

Harlow C. (1993). Towards a Theory of Access for the European Court of Justice. Yearbook of European Law, 12, 179.

Harlow C. (1996). Francovich and the Problem of the Disobedient State. European Law Journal, 199.

Hartley, D. (2001). Green citizenship, Social Policy and Administration, 35, 490.

Hartmann, J. (1992). Democracy, Development and Environmental Sustainability. In: H.O. Bergesen and G. Parmann (Eds.), Green Globe Yearbook of International Cooperation on Environment and Development (p. 49). Oxford, Oxford University Press.

Hauptmann, E. (2001). Can Less Be More? Leftist Deliberative Democrats. Critique of Deliberative Democracy. Policy, 397.

Hawken, P., Lovins, A. & Lovins, L. H. (2000). Natural Capitalism: Creating the next Industrial Revolution. Boston, Back Bay Books.

Hay, P. (2002). A companion to Environmental Thought. Edinburgh, Edinburgh University Press.

Hayton, R. D. (1993). The Matter of Public Participation. Natural Resources Journal. 275.

Hayward, T. (2000). Constitutional environmental rights: a case for political analysis. Political Studies, 48, 558.

Hayward, T. (2005). Constitutional environmental rights. Oxford, Oxford University Press.

Hectors, K. (2008). The Chartering of Environmental Protection: Exploring the Boundaries of Environmental Protection as Human Rights. European Energy and Environmental Law Review, June, 165.

Hedemann-Robinson M. (2007). Enforcement of European Union Environmental law. London, Routledge.

Hedemann-Robinson M. (2008). The EU and Environmental Crime: The Impact of the ECJ's Judgment of Framework Decision 2005/667 on Ship-Source Pollution. Journal of Environmental Law, 279.

Heilbroner, R. (1974). An Inquiry into the Human Prospect. New York, W.W. Norton.

Heinelt H., & Opladen A. (2002). Participatory Governance in Multi-Level Context: Concept and Experience. Leske + Budrich, Opladen.

Heinelt, H. (2007). Participatory Governance and European Democracy. In: B. Kohler-Kock, & B. Rittberger (Eds.), Debating the Democratic Legitimacy of the European Union (p. 219). Plymouth, Rowman & Littlefield.

Held, D. (1991). Political Theory Today. Cambridge, Stanford University Press.

Heldeweg, M. A. (2005). Towards Good Environmental Governance in Europe. European Environmental Law Review, 2 .

Heyward, C. (2008). Can the all-affected principle include future persons? Green deliberative democracy and the non-identity problem. Environmental Politics, 17, n. 4, 625.

Hilson, C. (2001). Greening citizenship: Boundaries of membership and the Environment. Journal of Environmental Law, 335.

Hinteregger, M. (2008a). Environmental Liability and Ecological Damage in European Law. Cambridge, Cambridge University Press.

Hinteregger, M. (2008b). International and Supranational Systems of Environmental Liability in Europe. In: M. Hinteregger (Ed.), Environmental Liability and Ecological Damage in European Law (p. 3). Cambridge, Cambridge University Press.

Hobbes, T. (1974). Leviathan. Harmondsworth, Penguin Classics.

Hobson, K (2001). Sustainable lifestyles: rethinking barriers and behaviour change. In: M. Cohen, & J. Murphy (Eds.), Exploring sustainable consumption: environmental policy and the social sciences (p. 191) Oxford, Emerald Group Publishing Limited.

Hobson, K. (2003). Thinking habits into action: the role of knowledge and process in questioning household consumption practices. Local Environment, 8 (1), 95.

Hodkova, I. (1991). Is There a Right to a Healthy Environment in the International Legal Order?. Connecticut Journal of International Law. 65.

Holder, J., & Lee M. (2007). Environmental Protection, Law and Policy. Cambridge, Aspen Publishers.

Holtz, U. (2008). Representative and participatory democracy. Colloquy of the European Association in Athens 02 May, Available at http://www.vemdb.de/files/rd_pd.pdf

Horn, L. (2004). The implications of the Concept of Common Concern of a Human Kind on a Human Right to a Healthy Environment. Macquarie Journal of International and Comparative EnvironmentalLaw, 1, 233.

Hostetler, E.G. (1995). Promoting the Effective Implementation of Multilateral Environmental Treaties: The Role of Non-Government organisations in Strategies For Environmental Enforcement. Stanford Environmental Law Society, 279.

Howard, W. (1996). Environmental democracy: Use it or lose it. National Wildlife, 34.

Hugo, G. (1996). Environmental concerns and international migration. International Migration Review, 105.

Hurrelmann, A. (2007). European Democracy, the 'Permissive Consensus' and the Collapse of the EU Constitution. European Law Journal, 343.

Jackson, T. (2005). Motivating Sustainable Consumption. Sustainable Development Research Network.

Jacobs, F. (2006). The Role of the European Court of Justice in the Protection of the Environment. Journal of Environmental Law, 18, 185.

Jacobs, F.G. (2007). Citizenship of the European Union–A Legal Analysis. European Law Journal, 591.

Jacobs, M. (1997). Environmental valuation, deliberative democracy and public decision-making institutions. In: J. Foster (Ed.),Valuing nature? Economics, ethics and environment (p. 211–231). London, Routledge.

Jacobs, M. (1999). Environmental democracy. In: A. Gamble, & T. Wright (Eds.), The New Social Democracy (p. 105). Oxford, Wiley .

Jacque, J.P. (1997). La protection de l'environnement au niveau européen ou régional. In: P. Kromarek (Ed.), Environnement et droits de l'homme (p. 65). UNESCO.

James, A. (1986). Sovereign statehood the basis of international society. London, Harper Collins Publishers Ltd.

Jans, H. (1996). Legal Protection in European Environmental Law: an overview. In: H. Somsen (Ed.), Protecting the European Environment: Enforcing EC Environmental Law. London, Blackstone Press.

Jans, J. H. (2006). Did baron von Munchhaausen ever visit Aarhus?. In: R. Macrony (Ed.), Reflection on 30 Years of EU Environmental Law (p. 447). Groningen, Europa Law Publishing.

Jans, J. H., & Vedder, H. (2008). European Environmental Law. Groningen, Europa Law Publishing.

Jasanoff, S. (1996). The dilemma of environmental democracy. Science and Technology, 13, 2.

Jayanti, S. (2009). Recognising Global Environmental Interests: A Draft Universal Standing Treaty for Environmental Degradation. Georgetown International Environmental Law Review, 1.

Jelin, E. (2000). Towards a Global Environmental Citizenship?. Citizenship Studies, 4, 47.

Jendroska, J. (2004). Towards implementation of the Aarhus Convention's third pillar: Draft Eu access to justice directive compared with the situation in Poland. Environmental Liability, 68.

Jendroska, J. (2005). Aarhus Convention and Community Law: The Interplay. Journal of European Environmental & Planning Law, 12.

Jendroska, J. (2006). Public Information and participation in EC Environmental Law. In: R. Macrony (Ed.), Reflections on 30 years of EU Environmental Law (p.63). Groningen, Europa Law Publishing.

Joerges, C. (2006). On the Disregard for History in the Convention Process. European Law Journal, 2.

Jóhannsdóttir, A. (2007). Considerations on the Development of Environmental Law in the Light of the Concept of Sustainable Development. YM, 27.

Jóhannsdóttir, A. (2008). Miljodemokrati–offentlighedens deltagelse i beslutningsprocessen. In: M. B. Andersen, & J. Christoffersen (Eds.), Forhandlingerne ved Det. nordiske Juristmode (p. 221), Copenhagen, University of Oslo Press.

Johnson, G. S. (2009). Environmental Justice, A brief history and overview. In: F. Chioma Steady (Ed.), Environmental justice in the new millennium: global perspectives on race, ethnicity and human rights (p. 17). New York, Palgrave Macmillan.

Johnson, G.F. (2007). Discursive democracy in the transgenerational context and a precautionary turn in public reasoning. Contemporary Political Theory, 6 (1), 67.

Jonas, H. (1979). Das Prinzip Verantwortung. Frankfurt, Königshausen & Neumann.

Jordan, L. (2000). Civil Society's Role In Global Policymaking. Alliance, March 2000. Available at www.globalpolicy.org/ngos/intro/general/2003/0520role.htm

Jørgensen, K.E. (1997). Reflective Approaches to European Governance. London, St. Martin's Press.

Kaelble, H. (1994). L'Europe "vécue" et l'Europe "pensée" aux XXe siècle: Les spécificités sociales de l'Europe. In: R. Girault (Ed.), Identité et conscience européennes aux XXe siècle (p. 27). Paris, Publications de la Sorbonne.

Kaika, M. (2003). The Water Framework Directive, a new directive for a changing social political and economic European framework. European Planning Studies, 11(3), 303.

Kaika, M., & Page, B. (2003). The EU water Framework directive: Part 1. European policy-making and the changing topography of lobbying. European Environment, 314.

Kanie, N. & Haas, P.M. (2004). Emerging Forces in Environmental Governance. United Nations New York, Bookwell Publications.

Karakostras, I. K. (2008). Greek and European Environmental law. Athens, Bruylant.

Karassin, O. (2010). Mind the Gap: Knowledge and Need in Regulating Adaptation to Climate Change. Georgetown International Environmental Law Review, 383.

Keessen, A. (2007). Reducing the Judicial Deficit in Multilevel Environmental Regulation: the Example of Plant Protection Products. European Environmental Law Review, 26.

Kelsen, H. (1961). General Theory of Law and State. New York, Lawbook Exchange, Ltd.

Kenny, M. (1996). Paradoxes of Community. In: B. Doherty and M. De Geus (Eds.), Democracy and Green Political Thought (p. 23). London, Routledge.

Kenyon, W., Nevin, C., & Hanley N. (2003). Enhancing Environmental Decision-making Using Citizens' Juries. Local Environment, 8, 22.

Ker Rault A., & Jeffrey, P. J. (2008). Deconstructing public participation in the Water Framework Directive: implementation and compliance with the letter or with the spirit of the law?. Water and Environment Journal, 22, 241.

Kingsbury, B. (2007). Global Environmental Governance as Administration: Implications for International Law. In: D. Bodansky, & J. Brunnée (Eds.), International Environmental Law (p. 63). Oxford, Oxford University Press.

Kiss, A. (1976). Peut-on définir le droit de l'homme à l'environnement?. Revue Juridique de L'Environnement, 9.

Kiss, A. (1990). Le droit de la conservation de l'environnement. Revue Universelle Des Droits De L'Homme, 445.

Kiss, A. (1992). An introductory note on a human right to environment. In: E. B. Weiss (Ed.), Environmental Change and International Law (p. 1992). Hong Kong, United Nations University Press.

Kiss, A. (2003). European Environmental Law and the Constitution. Pace Environmental Law Review, 103.

Kiss, A. (2005). De la protection intégrée de l'environnement à l'intégration du droit international de l'environnement. Revue Juridique de l'Environnement, 261.

Kiss, A. (2008). Does the European Charter of Fundamental Rights and Freedoms Guarantee a Right to Environment. In: A. Postiglione (Ed.), The role of the judiciary in the implementation and enforcement of environmental law (p. 161). Brussels, Bruylant.

Kiss, A., & Shelton, D. (1991). International Environmental Law. New York, Transnational Publishers Inc.,U.S.

Kiss, A., & Shelton, D. (1993). Manual of European Environmental Law. Cambridge. Cambridge University Press.

Kiss, A., & Shelton, D. (2000). International Environmental Law. New York, Transnational Publishers Inc.,U.S.

Kiss, A., & Shelton, D. (2007). International Environmental Law. New York, Brill.

Kitchen, L., Milbourne, P., Marsden, T., & Bishop, K. (2002). Forestry and Environmental Democracy: The Problematic Case of the South Wales Valleys. Journal of Environmental Policy and Planning, 4, 139.

Koester, V. (2005). Review of Compliance Under the Aarhus Convention: A Rather Unique Compliance Mechanism. Journal for European Environmental Planning Law, 31.

Kohler-Kock, B. (2004). Synthesis of the Debates. Conference on Participatory democracy: current situation and opportunities provided by the European Constitution. Brussels 8-9 March, text online.

Kohler-Kock, B. (2007). The Organization of Interests and Democracy in the European Union. In: B. Kohler-Kock & B. Rittberger (Eds.), Debating the Democratic Legitimacy of the European Union (p. 255). Plymouth, Rowman & Littlefield.

Kohler-Kock, B. & Rittberger, B. (2007a). Charting Crowded territory: Debating the Democratic Legitimacy of the European Union. In: B. Kohler-Kock & B. Rittberger (Eds.), Debating the Democratic Legitimacy of the European Union (p. 4). Plymouth, Rowman & Littlefield.

Kohler-Kock, B. & Rittberger, B. (2007b). Debating the Democratic Legitimacy of the European Union. Plymouth, Rowman & Littlefield.

Kokott, J. and Rüth, A. (2003). The European Convention and its Draft Treaty Establishing a Constitution for Europe: appropriate answers to the Laeken questions?. Common Market Law Review, 1315.

Koons, J. E. (2008). Earth Jurisprudence: the Moral Value of Nature. Pace Environmental Law Review, 263.

Kostakopoulos, D. (2007). European Union Citizenship: Writing the Future. European Law Journal, 623.

Kostas Bithas (2008). The European Policy on Water Use at the Urban Level in the Context of the Water Framework Directive. Effectiveness, Appropriateness and Efficiency. European Planning Studies, 16.

Kotov, V., & Nikitina, E. (1995). Russia and International Environmental Cooperation. In: H.O. Bergesen, & G. Parmann (Eds.), Green Globe Yearbook of International Cooperation on Environment and Development (p. 17). Oxford, Oxford University Press.

Krämer L. (2003a). Access to Letters of Formal Notice and Reasoned Opinions in Environmental Law Matters. European Environmental Law Review, 197.

Krämer L. (2003b). EC Environmental Law. London, Sweet & Maxwell.

Krämer L. (2004). Access to information in an Open European Society – Directive 2003/4 EC, in EC Environmental Law. Yearbook European Environmental law, 1.

Krämer L. (2006a). Directive 2004/35/EC on Environmental Liability. In: G. Betlem, & E. Brans (Eds.), Environmental Liability in the EU – The 2004 Directive compared with US and Member States Law (p. 29). London, Cameron May.

Krämer L. (2006b). Thirty Years of Environmental Governance in the European Union. In: R. Macrony (Ed.), Reflection on 30 Years of EU Environmental Law (p. 555). Groningen, Europa Law Publishing.

Krämer L. (2007). EC Environmental Law. London, Sweet & Maxwell.

Krämer L. (2008). The Environment and the Ten Commandments. Journal of Environmental Law, 20, 7.

Krämer L. (2009). Environmental Justice in the European Court of Justice. In: J. Ebbesson and Okowa P. (Eds.), Environmental law and Justice in the Context (p. 195). Cambridge, Cambridge University Press.

Kravchenko, S. (2007). The Aarhus Convention and Innovations in Compliance with Multilateral Environmental Agreements. Colorado Journal International Environmental Law and Policy, 18, 1.

Kravchenko, S., Skrylnikov, D., & Bonine, J. E. (2003). Access to justice in cases involving public participation in decision-making. In: S. Stec (Ed.), Handbook on Access to Justice under the Aarhus Convention (p. 27). Szentendre, Unites Nation Publication.

Krisch, N., & Kingsbury, B. (2006). Introduction: Global Governance and Global Administrative Law in the International Legal Order. European Journal International Law, 1.

Krutilla, K., & Reuveny, R. (2002). The Quality of Life in the Dynamics of Economic Development. Environment and Development Economics, 7, 23.

Kumar, R. (2003a). Reasonable reasons in contractualist moral arguments. Ethics, 114.

Kumar, R. (2003b). Who can be wronged?. Philosophy and Public Affairs, 31, 99.

Laavrysen, L. (2008). The European Court of Justice and the Implementation of Environmental Law. In: A. Postiglione (Ed.): The role of the judiciary in the implementation and enforcement of environmental law (p. 25). Brussels, Bruylant.

Lador, Y. (2010). Time for a Universal Declaration on Environmental Rights. Available at www.partnerships4planet.ch/en/environmental-rights.php

Larsson, M.L. (1999). The Law of Environmental Damage – Liability and Reparation. Cambridge, Brill.

Latouche, S. (2004). Survivre au développement. Paris, Mille et une nuits.

Latta, P. A. (2007). Locating Democratic Politics in Ecological Citizenship. Environmental Politics, 16, 377.

Layard, A. (2006). The Europeanisation of Contaminated Land. In: Betlem, G., & Brans, E.H.P. (Eds.), Environmental Liability in the EU – The 2004 Directive compared with US and Member States Law (p. 129). London, Cameron May.

Lee M., & Macrory, R. (2007). Environmental Liability Directive – UK (England and Wales). Paper for the Avosetta Group Meeting 1-2 June. Available at www.avosetta.org/.

Lee, M. (2001). From Private to Public: The Multiple Faces of Environmental Liability. European Public Law, 7, 375.

Lee, M. (2002a). New Generation regulation? The case of end-of-life vehicles. European Environmental Law Review, 114.

Lee, M. (2002b). The Changing Aims of Environmental Liability. Environmental Law and Management, 14, 189.

Lee, M. (2003). Public Participation, Procedure and Democratic Deficit in EC Environmental Law. Yearbook European Environmental law, 195.

Lee, M. (2005). EU Environmental Law: Challenges, Change and decision-Making. Oxford, Hart Publishing.

Lee, M. (2008). The Environmental Implications of the Lisbon Treaty. Environmental Law Review, 10, 131.

Lee, M., & Abbot, C. (2003). The Usual Suspects? Public Participation Under the Aarhus Convention. The Modern Law review, 80.

Leopold, A. (1949a). A Sand Country Almanac and Sketches Here and There. Oxford, Oxford University Press.

Leopold, A. (1949b). The Land Ethic. A sand County Almanac, 204.

Lessig, L. (1995). The Regulation of Social Meaning. University of Chicago Law Review, 62, 943.

Levi, L. (2006). Access to justice at the level of the EU: a practitioner's perspective. In: A. Gourtin (Ed.), The Aarhus Regulation: New Opportunities for Citizens in the EU and Beyond? Report of the ECOSPHERE Forum held in Brussels, 27 October 2006. Brussels, ECOSPHERE.

Li, Q., & Reuveny, R. (2003). Economic Globalisation and Democracy: An Empirical Analysis. British Journal of Political Science, 29.

Lietzmann, K. M., & Gary Vest D. (1999). Environment & Security in an International Context. North Atlantic Treaty organisation, Committee on the Challenges of Modern Society, Report 232.

Lindberg, L.N., & Scheingold, S.A. (1970). Europe's World-Be Policy: Patterns of Change in the European Community. New York, Prentice-Hall.

Lindblom, C. (1965). The Intelligence of Democracy: Decision Making Through Mutual Adjustment. New York, The Free Press.

Linklatera, A. (1998). The transformation of political community. Cambridge, Polity Press.

Locke, J. (1968). An Essay Concerning the true Original, Extent and End of Civil Government. Social Contract, p. 5.

Loibl, G. (2004). The Evolving Regime on Climate Change and Sustainable Development. In: N. Schrijver, & F. Weiss (Eds.), International Law and Sustainable Development, Principles and Practice (p. 97). Leiden, Brill.

Lopatta, H. (2009). Perspectives from the European Commission – Overview and State of Play of the ELD, 3rd CEA Environmental Liability Workshop of 27 April. Available at www.cea.eu/uploads/DocumentsLibrary/documents/1240821878_eld-overview-and-state-of-play-hans-lopatta.pdf.

Lorenz, P. (2007). Press officer Global 2000 – Initiative "1 Million against Nuclear Power. June 26.

Louka, E. (2004). Conflicting Integration – Environmental Law of the European Union. Cambridge, Cambridge University Press.

Low, N., & Gleeson, B. (1998). Justice, society and nature. London, Routledge.

Luque, E. (2005). Researching Environmental Citizenship and its Publics. Environmental Politics, 211.

Macdonald, K. E. (2008). A Right to a healthful Environment – Humans and Habitants: Re-thinking Rights in an Age of Climate Change. European Energy and Environmental Law review, 213.

Macedo, S. (1999). Introduction. In: S. Macedo (Ed.), Deliberative politics: essays on democracy and disagreement (p. 3). New York, OUP USA.

MacGregor, S. (2004). Reading the Earth Charter: Cosmopolitan Environmental Citizenship or Light Green Politics as Usual?. Ethics, Place and Environment, 90.

Macguire, C. R. (2005). The Constitution of the European Union: Content, Prospects, and Comparison to the US Constitution. Tulsa Journal Comparative and International Law, 307.

MacPherson, C. B. (1977). The Life and Times of Liberal Democracy. Oxford, OUP Canada.

Macrony, R. (2006). Reflection on 30 Years of EU Environmental Law. Groningen, Europa Law Publishing.

MacRory R. (1996). Environmental citizenship and the law: Repairing the European Road. Journal of Environmental law, 219.

MacRory R. (1999). Subsidiary and European Environmental Law. Revue des Affaires Européennes, 363.

Magnette, P. (2007). How can one be European? Reflections on the Pillars of European Civic Identity. European Law Journal, 664.

Mahoney, J. (2002). Perpetual restrictions on land the problem of the future. Virginia Law Review, 88.

Majone, G. (1996). Regulating Europe. London, Routledge.

Majone, G. (1998). Europe's Democratic Deficit: the question of standards. European Law Journal, 5.

Majone, G. (2000). The Credibility Crisis of Community Regulation. Journal of Common Market Studies, 2, 273.

Majone, G. (2002). Delegation of Regulatory Powers in a Mixed Policy. European Law Journal, 3, 319.

Makuch, Z. (2004). TBT or not TBT, That is the Question: The international Trade Law Implication of European Community Gm Traceability and Labelling Legislation. European Environmental Law Review, 226.

Maljean-Dubois, S. & Lecucq, O. (2008). Le rôle du juge dans le développement du droit de l'environnement. Bruxelles, Bruylant.

Maljean-Dubois, S. & Mehdi, R. (1999). Les Nations Unies et la protection de l'environnement: la promotion d'un développement durable. Paris, Pedone.

Manin, B. (1997). The principles of representative government. Cambridge, Cambridge University Press.

Mank, B. (1996). Protecting the environment for future generations: a proposal for a republican superagency. New York University Environmental Law Journal, 5, 445.

Markey, B. (2004). The Earth Charter and Ecological Integrity – Some Policy implications. World View, 76.

Marks, S. (2004). The Human Right to Development: Between Rhetoric and Reality. Harvard Human Rights, 17, 137.

Marsden, S., & De Mulder, J. (2005). Strategic Environmental Assessment and Sustainability in Europe – how bring is the Future?. Review of European Community and International Environmental Law, 50.

Marsh, G. P. (1864). Man and Nature. New York, Kessinger Publishing.

Marshall, F. (2006). Two Years in the Life: The Pioneering Aarhus Convention Compliance Committee 2004–2006. International Community Law Review, 8, 123.

Martens, M. (2007). Constitutional Right to a Healthy Environment in Belgium. Review of European Community and International Environmental Law, 287.

Mason, M. (1999). Environmental Democracy. London, Routledge.

Mathiesen, A. (2003). Public Participation in Decision-making and Access to Justice in EC Environmental Law: the Case of Certain Plans and Programmes. European Environmental Law Review, 36.

Maurer, A. (2007). The European parliament between Policy-Making and Control. In: B. Kohler-Kock, & B. Rittberger (Eds.), Debating the Democratic Legitimacy of the European Union (p. 75). Plymouth, Rowman & Littlefield.

May, J. R. (2005-2006). Constituting Fundamental Environmental Rights Worldwide. Pace Environmental Law Review. 113.

McAdams, R. (1997). The Origin, Development, and Regulation of Norms. Michigan Law Review, 96, 338.

McCaffrey, S. C., & Lutz, R.E. (1978). Environmental pollution and individual rights: an international symposium. London, Kluwer.

McCormick, J. (1995). The Global Environment Movement. Wiley, Wiley-Blackwell.

McGillivray, D., & Holder, J. (2001). Locating EC Environmental Law. Yearbook of European Law, 139

Mckenna, C. (1995). Study of Civil Liability Systems for Remedying Environmental Damage, Final Report EU White Paper on Environmental Liability of 31 December. Available at www.ec.europa.eu/environment/legal/liability/pdf/civiliability_ finalreport.pdf, 11-12.

McManus, F. (2005). Noise Pollution and Human Rights. European Human Rights Law Review. 575.

Meadowcroft, J. (1997). Planning, democracy and the challenge of sustainable development. International Political Science Review, 2, 167.

Mega, V. P. (1997). Fragments of an Urban Discourse in Europe: Utopias and Europias. A sustainability-friendly ABC. In: V. P. Mega, & R. Petrella (Eds.), Utopias and Realities of Urban Sustainable Development, New Alliances between Economy, Environment, and Democracy for small and Medium-sized Cities (p. 47). Dublin, European Foundation for the Improvement of Living and Working Conditions.

Mega, V. P. & Petrella R. (1997). Utopias and Realities of Urban Sustainable Development, New Alliances between Economy, Environment, and Democracy for small and Medium-sized Cities. Dublin, European Foundation for the Improvement of Living and Working Conditions.

Melle, U. (1998). Responsibility and the Crisis of Technological Civilization: A Husserlian Meditation on Hans Jonas. Human Studies, 21, 329.

Melo-Escrihuela, C. (2008). Promoting Ecological Citizenship: Rights, Duties and Political Agency. An International E-Journal for Critical Geographies, 113.

Mendez, A. J. (2005). Between Laeken and the Deep Blue Sea. An Assessment of the Draft Constitutional Treaty from a Deliberative-Democratic Standpoint. European Public Law, 105.

Merchant, C. (2005). Radical Ecology: The Search for a Livable World. London, Routledge.

Mersel, Y. (2006). The dissolution of political parties: the problem of internal democracy. International Journal of Constitutional law, 84.

Mestmacker, E. J. (1994). On the Legitimacy of European Law. Rabels Zeitschrift fur Auslandisches und Internationales prvatrecht, p. 622.

Midlarsky, M. (1998). Democracy and the Environment: An Empirical Assessment. Journal of Peace Research, 35, 341.

Miller, C. (1995). Environmental Rights: European Fact or English Fiction?. Journal of Law and Society, 3, 374–389.

Milton, K. & Curtin, D. (2002). Ecological Citizenship. In: F. Engin, & S. Turner (Eds.), Handbook of Citizenship Studies (293). London, SAGE Publications Ltd..

Ming-Zhi Gao A. (2006). SEA Guidance: A Reinterpretation of the SEA Directive and its Application to the Energy Sector. European Environmental Law Review, 129.

Ming-Zhi Gao A. (2008). The Application of the European SEA Directive to Carbon Capture and Storage Activities: The Issue of Screening. European Energy and Environmental law Review, 341.

Minteer, B. A., & B. Pepperman Taylor. Democracy and the Claims of Nature: Critical Perspectives for a New Century. Oxford, Rowman & Littlefield Publishers Inc.

Möllers, C. (2006). European Governance: Meaning and Value of a Concept. Common Market Law Review, 313.

Mollo, M. (2005). Environmental Rights Report: Human Rights and the Environment. (Materials for the 61st Session of the United Nations Commission on Human Rights, Geneva, March 14-April 22,). online: Earthjustice Legal Defense Fund.

Montanari, P. & Corradini, A. (2008). Women and Environment: women's sensibility in Innovative environmental projects. In: A. Postiglione (Ed.), The Protection and Sustainable Development of the Mediterranean Black Sea Ecosystem (p. 863). Bruxelles, Bruylant.

Montaro, R. (2002). L'ambiente e i nuovi istituti della partecipazione. In: A. Crosetti, & F. Fracchia, Procedimento amministrativo e partecipazione. Problemi, prospettive ed esperienze (p. 114). Milano, Giuffré.

Montefiore, H. (1970). Can Man Survive?. London, Fontana.

Montini, M. (2007). Environmental Liability Directive – Report for Italy", Paper for the Avosetta Group Meeting 1-2 June. Available at www.avosetta.org/.

Moreno, A.M., & García Ureta, A. (2007). Implementation of the Environmental Liability Directive in Spain. Paper for the Avosetta Group Meeting 1-2 June. Available at www.avosetta.org/.

Morgera, E. (2005). An Update on the Aarhus Convention and its Continued Global Relevance. Review of European Community and International Environmental Law, 138.

Mori, S. (2004). Institutionalization of NGO involvement in policy functions for global environmental governance. In: N. Kanie, & P.M. Haas (Eds.), Emerging Forces in Environmental Governance (157). New York, United Nations.

Morrison, R. (1995). Ecological Democracy. Boston, South End Press.

Morrow, K. (2004). Public Participation in the Assessment of the Effects of Certain plans and Programmes on the Environment – Directives 2001/42/EC, the UN/ECE Espoo Convention, and the Kiev protocol. Yearbook European Environmental law, 49.

Moss, B. (2008). The Water Framework Directive: Total environment or political compromise?. Science of the total environmental, 3.

Moussis, N. (2009). Guide to European Policies. European Study Service.

Mularoni, A. (2008). The Right to a safe environment in the case-Law of the European Court of human rights. In: Postiglione A. (Ed.), The role of the judiciary in the implementation and enforcement of environmental law (p. 231). Brussels, Bruylant.

Mullerat, B. (2005). European Environmental Liability: One Step Forward. International Company and Commercial Law Review, 16, 263.

Murphi, J., & Cohen, M. (2001). Sustainable consumption: environmental policy and the social sciences. In: M. Cohen, & J. Murphi (Eds.), Exploring sustainable consumption: environmental policy and the social sciences (p. 225). Oxford, Emerald Group Publishing Limited.

Myers, N. (1993). Environmental refugees in a globally warmed world. Bioscience, 43, 752.

Myers, N. (1997). Environmental refugees. Population and Environment, 19, 167.

Myint, T. (2003). Democracy in Global Environmental Governance: Issues, Interests, and Actors in the Mekong and the Rhine. Indiana Journal of Global Legal Studies, 10, 287.

Nadal, C. (2008). Pursuing Substantive Environmental Justice: The Aarhus Convention as a Pillar of Empowerment. Environmental Law Review, 10, 28.

Naddeo, V., Zarra, N., & Belgiorno, V. (2007). Optimisation of sampling frequency for river water quality assessment according to Italian implementation of the EU Water Framework Directive. Environmental Science and policy, 10, 243.

Naess, A. (1956). Democracy, Ideology and Objectivity. Oslo, Published for the Norwegian Research Council for Science and the Humanities by Oslo U.P; Blackwell.

Naess, A. (1990). Ecology, Community, and Lifestyle. Cambridge, Cambridge University Press.

Nagel, T. (1986). The view from nowhere. New York, OUP USA.

Najam, D., Papa, M. & Taiyab, N. (2006). Global Environmental Governance: A Reform Agenda. Winnipeg, International Institute for Sutainable Development (IISD).

Nanda, P., & Pring, G. (2003). International Environmental law for the 21st Century. New York, Transnational Publishers Inc.

Nascimento, A. (2009). Global frameworks for environmental justice: Searching for global responses to global problems, 8th Global Conference „Environmental

Justice and Global Citizenship". 10th – 12th July Oxford. Available at www. inter-disciplinary.net/critical-issues/ethos/environmental-justice-and-global-citizenship /project-archives/8th/.

Nash, H. A. (2009). The Revised Directive on Waste: Resolving Legislative Tension in Waste Management?. Journal of Environmental law, 140.

Nelson, J. (2002). Building Partnerships: Cooperation between the United Nations System and the Private Sector. New York, United Nations.

Neumayer, E. (2002). Do Democracies Exhibit Stronger International Cross Sectional Analysis. Journal of Peace Research, 139.

Newigl, J., & Fritsch O. (2009). Environmental Governance: Participatory, Multi-Level – and Effective?. Environmental Policy and Governance, 19, 197.

Nickel, J. W. (1993). The Human Right to a Safe Environment: Philosophical Perspectives on Its Scope and Justification. Yale Journal International Law, 18, 281.

Nicolet,C. (1978). Le métier de citoyen dans la Rome antique. Paris, Gallimard.

Nino, C. S. (1996). The Constitution of Deliberative Democracy, Oxford, Oxford University Press.

Norton, B. (2000). Biodiversity and Environment Values: In Search of a Universal Earth Ethic. Biodiversity and Conservation, 1029.

Noss, R. F. (1994). Some Principles of Conservation Biology, as They Apply to Environmental Law. Chicago Law Review, 893.

O'Neill, J. (2002). Deliberative Democracy and Environmental Policy. In: B. A. Minteer & B. Pepperman Taylor (Eds.), Democracy and the Claims of Nature (p. 257). Oxford, Rowman & Littlefield Publishers Inc..

Offe, C. & Preuss, U. K. (1991). Democratic institutions and Moral Resources. In: D. Held (Ed.), Political Theory Today (p. 165). Cambridge, Stanford University Press.

Ollennu, N.A. (1962). Principles of Customary Land Law in Ghana. London, Sweet & Maxwell.

Ophuls, W. (1973). Leviathan or Oblivion?. In: H. E. Daly (Ed.), Toward a Steady State Economy (p. 224). San Francisco, W.H.Freeman & Co Ltd..

Ophuls, W. (1977). Ecology and the Politics of Scarcity: A Prologue to a Political Theory of the Steady State. San Francisco, W.H.Freeman & Co Ltd.

Ostrogorski, M. (1992). Democracy and the organisation of political parties. New York, Forgotten Books.

Pace, V. (2001). La comunità religiosa internazionale e l'ambiente. In: A. Postiglione, & A. Pavan,(Eds.) Etica Ambiente Sviluppo (p. 15). Napoli, Edizioni Scientifiche Italiane.

Page, E. (2007). Climate change, justice and future generations. Cheltenham, Edward Elgar Publishing Ltd.

Pagh, P. (2007). Environmental Liability Directive – Danish Report. Paper for the Avosetta Group Meeting 1-2 June. Available at www.avosetta.org/, 1.

Pallemaerts, M. (2002). Introduction: human rights and environmental protection. In: M. Déjeant-Pons, & M. Pallemaerts (Eds.), Human Rights and the environment (p. 11). Strasbourg, Council of Europe.

Pallemaerts, M. (2003a). Human rights and democracy in the face of international environmental issues, available at www.coe.int/T/E/Com/Press/colloquies/2003/Pallemaerts_report.asp.

Pallemaerts, M. (2003b). Is Multilateralism the Future? Sustainable Development or Globalisation as ‚A Comprehensive Vision of the Future of Humanity. Environment, Development and Sustainability, 275.

Pallemaerts, M. (2004). Proceduralising environmental rights: the Aarhus Convention on Access to Information, Public Participation in Decision-Making and Access to Justice in Environmental Matters in a Human Rights Context. In: Human Rights and the Environment Proceedings of a Geneva Environment Network roundtable (p.14). Geneve, Geneva Environment Network.

Pallemaerts, M. (2009). Compliance by the European Community with its obligations on Access to Justice as a Party to the Aarhus Convention. London, IEEP Report (Institute for European Environmental Policy).

Pallemaerts, M., & Moreau, M. (2004). The role of « stakeholders » in international environmental governance. Global Governance, 15.

Panayoto, T. (2000). Economic Growth and the Environment. Cambridge. University of Cambridge Press.

Paper, E. & Redclift, M. (2003). Human Security and the Environment: International Comparisons. London, Edward Elgar Publishing.

Parfit, D. (1987). Reasons and persons. Oxford, Oxford University Press.

Park, J., Conca, K., & Finger M. (2008). The crisis of Global Environmental Governance. London, Routledge.

Parker, K. (1992). State Liability in Damages for Breach of Community Law. Law Quarterly Review, 181.

Parola, G. (2013). Environmental Democracy at Global Level, London, Versita.

Parry, J. (2010). Participatory democracy in the EU. Available at www.federalunion. org.uk/europe/participatorydemocracy.shtml.

Pasques, M. (2006). L'Environnement, un certain droit de l'homme. Administration Publique, 40.

Passmore, J. (1974). Man's Responsibility for Nature: Ecological Problems and Western Traditions. London, Macmillan Pub Co.

Passmore, J. (1975). Attitude to Nature. Nature and Conduct, 251.

Pateman, C. (1970). For a democratic polity to exist it is necessary for a participatory society to exist. In: C. Pateman (Ed.), Participation and Democratic Theory (p. 43). Cambridge, Cambridge University Press.

Pateman, C. (1970). Participation and Democratic Theory. Cambridge, Cambridge University Press.

Pathak, R.S. (1992). The Human Rights System as a Conceptual Framework for Environmental Law. In E. B. Weiss (Ed.), Environmental Change and International Law: New Challenges and Dimensions (p. 205). Hong Kong, United Nations University.

Paul, J. A. (2000). NGOs and Global Policy-Making, Global Policy Forum, June 2000. Available at www.globalpolicy.org/ngos/analysis/anal00.htm.

Payne, R. A. (1995). Freedom and the Environment. Journal of Democracy, 6, 41.

Pedersen, O. W. (2010). European Environmental Human Rights and Environmental Rights: A Long Time Coming?. Available at www.ssrn.com/abstract=1122289.

Peel, J. (2001). Giving the public a voice in the protection of the global environment: avenues for participation by NGOs in dispute resolution at the European Court of Justice and World Trade Organization. Colorado Journal International Law Environmental Law and Policy, 47.

Pennera, C., & SchooSchoo, J. (2004). La Codécision–dix ans d'application. Cahiers de droit européen, 531.

Pennock, J.R. & Chapman, J.W. (1983). Liberal democracy. New York, New York University Press.

Pereira, R. (2007). Environmental Criminal Law in the First Pillar: A positive Development for Environmental Protection in the European Union?. European Environmental Law Review, 254.

Peters, A. (2004). European Democracy After the 2003 Convention. Common Market Law Review, 37.

Petit, B. (2004). La dimension sociale du développement durable: le parent pauvre du concept. Les Petites Affiches, n° 12, 8.

Petit, Y. (2009). Droit et politiques de l'environnent. Paris, La documentation Française.

Petkova, E., & Veit, P. (2000). Environmental Accountability Beyond the Nation – State: The implications of the Aarhus Convention. Washington, World Resources Institute.

Peuhkuri, T. (2006). Knowledge production and citizens' participation in the implementation of the EU Water Framework Directive in Finland, 5th Global Conference: Environmental Justice and Global Citizenship, July 3–6 2006. Oxford, Oxford University Press.

Pevato, P. (1989). A Right to Environment in International Law: Current Status and Future Outlook. Review of European Community and International Law, 8, 309.

Pichler, J. W. (2008). Revolt of the stars. The 'European Citizens' Initiative. In: J. W. Pichler (Ed.), We Change Europe, The European Initiative- Art. 8b(4) Treaty of Lisbon (p. 32). Vienna, BWV Berliner Wissenschafts-Verlag.

Pichler, J. W., & Giese, K. (2008). Proposition for a European Initiative procedure-Incentives of founding Art. 8b (4) Treaty of Lisbon. In: J. W. Pichler (Ed.), We Change Europe, The European Initiative- Art. 8b(4) Treaty of Lisbon (p. 117). Vienna, BWV Berliner Wissenschafts-Verlag.

Pieratti, G., & Prat, J.-L. (2000). Droit, économie, écologie et développement durable: des relations nécessairement complémentaires mais inévitablement ambiguës. Revue Juridique de l'Environnement, 422.

Pildes, R. H., & Niemi, R.G. (1993). Expressive Harms, "Bizarre Districts," and Voting Rights: Evaluating Election-District Appearances After Shaw v. Ren. Michigan Law Review, 92, 438.

Pirotte, C. (2004). A Brief Overview of Directive 2004/35/EC on Environmental Liability. Paper to be presented at the time of the conference organised in Brussels on October 22, by Eagle International on the theme of environmental liability. Available at www.eagle-law.com/papers/brussels2004_en-06.pdf, 1.

Plumwood, V. (1999). Inequality, ecojustice and ecological rationality. Ecotheology, 5/6, 185.

Posner, E. A. (2000). Law and Social Norms: The Case of Tax Compliance. Virginia Law Review, 86, 1781.

Postiglione, A. (2008). The role of the judiciary in the implementation and enforcement of environmental law. Brussels, Bruylant.

Poujade, B. (2007). La Protection du droit à l'environnement par le juge administratif: l'exemple du contrôle juridictionnel des grands équipements public. In. A. Chamboredon (Ed.), Du Droit de l'Environnement au droit à l'Environnement, A la recherche d'un juste milieu (p.123). Paris, L'Harmattan.

Powell, F.M. (1995). Environmental Protection in International Trade Agreements: The Role of Public Participation in the Aftermath of NAFTA. Colorado Journal International Law Environmental Law and Policy, 109.

Prechal, S., & Hancher, L. (2002). Individual Environmental Rights: Conceptual Pollution in EU Environmental Law. Yearbook European Environmental Law, 89.

Prieur, M. (1993). Démocratie et droit de l'environnement et du développement. Revue Juridique de l'Environnement, 23.

Prieur, M. (2005). Les nouveaux droits. Actualité Juridique Droit Administratif, 1157.

Ramlogan, R. (1996). Environmental refugees. Review Environmental Conservation, 23, 81.

Raustiala, K. (1997). The Participatory Revolution in International Environmental Law. Harvard Journal International Law Environmental Law and Policy, 537.

Rawls, J. (1971). A theory of justice. Oxford, Harvard University Press.

Rawls, J. (1993). Political liberalism. New York, Columbia University Press.

Razaque, J. (2002). Background Paper Number 4: Human Rights and the Environment: The National Experience of South Asia and Africa, 2002. Available at www.unhchr.ch/environment/bp4.html.

Redgwell, C. (2007). Access to Environmental Justice. In: F. Francioni (Ed.), Access to Justice as a Human Right (p. 153). Oxford, Oxford University Press.

Reich, N. (1997). A European Constitution for Citizens: reflections on the rethinking of Union and Community law. European Law Journal, 155.

Reiman, J. (2007). Being fair to future people: the non-identity problem in the original position. Philosophy and Public Affairs, 35, 69.

Reiners, K. (2009). The Environmental Liability Directive of 2004, Traditional Administrative Mechanisms with a New Name, LL.M. Thesis. Reykjavik.

Renn, O. (1995). Fairness and competence in citizen participation: Evaluation models for environmental discourse, Dordrecht, Springer.

Rensi, G. (1995). La Democrazia Diretta. Milano, Adelphi.

Rest, A. (2008). Access to justice in international environmental law for individuals an NGOs: Efficacious enforcement by the Permanent Court of Arbitration. In: A.

Postiglione (Ed.), The role of the judiciary in the implementation and enforcement of environmental law (p. 56). Bruxelles, Bruylant.

Reuveny, R. (2003). Economic Growth, Environmental Scarcity and Conflict. Global Environmental Politics, 83.

Richardson, B. J. & Wood, S. (2006). Environmental Law for Sustainability. Oxford, Hart Publishing.

Risse, T. (2002). Nationalism and Collective Identities: Europe versus the Nation-State. In: P. Heywood, E. Jones, & M. Rhodes (Eds.), Developments in Western European Politics, Basingstoke, Palgrave.

Rittberger, B. (2007). Constructing Parliamentary Democracy in the European Union: How Did It Happen?. In: B. Kohler-Kock, & B. Rittberger, (Eds.), Debating the Democratic Legitimacy of the European Union (p. 111). Plymouth, Rowman & Littlefield.

Roberts, A. (2001). Structural Pluralism and the Right to Information. University of Toronto Law Journal, 243.

Roberts, A. (2002). Multilateral Institutions and the Right to Information – Experience in the European Union. European Public Law, 8, 255.

Robinson, N. A. (1972). Problems of definition and scope. In: J. L. Hargrone, (Ed.), Law Institutions and global environment (p. 44). New York, Kluwer Academic Publishers.

Robinson, N. A. (2003). Enforcing Environmental Norms: Diplomatic and Judicial Approaches. Hastings International and Comparative Law Review, 387.

Rocheleau, J. (1999). Democracy and Ecological Soundness. Ethics and the Environmental, 4, 38.

Rodenhoff, V. (2002). The Aarhus Convention and its Implications for the 'Institutions' of the European Community. Review of European Community and International Environmental Law, 11, 343.

Rodgers, W.H. (1977). Environmental Law. London, West Publishing Co.

Rodriguez, X. (2006). The Water Framework directive and the polluter pay principle, LLM Thesis 2006, University of Iceland.

Rodriquez, S. (2008). Representative democracy Vs. Participatory democracy in the EU and the US. In: R. Caranta (Ed.), Interest representation in administrative proceeding (p. 24). Napoli, Jovene.

Roller, G. (2006). Liability. In: R. Macrory (Ed.), Reflection on 30 Years of EU Environmental Law – A High Level of Protection (p. 127). Groningen, Europa Law Publishing.

Rolson, H. (1988). Environmental Ethics: Duties to and Values in the Natural World. Philadelphia, 143.

Rolston, H. (1993). Rights and Responsibilities on the Home Planet. Yale Journal International Law, 251.

Romi, R., Bossis, G., & Rousseau, S. (2005). Droit international et européen de l'environnement, Paris, Montchrestien.

Rose-Ackerman, S., & Halpaap, A. A. (2001). The Aarhus Convention and the Politics of Process: The Political Economy of Procedural Environmental Rights, Draft paper for The Law and Economics of Environmental Policy: A Symposium, Faculty of Laws, University College London, September 5-7, 2001. Available at www.cserge.ucl.ac.uk/Ackerman_and_Halpaap.pdf.

Rosenne, S. (1986). Exploitation and Protection of the Exclusive Economic Zone and the Continental Shelf. Yacht Brokers Association of America, 63.

Ross, M. (1993). Beyond Francovich. Modern Law Review, 56, 55.

Roston, H. (1993). Rights and Responsibilities on the Home Planet. Yale Journal International Law, 251.

Rousseau, J. J. (1913). The Social Contract. Oxford, Oxford Paperbacks.

Rousseau, J. J. (1992). Du contrat social. Paris, Bréal.

Roy, W.W. (2006). The Environmental Information regulation 2004: Limiting exceptions, Widening Definitions and Increasing access to Information. Environmental Law Review, 8, 51.

Ruster, B., & Simma, B. (1990). International Protection of the Environment. New York, Oceana Pubns.

Ryall, A. (2007). EIA and Public participation: Determine the limits of Members State Discretion, Case law analysis, Case C-216/05, Commission v. Ireland, judgement of 9 November 2006. Journal of Environmental Law, 247.

Sáiz, A.V. (2005). Globalisation, Cosmopolitanism and Ecological Citizenship. Environmental Politics, 14(2), 163.

Salter, J. R. (1995). European Environmental Law. London, Graham & Trotman/ Martinus Nijhoff.

Sanchez, R. (1993). Public Participation and the IBWC: Challenges and Options. Natural Resources Journal, 283.

Sands, P. (1991). The Role of Non-Governmental Organisations in Enforcing International Environmental Law. In: W. E. Butler (Ed.), Control Over Compliance With International Law. London, Kluwer Academic Publishers.

Sands, P. (1995). Principle of International Environmental Law. Cambridge, Cambridge University Press.

Sands, P. (1999). Sustainable Development: Treaty, Custom, and the Cross-Fertilisation of International Law. In: A. Boyle, & D. Freestone (Eds.), International Law and Sustainable Development (p. 43). Oxford, Brill.

Sands, P. (2004). Human rights and the environment. In M. Pallermarts, Human Rights and the Environment Proceedings of a Geneva Environment Network roundtable. Geneva, Geneva Environment Network.

Savoia, R. (2003). Administrative, judicial and other means of access to justice. In: S. Stec (Ed.), Handbook on Access to Justice under the Aarhus Convention (p. 39). Szentendre, Unites Nation Publication.

Saward, M. (1998). Green state/democratic state. Contemporary Politics, 4, 345.

Saward, M. (2001). Reconstructing democracy: Current thinking and new directions. Government and Opposition, 36, 559.

Sax, J. L. (1972). Defending the Environment, A Handbook for Citizen Action. New York, Vintage Books.

Scanlon, T.M. (1999). What we owe to each other. Cambridge, Belknap Pr.

Schachter, O. (1997). The Decline of the Nation-State and its Implications for International Law. In: J. I. Charney, D. K. Anton, & M. E. O'Connell (Eds.), Politics, Values And Functions: International Law In The 21st Century: Essays In Honor Of Professor Louis (p. 26). Henkin, Martinus Nijhoff Publishers.

Schall, C. (2008). Public Interest Litigation Concerning Environmental Matters before Human Rights Courts: A Promising Future Concept?. Journal of Environmental Law, 417.

Schechter, M.G. (2001). Making meaningful UN-sponsored world conferences of the 1990s: NGOs to the rescue?. In: M.G. Schechter (Ed.), United Nations-Sponsored World Conferences: Focus on Impact and Follow-up (p. 184). Tokyo, United Nations.

Schlosberg, D., Shulman, S.,& Zavetoski, S. (2006). Virtual environmental citizenship: Web-based public participation in rule making in the United States. In: A. Dobson, & D. Bell (Eds.), Environmental Citizenship (p. 207). Cambridge, Cambridge University Press.

Schmalz-Bruns, R. (2002). Normative Desirability of Participatory Democracy. In: H. Heinelt, & A. Opladen (Eds.), Participatory Governance in Multi-Level Context: Concept and Experience (p. 59). Leverkusen, Leske + Budrich.

Schmalz-Bruns, R. (2007). The Euro-polity in Perspective: Some Normative Lessons from Deliberative Democracy, In: B. Kohler-Kock & B. Rittberger (Eds.), Debating the Democratic Legitimacy of the European Union (p. 281). Plymouth, Rowman & Littlefield.

Schmitt, C. (1999). Parlamentarismo e democrazia, Lungro, Marco.

Schmitter, P. C., & Lehmbruch G. (1979). Trends Toward Corporatist Intermediation. Sage, SAGE Publications Ltd.

Schout, A., & Jordan, A. (2005). Coordinated European Governance: self-organizing or centrally steered?. Public Administration, 201.

Schram, F. (2005). Public Access to EU Environmental documents – Regulation (EC no. 1049/2001). Yearbook European Environmental Law, 52.

Schrijve, N. (2008). The evolution of sustainable development in international law: inception, meaning and status. Boston, The Hague Academy of International Law.

Schrijver, N. (1995). Sovereignty Over Natural Resources – Balancing Rights and Duties in an Independent World. Groningen, Europa Law Publishing.

Schrijver, N. & Weiss, F. (2004). International Law and Sustainable Development, Principles and Practice. Leiden, Brill.

Schultz, C. B., & Crockett, T.R. (1990). Economic Development, Democratisation, and Environmental Protection in Eastern Europe. Boston College Environmental Affairs Law Review, 18, 53.

Schwarze, J. (2006). The Treaty establishing a Constitution for Europe – Some general Reflections on its Character and its Chances of Realisation. European Public Law, 199.

Sedjari, I A. (2008). Droits de l'homme et développement durable. Paris, L'Harmattan.

Sen, A. (1994). Liberty and Poverty: Political Rights and Economics. New Republic, 31.

Sensi S. (2004). Human Rights and the Environment: The Perspective of the Human Rights Bodies. In UN Environment Programme, Human Rights and the Environment, Proceedings of a Geneva Environmental Network Roundtable (UNEP, 2004). Available at www.environmenthouse.ch/docspublications/ reportsRoundtables/Human%20/Rights%20Env%20Report.pdf>.

Seyfang, G. (2005). Shopping for Sustainability: Can Sustainable Consumption Promote Ecological Citizenship?. Environmental Politics, 14, 290.

Shama, S. (1995). Landscape and memory. Fontana, Harper Perennial.

Sharander-Frechette, K. (2002). Environmental justice: creating equality, reclaiming democracy. Oxford, OUP USA.

Shaw, J. (2000). Law of the European Union. Basingstoke, MacMillan.

Sheate, W. R. (2003). The EC Directive on Strategic Environmental Assessment: A Much-Needed Boost for Environmental Integration. European Environmental Law Review, 334.

Shelton, D. (1991). Human Rights, Environmental Rights and the Right to Environment. Stanford Journal of International Law, 28, 103.

Shelton, D. (1992). What happened in Rio to human rights?. Yearbook International Environmental Law, 82.

Shelton, D. (1993). Environmental Rights in the European Community. Hastings International and Comparative Law Review, 557.

Shelton, D. (2005) Environmental Rights. In: P. Alston (Ed.), People's Rights (p. 185). Oxford, OUP.

Shelton, D. (2007). Human rights and the environment: what specific environmental rights have been recognised?. Denver Journal of International Law and Policy, 35, 129.

Shelton, D., & Memon, A. (2002). Adopting Sustainability as an Overarching Environmental Policy: A review of Section 5 of the RMA. Resource Management Journal, March, 8.

Sieghart, P. (1985). The Lawful Rights of Mankind: An introduction to the International Legal Code of Human Rights. Oxford, Oxford University Press.

Sjafjell, B. (2009). Towards a Sustainable European Company Law. A Normative Analysis of the Objectives of EU Law, with the Takeover Directive as a Test Case. New York, Kluwer Law International.

Sjafjell, B. (2010). The Very Basis of Our Existence Labour and the Neglected Environmental Dimension of Sustainable Development. Available at www.ssrn.com/abstract=1517393.

Skagen, K. (2005). Giving a voice to posterity – deliberative democracy and representation of future people. Journal of Agricultural and Environmental Ethics, 18, 429.

Skinner, J.B. (1988). Earth Resources. New Jersey, Prentice Hall.

Smismans, S. (2003). European Civil Society: Shaped by Discourses and Institutional Interests. European Law Journal, 9, 473.

Smismans, S. (2004). The Constitutional Labelling of "the democratic life of the EU": representative and participatory democracy. In: A. Follesdal, & L. Dobson (Eds.), Political Theory and the European Constitution (p. 122). Cambridge, Cambridge University Press.

Smismans, S. (2009). Should participatory democracy become the normative model for EU governance?. Available at www.re-public.gr/en/?p=481.

Smith, G. (2002). The European Union's Commitment to Sustainable Development: Is the Commitment Symbolic or Substantive in the Context of Transport Policy. Colombia Journal International Environmental Law and Policy, 241.

Smith, G. (2003). Deliberative democracy and the environment. London, Routledge.

Smith, G. (2005). Green Citizenship and the Social Economy. Environmental Politics, 14, 273.

Smith, G., & Wales, C. (2000). Citizens' juries and deliberative democracy. Political Studies, 1, 51.

Smith, M.J. (1998). Ecologisme–Towards Ecological Citizenship. London, Open University Press.

Snyder, F. (2004). Editorial: Is the European Constitution Dead?. European Law Journal, 255.

Sohn, L. (1973). The Stockholm Declaration on the Human Environment. Harvard International Law Journal, 455.

Solum, L. (2001). To our children's children: The problem of intergenerational ethics. Loyola of Los Angeles law Review, 35.

Somsen, H. (2002). Editor's Preface. Yearbook of European Environmental Law, 1.

Soveroski, M. (2007). Environment Rights versus Environmental Wrongs: Forum over Substance?. Review of European Community and International Environmental Law, 16, 261.

Spaulding, M. J. (1995). Transparency of Environmental Regulation and Public Participation in the Resolution of International Environmental Disputes. Santa Clara Law Review, 1127.

Speeckaert, G. P. (1956). Les fonctions, les méthodes et la valeur du travail international non gouvernemental. In: L'avenir des organisations non gouvernementales (p. 39). Brussels, Union des Associations internationales.

Speth, J.G. (2009). The Bridge at the Edge of the World: Capitalism, the Environment, and Crossing from Crisis to Sustainability. London, Yale University Press.

Spyke, N.P. (1999). Public Participation in Environmental Decision-making at the New Millennium: Structuring New spheres of Public Influence. Boston College Environmental Affairs Law Review, 26, 263.

Stange, T., & Baylet, A. (2008). Le développement durable à la croisée de l'économie, de la société et de l'environnement. Paris, La Documentation Française.

Staveley, E.S. (1972). Greek and Roman Voting and Elections. New York, Cornell Univ Pr.

Stec, S. (2003). Handbook on Access to Justice under the Aarhus Convention. Szentendre, Unites Nation Publication.

Stec, S. & Casey-Lefkowitz S. (2000). The Aarhus Convention: An Implementation Guide. New York and Geneva, United Nations.

Steele, J. (2001). Participation and Deliberation in Environmental Law: Exploring a problem-solving approach. Oxford Journal of Legal Studies, 21, 415.

Stein, T. (1998). The Ecological Crisis – A Challenge to Constitutional Democracy? Does the Constitutional and Democratic System Work?. Constellations, 4, 420.

Stephenson, W. (1978). Concourse theory of communication. Communication, 3, 21.

Stoczkiewicz, M. (2009). The polluter pay principle and State aid for environmental protection. Journal of European Environmental and Planning Law, 171.

Stone, C. (1972). Should threes have Standing? Towards Legal Rights for Natural Objects. S. Cal. Law Review, 450.

Stone, C. (1988). The Environment in Moral Thought. Tennessee Law Review, 56.

Stone, C. (2007). Ethics and International Environmental Law. In: D. Bodansky, & J. Brunnée (Eds.), International Environmental Law (p. 291). Oxford, Oxford University Press.

Sudre,F. (2001). Droit International et Européen des Droits de L'Homme. Paris, Pr. Univ. de France.

Suhrke, A. (1994). Environmental degradation and population flows. Journal of International Affairs, 47, 473.

Sverker, C. J. (2009). In search of the ecological citizen. Environmental Politics, 18, 18.

Takacs, D. (2010). Forest Carbon Offsets and International Law: A Deep Equity Legal Analysis. Georgetown International Environmental Law Review, 521.

Tan Yan, Wang Yi Qian, (2004). Environmental Migration and Sustainable Development in the Upper Reaches of the Yangtze River. Population and Environment, 25, 613.

Taylor, M. (1982). Community, Anarchy and Liberty. Cambridge, Cambridge University Press.

Taylor, P. (1998). From Environmental to Ecological Human rights. A new Dynamic in International Law. Geo International Environmental Law Review, 10, 309.

Taylor, P. (2009). Ecological Integrity and Human Rights. In: L. Westra, K. Bosselmann, & R. Westra (Eds.), Reconciling Human Existence with Ecological Integrity (p. 89). London, Earthscan.

Taylor, P. W. (1986). Respect for nature: a theory of environmental ethics . Princeton, Princeton University Press.

Teubner, G., & Other (1994). Environmental Law and Ecological Responsibility: The concept and Practice of Ecological Self-Organisation, Chichester, Wiley-Blackwell.

Thieffry, P. (2008). Droit de l'environnement de l'Union Européenne. Bruxelles, Bruylant.

Thomas, D.S.G., & Twyman, C. (2005). Equity and justice in climate change adaptation amongst natural-resource-dependent societies. Global Environmental Change, 15, 115.

Thompson, B. (2004). The trouble with time: Influencing the Conservation Choices of Future Generations. Natural Resources Journal, 44.

Thompson, D. (2005). Democracy in time: popular sovereignty and temporal representation. Constellations, 12, 245.

Thornton, J., & Beckwith, S. (2004). Environmental Law. London, Sweet & Maxwell.

Thorvaldsson, Ó. B. (2002). Direct Effect, Supremacy and State Liability – A Comparison between EC Law and the EEA Agreement. Master thesis, Faculty of Law. Lund University.

Thoyer, S. & Martimort-Asso, B. (2005). Participation fort Sustainability in Trade. London, Ashgate.

Tizzano, A. (2003). Prime note sul progetto di Costituzione Europea. Diritto Unione Europea, 249.

Torgerson, D. (2008). Constituting Green Democracy: A political project. The Good Society, 17, 18.

Torras, M., & Boyce J. K. (1998). Income, Inequality, and Pollution: A Reassessment of the Environmental Kuznets Curve. Ecological Economy, 147.

Toth, A. G. (1992). The Principle of Subsidiary in the Maastricht Treaty. Common Market Law Review, 239.

Touzet, A. (2008). Droit et développement durable. Revue Droit Public, 453.

Tribe, L. H. (1974). Ways To Think About Plastic Trees: New Foundations for Environmental Law. The Yale Law Journal, 1315.

Tromans, S. (2001). Environmental Court Project: Final Report. Journal of Environment Law, 13, 423.

Tuesen, J., & Simonsen, J. (2000). Compliance with the Aarhus Convention. Environmental Policy and Law, 299.

Tully, J. (2002). The freedom of the moderns in comparison to their ideas of constitutional democracy. Modern Law Review, 65, 204.

Turner, S. J. (2008). A Substantive Environmental Right. Austin. Kluwer Law International.

Uerpmann-Wittzack, R. (2006). The Constitutional Role of Multilateral Treaty Systems. In: A. Von Bogdandy (Ed.), Principles of European Constitutional Law, Modern Studies of European Law. Oxford, Hart.

UNEP, (1991). Caring for the Earth: A Strategy for Sustainable Living, Gland, (Switzerland), IUCN, UNEP & WWF.

Valdivielso, J. (2005). Social Citizenship and the Environment. Environmental Politics, 14, 239.

Valvo, A. L. (2004). Governance e democrazia nell´Unione europea. Rivista della cooperazione giuridica internazionale, 18, 27.

Van Lang, A. (2007). La protection constitutionnelle du droit à l'environnement. In: A. Chamboredon (Ed.), Du Droit de l'Environnement au droit à l'Environnement, A la recherche d'un juste milieu (p. 123). Paris, L'Harmattan.

Van Zeben, J. (2010). The Untapped Potential of Horizontal Private Enforcement Within European Environmental Law. Georgetown International Environmental Law Review, 241.

Vedder, H. (2008). European Environmental Law. Groningen, Europa Law Publishing.

Veinla, H. (2007). Implementation of Environmental Liability Directive in Estonia. Paper for the Avosetta Group Meeting 1-2 June. Available at www.avosetta.org/

Verschuuren, J. (2004). Public Participation regarding the Elaboration and Approval of Projects in the EU after the Aarhus Convention. Yearbook European Environmental law, 35.

Vidalenc, G. (2008). Le développement durable: regards sur un droit en construction, et sur ses bâtisseurs. Les Petites Affiches, 22 avril, n° 81, 8.

Villani, U. (2005). Principi democratici e diritti fondamentali nella Costituzione europea, La comunità internazionale. La Comunità internazionale, 643.

Visalenc, G. (2008). Le développement durable: regards sur un droit en construction, et sur ses bâtisseurs. Les Petites Affiches, 22 avril, n° 81, 8.

Vitale, D. (2006). Between deliberative and participatory democracy: A contribution on Habermas. Philosophy Social Criticism, 32, 748.

Von Bogdandy, A. (2005). The Prospect of a European Republic: what European Citizens are voting on. Common Market Law Review, 913.

Von Unger, M. (2007). Access to Eu Documents: An End at Last to the Authorship Rule?. Journal for European Environmental and Planning Law, 440.

Vonkeman, G. (1997). Alliances between Economy, Ecology and Democracy: Integration or Separation? Proposals and Analysis on the Relations between the Three Spheres; Repercussions for the Small and Medium-Sized Cities of Europe. In: V. P. Mega & R. Petrella (Eds.), Utopias and Realities of Urban Sustainable Development, New Alliances between Economy, Environment, and Democracy for small and Medium-sized Cities (p. 319). Dublin, European Foundation for the Improvement of Living and Working Conditions.

Waak, P. (1995). Shaping a Sustainable Planet: The Role of Nongovernmental Organisations. Colorado Journal International Law Environmental Law and Policy, 345.

Waite, A. (2007). Sunlight through the trees, a perspective on environmental rights and human rights. In: Mélanges en l'Honneur de Michel Prieur, Pour un droit commun de l'environnement (p. 393). Paris, Dalloz.

Wälde, T. (2004). Natural Resources and Sustainable Development: From "Good Intentions" of "Good Consequences". In: N. Schrijner & F. Weiss (Eds.), International Law and Sustainable Development, Principles and Practice (p. 119). Leiden, Brill.

Walker, K.J. (1988). The Environmental Crisis: A Critique of Neo-Hobbesian Responses. Polity, 21, 67.

Wang, X., & Wart, M.W. (2007). When Public Participation in Administration Leads to Trust: An empirical Assessment of Managers' Perception. Public Administration Review, 265.

Ward, A. (2000). Judicial Review of Environmental Misconduct in the European Community: problems, prospects and strategies. Yearbook of European Environmental Law, 137.

Warren, M. (1995). The self in Discursive Democracy. In: S. While (Ed.), The Cambridge Companion to Habermas (p. 181). Cambridge, Cambridge University Press.

Wates, J. (2005a). The Aarhus Convention: a Driving Force for Environmental Democracy. Journal of European Environmental Planning Law, 2.

Wates, J. (2005b). The Aarhus Convention: a new instrument Promoting Environmental Democracy. In: M.-C Cordonier Segger, & C.G. Weeramantry (Eds.), Sustainable Justice: Reconciling Economic, Social and Environmental Law (p. 393). London, Martinus Nijhoff.

Webler, T., & Renn, O. (1995). A brief primer on participation: philosophy and practice. Fairness and Competence in Citizen Participation: Evaluating Models for Environmental Discourse. Netherlands, Springer.

Weiler, J. (1997). Legitimacy and Democracy of Union Governance. In: G. Edwards, & A. Pijpers (Eds.), The Politics of European Treaty Reform (p. 249). London, Continuum International Publishing Group Ltd.

Weinburg, R. (2010). Review: future people: a moderate consequentialist account of our obligations to future generations. Notre Dame Philosophical Reviews Notre Dame University. Available at www.ndpr.nd.edu/review.cfm?id1/48165.

Weiss, E. B. (1984). Conservation and Equity between Generations. Contemporary Issues in International Law, 119.

Weiss, E. B. (1989). In Fairness to Future Generation: international Law, common patrimony and Intergeneration Equity. Tokyo, Transnational Publishers Inc.

Weiss, E. B. (1990). Our rights and obligations to future generations for the environment. American Journal of International Law, 198.

Weiss, E. B. (1992). Environmental Change and International Law. Hong Kong, United Nations University Press.

Weiss, E. B. (1992). Intergenerational equity: A legal framework for global environmental change. In: E. B. Weiss (Ed.), Environmental Change and International Law. Hong Kong, United Nations University.

Weiss, E. B. (2000). The Rise or the Fall of International Law?. Fordham Law Review, 345.

Wenk, M.S. (2005). The European Union's Eco-Management and Audit Scheme (EMAS), Dordrecht, Springer.

Wenneras, P. (2007). The Enforcement of EC Environmental law. Oxford, OUP.

Wessels, W., & Diedrichs, U. (1997). A New Kind of Legitimacy for a New Kind of Parliament–the Evolution of the European Parliament. Available at www.eiop. or.at, 1, 6.

Westerlund, E. (2008). A Sustainable Criminal Law–Criminal law for Sustainability. In: H. C. Bugge, & C. Voigt (Eds.), Sustainable Development in International and National Law (p. 503). Groningen, Europa Law Publishing.

Westing, A.H. (1992). Environmental refugees: A growing category of displaced persons. Environmental Conservation, 19, 20.

Westing, A.H. (1994). Population, desertification and migration. Environmental Conservation, 21, 110.

Westra, L. (2006). Environmental Justice and the Rights of Unborn and Future Generations. London, Routledge.

Westra, L. (2004). Ecoviolence and the Law, Supranational Normative Foundations of Ecocrime. New York, Transnational Publishers Inc.

Westra, L., Bosselmann, K. & Westra, R. (2009). Reconciling Human Existence with Ecological Integrity. London, Earthscan.

Wetterstein, P. (1997). A Proprietary or Possessory Interest: A Condition Sine Qua Non for Claiming Damages for Environmental Impairment. In: P Wetterstein (Ed.), Harm to the Environment: The Right to Compensation and the Assessment of Damages (p. 29). Oxford, Clarendon Press.

WHAT (2000). Governance for a sustainable future, Report by the World Humanity Action Trust, London, World Humanity Action Trust.

Whelan, F.G. (1983). Democratic theory and the boundary problem. In: J.R. Pennock, & J.W.Chapman (Eds.), Liberal democracy (p.13). New York, New York University Press.

Wilkinson, D. (2002). Environment and Law. London, Routledge.

Williams, A. (2008). Turning the Tide: Recognising Climate Change Refugees in International Law. Law and Policy, 30, 502.

Williams, M. (2000). The uneasy alliance of group representation and deliberative democracy. In: W. Kymlicka, & W. Norman (Eds.), Citizenship in diverse societies (p. 124). Oxford, OUP.

Wind, M. (2009). The Commission White Paper. Bridging the gap between the governed and the governing?. Available at www.jeanmonnetprogram.org.

Winter, G., Jans, J.H., Macrory, R., & Krämer, L. (2008). Weighing up the Liability Directive. Journal of Environmental Law, 20, 163.

Wissenburg, M. (2004). Fragmented citizenship in a global environment. In: J. Barry, B. Baxter, & R. Dunphy (Eds.), Europe, Globalisation and Sustainable Development (p. 73). London, Routledge.

Wolf, J. (2007). The ecological citizen and climate change. In: Prepared for the workshop "Democracy on the day after tomorrow" at the ECPR Joint Sessions. Helsinki.

Wolfe, M. W. (1897). The shadows of Future Generations. Duke Law Journal.

Wonga, S., & Sharpb, L. (2009). Making power explicit in sustainable water innovation: re-linking subjectivity, institution and structure through environmental citizenship. Environmental Politics, 18, 37.

Wood, M. C. (2009). Advancing the Sovereign Trust of Government of Safeguard the Environment for Present and Future Generations (Part I): Ecological Realism and the Need for a Paradigm Shift. Environmental Law, 43.

Wood, P. (2000a). Intergenerational justice and curtailments on the discretionary powers of Governments. Environmental Ethics, 411.

Wood, P. (2000b). Biodiversity and democracy: rethinking society and nature. Vancouver, University of British Columbia Press.

Woodward, J. (1986). The non identity problem. Ethics, 804.

World Commission On Environment and Development (1987). Our Common Future [Bruntland Report]. Oxford, Oxford Paperbacks.

Young, I.M. (1990). Justice and the politics of difference. Princeton, Princeton University Press.

Young, I.M. (1999). Justice, inclusion and deliberative democracy. In: S. Macedo (Ed.), Deliberative politics: essays on democracy and disagreement (p. 151). New York, OUP USA.

Young, I.M. (2000). Inclusion and democracy. Oxford,Oxford University Press.

Yourcenar, M. (1980). Les Yeux Ouverts. Paris, le Livre de Paris.

Zaccai, E. (2009). Développement durable: l'idéologie du XXIe siècle. Les Grands Dossiers des Sciences Humaines, n°14.

Zampetti, P.L. (1995). La democrazia partecipativa e il rinnovamento delle istituzioni. Genova, Edizioni Culturali Internazionali Genova.

Ziehm, C. (2005). Legal Standing for NGOs in Environmental Matters under the Aarhus Convention ad under Community and National law. Journal for European Environmental Planning Law, 287.

2. International Sources

2.1. Treaties

Cartagena Protocol on Biosafety to the Convention on Biological Diversity, Jan. 29, 2000, 39 I.L.M. 1027;

Convention for the Protection of the Marine Environment of the North-East Atlantic, Sept. 22, 1992, 32 I.L.M. 1069

Convention on Access to Information, Public Participation in Decision- Making and Access to Justice in Environmental Matters, Participants, June 25, 1998, 38 I.L.M. 517 (1999), entered into force Oct. 30, 2001.

Convention on Biological Diversity of 5 June 1992. 1760 UNTS, p. 79

Convention on Civil Liability for Damage Resulting from Activities Dangerous to the Environment, June 21, 1993, 32 I.L.M. 1228;

Convention on Cooperation and Sustainable Use of the Danube River, June 29, 1994, available at www.icpdr.org/ icpdr-pages/drpc.htm

Convention on Cooperation and Sustainable Use of the Danube River, June 29, 1994, available at www.icpdr.org/ icpdr-pages/drpc.htm

Convention on International Trade in Endangered Species of Wild Fauna and Flora, 3 March 1973 available at www.cites.org/

Convention on Long-range Transboundary Air Pollution, 13 November 1979. 18 ILM 1979, p. 1442

Convention on the Conservation of European Wildlife and Natural Habitats, 19 September 1979, ETS n. 104, UKTS n. 56 (1982)

Convention on the Protection and Use of Transboundary Watercourses and International Lakes, Mar. 17, 1992, 31 I.L.M. 1312

Convention on the Rights of the Child, 20 November 1989, 1577 UNTS 3

Convention on the Transboundary Effects of Industrial Accidents, Article 9, Mar. 17, 1982, 2105 U.N.T.S. 460

Convention to Combat Desertification in Those Countries Experiencing Serious Drought and/or Desertification, June 17, 1994, 33 I.L.M. 1328

Covenant on Civil and Political Rights, December 16, 1966, 999 UNTS, p. 171

Earth Charter, Mar. 2000, available at www.earthcharter.org/files/charter/charter.pdf

Energy Charter Treaty, Dec. 17, 1994; 33 I.L.M. 360

Framework Convention on Climate Change, May 9, 1992, 1771 UNTS 107, UN Doc. A/AC.237/18 (Part II)/Add.1

International Treaty on Plant Genetic Resources for Food and Agriculture, Nov. 3, 2001, available at ftp://ftp.fao.org/ag/cgrfa/it/ITPGRe.pdf

Kyoto Protocol to the United Nations Framework Convention on Climate Change, Dec. 11, 1997, 37 I.L.M. 22

Montreal Protocol on Substances that Deplete the Ozone Layer September 16, 1987 BGBl 1988 II, 1015; 26 ILM 1550 [1987]

North American Agreement on Environmental Cooperation, Sept. 14, 1993, 32 I.L.M. 1480

Protocol Concerning Specially Protected Areas and Biological Diversity in the Mediterranean, June 10, 1995, 1999 O.J. (L 322) 3

Protocol on Water and Health to the 1992 Convention on the Protection and Use of Transboundary Watercourses and International Lakes, June 17, 1999, available at www.euro.who.int/ Document/Pehehp/ ProtocolWater.pdf

Protocol to the 1979 Convention on Long-Range Transboundary Air Pollution Concerning the Control of Emissions of Volatile Organic Compounds or Their Transboundary Fluxes, Nov. 18, 1991, 31 I.L.M 568

PRTR Protocol May 2003, in Kiev, Ukraine available at www.unece.org/env/pp/ prtr.htm

Rotterdam Convention on the Prior Informed Consent Procedure for Certain Hazardous Chemicals and Pesticides in International Trade, Sept. 10, 1998, available at www.fco.gov.uk/Files/ kfile/CM%206119.pdf

Stockholm Convention on Persistent Organic Pollutants, Sept. 22, 2001, 40, I.L.M. 532

United Nations Declaration on the responsibilities of the present generations towards future generations UNESCO–United Nations Educational, Scientific and Cultural Organization, New York 1997

World Charter for Nature, Oct. 28, 1982, 37 UN – GAOR, Supp. No. 51, p. 17, UN Doc. A/37/51

2.2. Other International Sources

African Charter on Human and Peoples' Rights, adopted by the Organisation of African Unity, 27 June 1981, 21 I.L.M. 58 (1982)

Agenda 21 of the United Nations Division for Sustainable Development, adopted at the United Nations Conference on Environment and Development (UNCED), Rio de Janeiro, Brazil, 3-14 June 1992.

Bergen Ministerial Declaration on Sustainable Development in the ECE Region, 16 may 1990, UN Doc. A/CONF.151/PC/10; 1 Yearbook on International Environmental Law 429 (1990): 4312

Communication ACCC/C/2008/32, submitted on 1 December 2008 by ClientEarth and others, *available at available at www.unece.org/env/pp/compliance/C2008-32/DatasheetC-2008-32v2009.01.19.doc.*

Conference on Security and Co-Operation in Europe Final Act of 1 August 1975, 14 ILM 1992, p. 1292.

Conference Report: "Resolution of the Avosetta Conference 11-12 October 2002, Amsterdam", *European Environmental Law Review*, 2003, p. 34.

Declaration by the Environment Ministers of the region of the United Nations Economic Commission for Europe (UN/ECE), 4th Ministerial Conference „Environment for Europe", Aarhus, Denmark, 23-25 June 1998

Draft International Covenant on Environmental and Development, 1995 and update in 2000 and 2004, Cambridge

ECOSOC, ECE, Meeting of the Signatories to the Convention on Access to Information, Public Participation in Decision-making and Access to Justice in Environmental Matters, *Annex to the Addendum to the Report of the First Meeting of the Parties: Decision I/7 Review of Compliance* 4, U.N. Doc. ECE/MP.PP/2/Add.8 (Apr. 2, 2004), available at www.unece.org/env/pp/documents/mop1/ece.mp.pp.2.add.8.e.pdf

European Social Charter, adopted by the Council of Europe, 18 October 1961, entered into force 26 February 1965, European Treaty Series (ETS), No. 35

Fourth Ministerial Conference Environment for Europe, Åarhus, Denmark 23–25 June 1998 Declaration by the Environment Ministers of the region of the United Nations Economic Commission for Europe (UN/ECE), available at www.unece.org/env/efe/history%20of%20EfE/Aarhus.E.pdf

Johannesburg Declaration on Sustainable Development, adopted by the World Summit on Sustainable Development, 2-4 September 2002, U.N. Doc. A/CONF.199/20, §13.

Joint Communique and Declaration on the Establishment of the Arctic Council, Sept. 19, 1996, 35 I.L.M. 1382

Ksentini Report, Final Report, UN Doc. E/CN.4/Sub.2/1994/9

Report of the second meeting of the Task Force on Access to Justice, UN Doc. MP.PP/WG.1/2004/3, 8 January 2004, *available at www.unece.org/env/documents/2004/pp/mp.pp/wg.1/mp.pp. wg.1.2004.3.e.pdf*, Annex, p. 15, para. 17.

Report of the World Commission on Environment and Development: Our Common Future (Brundtland Report) of 1987, UN Doc. A/42/427, p. 40

Rio Declaration on Environment and Development, Report of the United Nations Conference on Environment and Development, Aug. 10, 1992, UN Doc. A/CONF.151/26 (Vol. I)

Stockholm Declaration of the United Nations Conference on the Human Environment, UN – Doc. A/CONF. 48/14 (1972), reprinted in (1972) 11 ILM 1416

Turin Council: White Paper on the 1996 Intergovernmental Conference, 29 March 1996, Vol. II

U.N. Econ. & Soc. Council [ECOSOC], Econ. Commission' for Europe, *Report of the Meeting of the Parties to the Protocol on Water and Health to the Convention on the Protection and Use of Transboundary Watercourses and International Lakes*, U.N. Doc. ECE/MP.WH/2/Add.3, *available at www.unece.org/env/documents/2007/wat/wh/ece.mp.wh.2_add_3.e.pdf.*

3. Documents of the European Union

3.1. European Treaties

Treaty of Lisbon, 13.12.2007, OJ 2007 C 306/01

Treaty establishing the European Economic Community (EEC), 25.03.1957

Single European Act, 28.02.1986, OJ L 169 of 29.06.1987

Treaty on European Union (Maastricht Treaty), 07.02.1992, OJ C 191 of 29.07.1992

Treaty of Amsterdam, 02.10.1997, OJ C 340 of 10.11.1997

Treaty of Nice, 26.02.2001, OJ C 80 of 10.03.2001

3.2. Regulations

Regulation (EC) N° 1049/2001 of the European Parliament and of the Council of 30 May 2001 regarding public access to European Parliament, Council and Commission documents, OJ L 145, 31.5.2001, p. 43,

Regulation (EC) No 1638/2006 of the European Parliament and of the Council of 24 October 2006 Laying Down General Provisions Establishing a European Neighbourhood and Partnership Instrument, OJ 2006, L 310/1

Regulation (EC) No 1905/2006 of the European Parliament and of the Council of 18 December 2006 Establishing a Financing Instrument for Development Cooperation, OJ 2006, L 378/41

Regulation (EC) No 889/2008 of 5 September 2008 Laying Down Detailed Rules for the Implementation of Council Regulation (EC) No 834/2007 on Organic production and Labelling of Organic Products with Regard to Organic Production, Labelling and Control, OJ 2008, L 250/1

Regulation (EEC) No 259/93 of 1 February 1993 on the Supervision and Control of Shipments of Waste within, into and out of the European Community, OJ 1993, L 30/1

Regulation 1367/2006 on the application of the provisions of the Aarhus Convention on Access to Information, Public Participation in Decision-making and Access to Justice in Environmental matters to Community institutions and bodies, OJ 2006L 264/13

Regulation 166/2006, the pollutant Release and Transfer Register Regulation. OJ 2006 L 33/1.

3.3. Directives

Directive 1999/32/EC of 26 April 1999 Relating to a Reduction in the Sulphur Content of Certain Liquid Fuels and Amending Directive 93/12/EEC, OJ 1999, L 121/13

Directive 2003/30/EC of the European Parliament and of the Council of 8 May 2003 on the Promotion of the use of Biofuels or other Renewable Fuels for Transport, OJ 2003, L 123/42

Directive 2003/4/EC of the European Parliament and of the Council of 28 January 2003 on Public Access to Environmental Information and Repealing Council Directive 90/313/EEC, OJ 2003, L 41/26

Directive 67/548/EEC of 27 June 1967 on the Approximation of Laws, Regulations and Administrative Provisions Relating to the Classification, Packaging and Labelling of Dangerous Substances, OJ 1967, L 196/1

Directive 96/61/EC of 24 September 1996 Concerning Integrated Pollution Prevention and Control, OJ 1996, L 257/26

Directive 1999/13/EC of 11 March 1999 on the Limitation of Emissions of Volatile Organic Compounds Due to the Use of Organic Solvents in Certain Activities and Installations, OJ 1999, L 85/1

Directive 1999/31/EC of 26 April 1999 on the Landfill of Waste, OJ 1999, L 182/1

Directive 1999/45/EC of the European Parliament and of the Council of 31 May 1999 Concerning the Approximation of the Laws, Regulations and Administrative Provisions of the Member States Relating to the Classification, Packaging and Labelling of Dangerous Preparations, OJ 1990, L 200/1

Directive 2000/16/EC of the European Parliament and the Council of 10 April 2000 amending Council Directive 79/373/EEC on the Marketing of Compound Feedingstuffs and Council Directive 96/25/EC on the Circulation of Feed Materials, OJ 2000, L 105/36

Directive 2000/60/EC of the European Parliament and of the Council of 23 October 2000 Establishing a Framework for Community Action in the Field of Water Policy, OJ 2000, L 327/1

Directive 2000/76/EC of the European Parliament and of the Council of 4 December 2000 on the Incineration of Waste, OJ 2000, L 332/91

Directive 2001/18/EC of the European Parliament and of the Council of 12 March 2001 on the Deliberate Release into the Environment of Genetically Modified Organisms and Repealing Council Directive 90/220/EEC, OJ 2001, L 106/1

Directive 2001/59/EC of 6 August 2001 Adapting to Technical Progress for the 28th time Council Directive 67/548/EEC on the Approximation of the Laws, Regulations and Administrative Provisions Relating to the Classification, Packaging and Labelling of Dangerous Substances, OJ 2001, L 225/1

Directive 2002/32/EC of the European Parliament and of the Council of 7 May 2002 on Undesirable Substances in Animal Feed, OJ 2002, L 140/10

Directive 2002/55/EC of 13 June 2002 on the Marketing of Vegetable Seed, OJ 2002, L 193/33

Directive 2002/91/EC of the European Parliament and of the Council of 16 December 2002 On the Energy Performance of Buildings, OJ 2003, L 1/65

Directive 2003/35/EC of 26 May 2003 providing for public participation in respect of the drawing up of certain plans and programmes relating to the environment and amending with regard to public participation and access to justice Council Directives 85/ 337/EEC and 96/61/EC, [2003] OJ L156/17

Directive 2003/4/EC of the European Parliament And Of The Council of 28 January 2003 On Public Access to Environmental Information and Repealing Council Directive 90/313/EEC, OJ 2003, L 41/26

Directive 2006/12/EC of the European Parliament and of the Council of 5 April 2006 on waste, OJ 2006, L 114/9

Directive 2006/21/EC of the European Parliament and of the Council of 15 March 2006 on the Management of Waste From Extractive Industries and Amending Directive 2004/35/EC, OJ 2006, L 102/15

Directive 2006/88/EC of 24 October 2006 on Animal Health Requirements for Aquaculture Animals and Products Thereof, and on the Prevention and Control of Certain Diseases in Aquatic Animals, OJ 2006, L 328/14

Directive 2008/1/EC of the European Parliament and of the Council of 15 January 2008 Concerning Integrated Pollution Prevention and Control, OJ 2008, L 24/8

Directive 2008/50/EC of the European Parliament and of The Council of 21 May 2008 On Ambient Air Quality and Cleaner Air for Europe, OJ 2008, L 152/1

Directive 2008/98/EC of the European Parliament and of the Council of 19 November 2008 on Waste and Repealing Certain Directives, OJ 2008, L 312/3

Directive 2009/13/EC of 16 February 2009 implementing the Agreement concluded by the European Community Shipowners' Associations (ECSA) and the European Transport Workers' Federation (ETF) on the Maritime Labour Convention, 2006, and amending Directive 1999/63/EC, OJ 2009, 124/30

Directive 2009/16/EC of the European Parliament and of the Council of 23 April 2009 on Port State Control, OJ 2009, L 131/57

Directive 2009/31/EC of the European Parliament and of the Council of 23 April 2009 On the Geological Storage of Carbon Dioxide and Amending Council Directive 85/337/EEC, European Parliament and Council Directives 2000/60/EC, 2001/80/EC, 2004/35/EC, 2006/12/EC, 2008/1/EC and Regulation (EC) No 1013/2006, OJ 2009, L 140/114

Directive 2009/33/EC of the European Parliament and of the Council of 23 April 2009 on the Promotion of Clean and Energy-Efficient Road Transport Vehicles, OJ 2009, L 120/5

Directive 2009/41/EC of the European Parliament and of the Council of 6 May 2009 on the Contained Use of Genetically Modified Micro-Organisms, OJ 2009, L 125/75

Directive 67/548/EEC of 27 June 1967 on the Approximation of Laws, Regulations and Administrative Provisions Relating to the Classification, Packaging and Labelling of Dangerous Substances, OJ 1967, L 196/1

Directive 67/548/EEC of 27 June 1967 on the approximation of laws, regulations and administrative provisions relating to the classification, packaging and labelling of dangerous substances, OJ p. 196 of 16.8.1967

Directive 76/160/EEC of 8 December 1975 concerning the quality of bathing water, OJ L 31 of 5.2.1976

Directive 76/464/EEC of 4 May 1976 on Pollution Caused by Certain Dangerous Substances, Discharged into the Aquatic Environment of the Community, OJ 1976, L 129/23

Directive 79/409/EEC of 2 April 1979 on the Conservation of Wild Birds, *OJ 1979, L 103/1*

Directive 80/68/EEC of 17 December 1979 on the Protection of Groundwater Against Pollution Caused by Certain Dangerous Substances, OJ 1980, L 20/43

Directive 84/360/EEC of 28 June 1984 on the Combating of Air Pollution from Industrial Plants, OJ 1984, L 188/20

Directive 90/219/EEC of 23 April 1990 on the Contained Use of Genetically Modified Micro-organisms, OJ 1990, L 117/1

Directive 90/313/EEC of 23 July 1993 on the freedom of access to information on the environment provided the legal basis for access to environmental information in the EC countries and in other countries in the UN/ECE region, OJ L158/56

Directive 91/156/EEC of 18 March 1991 Amending Directive 75/442/EEC On Waste, OJ 1991, L 78/32

Directive 91/414/EEC of 15 July 1991 Concerning the Placing of Plant Protection Products on the Market, OJ 1991, L 230/1; Directive 98/8/EC of the European Parliament and of the Council of 16 February 1998 Concerning the Placing of Biocidal Products on the Market, OJ 1998, L 123/1

Directive 91/689/EEC of 12 December 1991 on Hazardous Waste, OJ 1991, L 377/20

Directive 92/43/EEC of 21 May 1992 on the Conservation of Natural Habitats and of Wild Fauna and Flora, *OJ 1992, L 206/7*

Directive 93/75/EEC of 13 September 1993 Concerning Minimum Requirements for Vessels Bound for or Leaving Community Ports and Carrying Dangerous or Polluting Goods, OJ 1993, L 247/19

Directive 94/55/EC of 21 November 1994 on the Approximation of the Laws of the Member States with Regard to the Transport of Dangerous Goods by Road, OJ 1994, L 319/7

Directive 96/49/EC of 23 July 1996 on the Approximation of the Laws of the Member States with Regard to the Transport of Dangerous Goods by Rail, OJ 1996, L 235/25

Directive 98/8/EC of the European Parliament and of the Council of 16 February 1998 Concerning the Placing of Biocidal Products on the market, OJ 1998, L 123

3.4. Others EU Sources

Charter of Fundamental Rights of the EU, OJ C 364/1, 18 December 2000.

 Commission Decision 94/90/ECSC, Euratom of 8 February 1994. OJ 1997 L263/27.

 Commission Proposal on Environmental Liability in the Waste Sector on 22 May 1991 COM, 1991, 102 final – SYN 335

1st Environmental Action Programme, 1973-1976 (1973) OJ C112

25th Annual Report on monitoring the application of Community law [COM(2008) 777]

2st Environmental Action Programme, 1977-1981 (1977) OJ C 139

3st Environmental Action Programme, 1982-1986 (1981) OJ C46

4st Environmental Action Programme, 1987-1992 (1987) OJ C328

5st Environmental Action Programme 1993-2001 (1993) OJ C138

6st Environmental Action Programme, 2002-2012 (2002) OJ L242/1

Charter of Fundamental Rights of the European Union, Dec. 14, 2007, 1007 O.J. (C 303) 1

Commission Communication External Action of 16 February 2006, Thematic Programme for Environment and Sustainable Management of Natural Resources including Energy, COM(2006) 20

Commission Communication on Implementing European Community Environmental Law, COM (2008) 773 final, 18 November 2008

Commission, 'Communication on Promoting the role of voluntary organisations and foundations in Europe', 6 June 1997, COM (97), 241 final

Council Decision in 2005, 2005/370, Official Journal L 124 (2005), p. 1

Decision 93/731/EC on public access to Council documents (20 December 1993),Consolidated version of the Decision of the Council of the European Union of 20 December 1993 on public access to its documents, incorporating the amendments introduced by the Council Decision of 6 December 1996.

EEA: Environment in the European Union at the Turn of the Century, Copenhagen 1999

European Commission Work Programme, white Paper on European Governance: Enhancing Democracy in the European Union, SEC (2000) 1547/7, 11 October 2000

European Commission Work Programme, white Paper on European Governance: Enhancing Democracy in the European Union, SEC (2000) 1547/7, 11 october 2000

EUROPEAN ENVIRONMENT AGENCY, *The European Environment – State and Outlook 2005*, Copenhagen

Natura 2000, European Commission DG Env Nature Newsletter, no. 26, July 2009, available at *www.ec.europa.eu/environment/nature/info/pubs/docs/nat2000newsl/nat26_en.pdf*

Presidency Conclusions of the Brussels European Council 15–16 June 2006 (10633/1/06 REV 1)

Proposal for a Directive of the European parliament and of the Council on access to justice in environmental matters, COM (2003)624 of 23 October 2003

Protocol on the application of the Charter of Fundamental rights of the European Union to Poland and to the United Kingdom. Available at www.eur-lex.europa.eu/LexUriServ/LexUriServ.do?uri=OJ:C:2007:306:0156:0157:EN:PDF.

4. Jurisprudence

4.1. Cases of the European Court of First Instance

T-12/93, Comité Central d'Entreprise de la Société Anonyme Vittel and Comité d'Etablissement de Pierval and federation Générale Agroalimentaire v. Commission, [1995] ECR 11-1247

T-126/95 *Dumez v. Commission* (1996) ECR II- 2863.

T-168/02, IFAW Internationaler Tierschutz-Fonds gGmbH v. Commission of the European Communities, 30 November 2004

T-17/00 *Will Rothley v. Parliament* (2002) ECR II- 579

T-17/00 *Will Rothley v. Parliament* (2002) ECR II- 579

T-173/98 *Unión de Pequeños Agricultores v. Council* [1999] ECR II-3357

T-187/03, Isabella Scippacercola v. Commission of the European Communities, 17 March 2005

T-219/95 R, Marie-Thérèse Danielsson, Pierre Largenteau, Edwin Haoa v. Commission of the European Communities,[1995] ECR II-3051

T-236/04, *EEB and Stichting Natuur en Milieu v. Commission,* [1995] ECR II-3051

T-76/02, Mara Messina v. Commission of the European Communities, 17 September 2003

T-84/01 *Association contre l'heure d'été v Parliament and Council* (2002) ECH II-99.

T-91/07 *WWF-UK Ltd v. Council of the European Union*, 2 June 2008

T-177/01 *Jégo-Quéré v. Commission* [2002] ECR II-2365

4.2. Cases of the European Court of Justice

C- 142/95 *P Rovigo v. Commission* (1996) ECR I-6669.

C- 322/88 *Salvatore Grimaldi v. Fonds des maladies professionnelles* (1989) ECR 4407.

C- 365/97, *Commission v. Italy* (1997) ECR I-7773

C- 412/85, *Commission v. Germany* (1987) ECR 3503

C- 44/95, *R. v. Secretary of State for the Environment*, (1996) ECH I-3805.

C-106/77, *Amministrazione delle Finanze dello Stato v. Simmenthal SpA* [1978] ECR 629, [1978] 3

C-11/66 *Others v. Commission (Noordwijks Cement Accord)*, [1967] ECR 75, at 91

C-11/70 *Internationale Handelsgesellschaft mbH v. Einfuhr- und Vorratsstelle für Getreide und Futtermittel* [1970] ECR 1125

C-131/88, *Commission v. Germany* (1991) ECR I-825

C-14/83, *Von Colson v. Land Nordrhein-Westfalen*, [1984] ECR 1891

C-147/96 *Netherlands v. Commission* (2000) ECR I-4723

C-159/96 *Portugal v. Commission* (1998) ECR I- 7379.

C-16/88, *Commission v. Council*, ECR [1989] 3457

C-169/84 *COFAZ v. Commission* [1986] ECR 391

C-186/91, *Commission v. Belgium,* (1993) ECH I-185

C-191/82 *FEDIOL v. Commission* [1983] ECR 2913

C-239/03 *Commission v. France* [2004] ECR I-9325

C-240/83 *Procureur de la Règublique v. Association de défense des Bruleurs d'huiles Usagèe* (1983) ECR 531

C-26/62, NV *Algemene Transport- en Expeditie Onderneming van Gend en Loos v. Nederlandse Administratie der Belastingen* [1963] ECR 1

C-26/76 *Metro v. Commission I* [1977] ECR 1875

C-263/02P, Commission v. Jégo-Quéré and Cie SA, [2002] ECR II-2365

C-272/80, Biologische Produketen (1981) ECR 3277

C-301/03 *Italy v. Commission* (2005) ECR I-10217

C-321/95 P, Stichting Greenpeace Council and Others v. Commission, [1998] ECR 1-1651

C-322/86, *Commission v. Italy* (1988) ECR I-3995

C-33/70, *Spa SACE v. Italian Ministry of Finance,* [1970] ECR 1213

C-332/04 *Commission v. Spain* [2006] ECR I-0000

C-343/95 *Diego Calì and Figli v. Servizi ecologici porto di Genova SpA (SEPG),* Judgement of 18 March 1997, ECR [I-01574

C-355/90, *Commission v. Spain* (1993) ECR I-4221

C-36/75, *Roland Rutili v. Ministre de l'Intérieur,* [1975] ECR I-1219,

C-361/88, *Commission v. Germany* [1991] ECR I- 256

C-6 and 9/90 *Francovich and Bonifaci v. Italy* [1991] ECR I-5357

C-6/64 *Flamino Costa v. ENEL* [1964] ECR 585.

C-64/05P, *Kingdom of Sweden v. Commission of the European Communities*, 18 December 2007

C-8/66, *Société Anonyme Cimenteries C.B.R. Cementsbedrijven N.V.*, [1967] ECR 75, at 91.).

C-92/79 *Commission v. Italy* (1980) ECJ 1115

4.3. Case of European Court of Human Rights

Fadeyeva v. Russia, App. No 55723/ 00, 45 EHRR (2007)

Powell v. United Kingdom, (App. no. 9310/81), 172 Eur. Ct. H.R. (ser. A) 1 (1990)

S. v. France, App. No. 13728/88, 65 Eur. Comm'n H.R. Dec. and Rep. 250, 263-64 (1990)

Arrondelle v. United Kingdom, App. No. 7889/77, 26 Eur. Comm'n H.R. Dec. and Rep. 5, 8-9 (1983).

Athanassoglou v. Switzerland, (Appl no. 27644/95) 31 EHRR 13 (2001)

Buckley v. United Kingdom, App. No 20348/92, Eur. Ct. H.R. 1271, 1287 (1996)

Guerra and Others v. Italy (116/1996/735/932), (1998), www.hrcr.org/safrica/environmental/guerra_italy.html

Hatton v. United Kingdom, 2003-VIII Eur. Ct. H.R. 189, 228 (2003)

Johannische Kirche v. Germany, App. No. 41754/98 (2001), 2001-VIII Eur. Ct. H.R.

Moreno Gómez v. Spain, 2004-X Eur. Ct. H.R. 327, 343 (2005).

Taskin v. Turkey, 10 November 2004, 2004-X Eur. Ct. H.R. 145 (2005).

X. v. Germany, App. No. 7407/76, 5 Eur. Comm'n H.R. Dec. and Rep. 161, 161 (1976)

Detailed Table of Content

Abbreviations 9

Introduction 12

Environmental Democracy in a European Context 15

Chapter 1
1. **"Democracy" and "Environment" in the European Union** 15

1.1. "Democracy" 15
1.1.1. Democratic Deficit in the EU...................................16
1.1.2. The Remedies of Democratic Deficit........................20
1.1.2.1. Representative Democracy Tools....................21
1.1.2.2. Participatory and Deliberatory Tools.............23
1.1.3. The Treaty Instruments to Participate 26
1.1.3.1. Access to Environmental Information............28
1.1.3.2. Public Participation in Environmental Matters....29
1.1.3.2.1. White Paper on European Governance 29
1.1.3.2.2. Constitution for Europe and the Following Plan "D"...........30
1.1.3.2.3. Treaty of Lisbon 32
1.1.3.3. Access to Justice: Former Article 230........34

1.2. "Environment" in the European Community 36
1.2.1. The Definition of the Term "Environment" in Europe...........36
1.2.1.1. Wide Definition of "Environment"...................38
1.2.1.2. Narrow Definition of "Environment"................40
1.2.2. Anthropocentric and Ecocentric Character of Environment in Europe................42
1.2.3. Protection of Environment in the Treaty..................43
1.2.3.1. Single European Act....................45

1.2.3.2.   The Treaty of Amsterdam..47
1.2.3.3.   The Constitution for Europe..48
1.2.3.4.   The Lisbon Treaty...49

2.   Environmental Democracy in Europe 53

2.1.   Dimensions of European Environmental Democracy: Form and Space 53
2.1.1.   Form...53
2.1.2.   Space...55

2.2.   Actors of Environmental Democracy at a European Level: the Role for
        European citizens...57
2.2.1.   European Environmental Rights..59
2.2.1.1.   Substantive Environmental Rights 60
2.2.1.1.1.   Article 37 Codifies an Environmental Human Right...........61
2.2.1.1.2.   Article 37 Does Not Codify an Environmental Human
            Right 63
2.2.1.1.3.   Where Can We Find the European Environmental Substantive
            Rights?..66
2.2.1.1.4.   ECHR Jurisprudence: Environmental Protection "Par
            Ricochet"...67
2.2.1.1.4.1.   Jurisprudences of ECHR in Environmental matters 68
2.2.2.   Ecological European Citizens 71
2.2.2.1.   Ecological Duties 75
2.2.2.1.1.   Preventive Principle and Precautionary Principle 76
2.2.2.1.2.   Sustainable Development..77
2.2.2.1.3.   Polluter Pays Principle 79
Conclusion of Chapter 1...80

Chapter 2
Implementation of Environmental Rights and Duties in Europe.......... 82

1.   Environmental Democracy at the EU Level................................ 84

1.1.   Procedural Rights: Implementation of the Aarhus Convention................84
1.1.1.   First Pillar: Access to Environmental Information........................86
1.1.1.1.   Background on Public Access to Information in Europe..............86
1.1.1.2.   Passive Access to Environmental Information 89
1.1.1.2.1.   General Rules 89
1.1.1.2.2.   Exceptions of the Access to Information 91
1.1.1.3.   Active Access to Environmental Information 94

1.1.2.   Second Pillar: Environmental Participation..........................96
1.1.3.   Third Pillar: Access to Justice in Environmental Matters 98
1.1.3.1.   Background on Former Article 230 EC 99
1.1.3.2.   Implementation of Article 9(1) of the Aarhus Convention.......105
1.1.3.3.   Implementation of Article 9(2) of the Aarhus Convention.......106
1.1.4.   Fourth Pillar: Implementation of Article 9(3) of the Aarhus Convention..108
1.1.4.1.   Internal Review Process by a Community Institution or Body..110
1.1.4.1.1.   Article 10 Request for Internal Review of Administrative Act...111
1.1.4.1.2.   Article 11 Criteria for Entitlement at Community Level...116
1.1.4.2.   Proceeding Before the Court of Justice 117
1.1.4.3.   Limits of Aarhus Regulation Compared to the Aarhus Convention..118
1.1.4.4.   "Individual Concern" After the Entry into Force of the Aarhus Regulation...120
1.1.4.5.   Communication to the Aarhus Convention's Compliance Committee..122

2.   **Environmental Democracy at National Level 126**

2.1.   Procedural Environmental Rights...127
2.1.1.   First Pillar: Access of Environmental Information..........................127
2.1.1.1.   Directive 2003/4/EC on Public Access to Environmental Information..128
2.1.2.   Second Pillar: Participation in Environmental Matters 131
2.1.2.1.   Directive 2003/35/EC...132
2.1.2.2.   Implementation of Article 6 of Aarhus Convention: EIA Directive and IPPC Directive 133
2.1.2.3.   Implementation of Article 7 of Aarhus Convention....................135
2.1.3.   Third Pillar: Access to Justice in Environmental Matters 137
2.1.3.1.   Implementation of Article 9 (1).................................137
2.1.3.2.   Implementation of Article 9 (2).................................138
2.1.4.   Fourth Pillar: Implementation of Article 9 (3)............................139
2.1.4.1.   The Proposal on Access to Justice in Environmental Matters..139
2.1.4.2.   The Main Novelties of the Proposal on Access to Justice..........141

2.2.   Ecological Duties..143
2.2.1.   Implementation by Waste Legislation 143
2.2.2.   Implementation by Environmental Criminal Law............................144
2.2.3.   Implementation by Environmental Liability Directive......................147

2.2.3.1.   The Polluter Pays Principle and the Preventive Principle in the
Directive 150

2.2.3.2.   The Personal, Material and Temporal Scope of the Liability
Directive 151

2.2.3.3.   Ecological Duties Under the Liability Directive 155

2.2.3.4.   Access to Justice in the Liability Directive 157

Conclusion of Chapter 2 158

Conclusion...160

Index 164

Bibliography..168

1. Books and Articles **168**

2. International Sources..**236**

2.1. Treaties...236

2.2. Other International Sources 238

3. Documents of the European Union..**240**

3.1. European Treaties 240

3.2. Regulations..241

3.3. Directives 242

3.4. Others EU Sources 246

4. Jurisprudence **248**

4.1. Cases of the European Court of First Instance...............................248

4.2. Cases of the European Court of Justice..249

4.3. Case of European Court of Human Rights.......................................251

Detailed Table of Content 252